MATTER AND INFINITY IN THE PRESOCRATIC SCHOOLS AND PLATO

WIJSGERIGE TEKSTEN EN STUDIES
PHILOSOPHICAL TEXTS AND STUDIES

onder redactie van
edited by

PROF. DR. C. J. DE VOGEL EN PROF. DR. K. KUYPERS

Uitgaven van de Filosofische Instituten der Rijksuniversiteit te Utrecht

MATTER AND INFINITY
IN THE PRESOCRATIC SCHOOLS
AND PLATO

by

THEO GERARD SINNIGE, Ph. D.

ASSEN - MCMLXVIII

VAN GORCUM & COMP. N.V. - DR. H. J. PRAKKE & H. M. G. PRAKKE

Printed in the Netherlands by Royal VanGorcum Ltd., Assen

CONTENTS

CHAPTER I

ANAXIMANDER

In the *Lives of the Illustrious Philosophers* by Diogenes Laertius, six so-called ἀποφθέγματα or 'proverbial sayings' are found, which are ascribed to Thales of Miletus (I 35). They have the form of condensed expressions, more or less in a popular tone, and each of them consists of two parts, which together form a kind of verse. Each of these verses starts with a superlative:

πρεσβύτατον τῶν ὄντων θεός· ἀγένητον γάρ.

κάλλιστον κόσμος· ποίημα γὰρ θεοῦ.

μέγιστον τόπος· ἅπαντα γὰρ χωρεῖ.

τάχιστον νοῦς· διὰ παντὸς γὰρ τρέχει.

ἰσχυρότατον ἀνάγκη· κρατεῖ γὰρ πάντων.

σοφώτατον χρόνος· ἀνευρίσκει γὰρ πάντα.

The character of the lines makes it clear that they must be classified in the category of age-old wisdom-expressions, transmitted from generation to generation. We may safely suppose that neither their form nor their contents can be ascribed to Thales. Each of the lines treats of a cosmic principle: god, the cosmos, space, intelligence, fate, and time, and of each of these principles a very short description is given, mostly in terms that indicate a divine power. The superlatives with which they begin make it probable, as Otto Brendel (1936) stated, that those proverbs circulated in the oral form as riddles, e.g. 'what is most ancient?', the answer 'God', the reason given 'he is unborn', and so on.

To the collection of six proverbial sayings, all having the form here described, a seventh line is added, in which the expression is different but which nevertheless runs parallel to the others:

τί τὸ θεῖον; τὸ μήτε ἀρχὴν ἔχον μήτε τελευτήν.

"what is it that is called divine? that which has neither beginning nor end."

Taken together the seven proverbs may have formed a whole of wisdom-proverbs, in which ancient cosmological myths found expression. They represent, as we shall see, a coherent set of theological principles, all centered on the idea of an all-embracing, unborn, eternal, omnipresent divine power ruling the whole of things. The seven proverbs are distinguished from other formulas that occur in the same context by their theological contents. Those other formulas have an ethical character, as most sayings have, pronounced by the most ancient 'wise men' the Greek knew of (DK 10). The proverbs ascribed to Thales are accompanied, in the text of Diogenes Laertius (I 35), by a series of ethical sentences. Parallels of the theological ones are mentioned by Plutarch (*Conv. Septem Sap.*, IX 135 C) and by Stobaeus (*Eclogae* I, 29 a, - I, 4, 7 a, - I 8, 40 a, - I 18, 1 e). A more detailed survey of them is given by Diels, *Doxographi* 555, in a note on Hippolytus' *Philosophoumena* I 3, where the same theological aphorism is ascribed to Thales: God is that which has neither beginning nor end.

As Brendel noticed, the theological character of our seven proverbs distinguishes them from the other sayings, which remain within the ethical way of thinking of the first Greek 'sages'. Brendel refers to the great work of Eisler (1910, 662), who must have been the first to see the ancient traditions hidden in the ἀποφθέγματα ascribed to Thales.

The proverbs mentioned may be considered more or less as forming a whole. There is a trace of systematical ordering in the sequence in which they are given. The first two talk about God in contrast to the cosmos or to 'things being' (τὰ ὄντα). The next two mention cosmic space and the intelligible principle omnipresent in it. The fifth line says that 'all things' i.e. things being or the cosmos have a ruling principle in it: ineluctable ἀνάγκη. In the sixth line Time is introduced as an omniscient principle, and in the seventh aphorism the whole cycle returns to its starting-point: the unborn godhead, the most ancient of all things, having neither beginning nor end.

The sixth in our series of ἀποφθέγματα asks for a more detailed discussion. The text reads: σοφώτατον χρόνος· ἀνευρίσκει γὰρ πάντα, "Time is what is wisest; for it finds out all things". In the motivation 'it finds out all things' we may see a trace of old traditions about divine wisdom, if it can be stated first that the subject of the sentence 'χρόνος' really represents a divine principle. The predicate 'wisest of all' does point in this direction, as does the parallelism of the proverbs. An indication that Time was considered a deity may be found in the later identification of Κρόνος with Χρόνος, in the context of a myth which is said to be of eastern origin. A more decisive proof, however,

2

can be found in some lines of Aristotle's and in very early, Orphic traditions.

When treating the problem of how to define the concept of time, Aristotle says: (*Phys.* Δ 10, 218 a 34 - 35): οἱ μὲν γὰρ τὴν τοῦ ὅλου κίνησιν εἶναί φασιν, οἱ δὲ τὴν σφαῖραν αὐτήν, "some say it is the movement of the whole, others that it is the sphere itself." The first part of this remark refers principally to the doctrines developed by Plato in his *Timaeus* (37 A - 39 E), the second part probably to a theory of the Pythagoreans. At any rate, Aristotle knew of a theory in which Time and the heavenly sphere were explained as one and the same divinity. Even the reasons given for this are mentioned by Aristotle (218 b 5 - 7): it is "because all things are at once in Time and in the cosmic sphere". In Simplicius' comments on these lines, it is suggested that Aristotle may have been mistaken in writing this, but the wording of this comment easily shows that Simplicius did not suspect that any meaning could be given to what he found in Aristotle's text. Therefore Simplicius tries to explain this as an obscure way of saying that Time is that which measures the cosmos (cf. Ross a.l.). Now even Simplicius says, it was the Pythagoreans who had this theory. As in ancient traditions Time is considered a divine, all-embracing power, the mention that Time was the sphere itself, is much easier to understand when we suppose that both Time and the cosmic sphere stand for the same ancient cosmic divinity. It was Eisler and, following him, Brendel, who worked out this explanation. The first intuition of it had been formulated by Zeller (*Philos. d. Griechen* I 1, 6. Aufl., 1919, S. 546, 1): "Ich möchte vermuten, ursprünglich sei χρόνος ein symbolischer Name für den Himmel". It is confirmed by a passage in Aëtius (DK 58 B 33):

Πυθαγόρας τὸν χρόνον τὴν σφαῖραν τοῦ περιέχοντος εἶναι, "Pythagoras says that Time is the encircling sphere of the universe."

Several other texts can be adduced to confirm the interpretation of χρόνος with its quality of 'finding out all things' as representing an ancient mythical being that embraced the cosmos by its power. One of our sources for the oldest Orphic theology (DK 1 B 13) says that the Orphics held that the first principles of things were three: water, earth and time. Time was represented as a monster with the heads of a god, a lion and a bull, and it had the name of Χρόνος ἀγήραος, never-aging Time. This Χρόνος was attended by Ἀνάγκη and Ἀδράστεια, Fate and Ineluctability, the latter being described as "embracing the whole universe, keeping hold of its boundaries".

3

This description of Χρόνος reminds us of the Mesopotamian divine monsters with numerous heads and bodies. The heads of a lion and a bull may well have been the symbols of resp. supreme power and vegetative power penetrating all things. In course of time then this pictorial expression must have given way to a more abstract wording in terms of 'Ανάγκη and 'Αδράστεια, concepts which in later centuries developed into the concepts of 'causality' and 'law of nature'. Without anticipating later developments we may state that a very ancient mythical symbol existed representing Χρόνος as omnipotent and active Ruler, embracing the universe.

Furthermore there is a fragment of Aristotle's which has been preserved by Stobaeus (*Ecl.* I 18, 1 c):

'Εν δὲ τῷ περὶ τῆς Πυθαγόρου φιλοσοφίας πρώτῳ γράφει (sc. ὁ 'Αρ.) τὸν οὐρανὸν εἶναι ἕνα, ἐπεισάγεσθαι δ' ἐκ τοῦ ἀπείρου χρόνον τε καὶ πνοήν. (= *Fragmenta selecta* ed. Ross, p. 137).

"In the first book on the philosophy of Pythagoras Aristotle writes that the heaven is one, and that time and breath are being drawn from the unbounded."

The description is that of a breathing universe, which is known from several other sources to have formed part of the Pythagorean doctrines (Ar. *Phys.* 213 b 22, Diels *Doxographi* 338). The universe is taking breath from the surrounding endless space and inhales from it 'unbounded Time'. Once more that which surrounds the universe is identified with 'unbounded Time'; in other words: the surrounding Heaven and Time as an all-embracing divinity are one and the same.

Just as we have seen that in the Orphic symbols Time has as its attribute 'Ανάγκη, so we recognize the same idea when finding in Stobaeus (I 4, 7 = *Doxographi* 321):

Πυθαγόρας 'Ανάγκην ἔφη περικεῖσθαι τῷ κόσμῳ

"Pythagoras said that 'Ανάγκη surrounds the universe."

In this line it is not Time, but one of the attributes of Time, 'Ανάγκη, that is considered identical with the outmost Heaven. This does not differ much from the saying of Pythagoras, quoted above, in which Time was described as a sphere of infinity surrounding all things.

Theophrastus, in his account of Anaximander (DK 12 A 10), says that Anaximander considered τὸ ἄπειρον as the cause of coming-to-be and passing-away in the universe. Explaining this Theophrastus says that Anaximander had pointed out that passing-away and coming-to-be occurred by way of a cyclic process, in consequence of which all things from eternity returned into their former state. This means that, to

4

Anaximander, the ἄπειρον had to be described as exercising its function by means of cyclic time. The same note is struck in the account by Hippolytus (DK 12 A 11), who informs us that, according to Anaximander, the ἄπειρον as a principle of all things is ἀΐδιον καὶ ἀγήρω, eternal and never-aging. Once more the ἄπειρον is bearer of the attributes of eternal Time, and, like the ancient divinity Time, it is a power ruling the universe: ἣν καὶ πάντας περιέχειν τοὺς κόσμους.

It is interesting to note that, in Hippolytus' account the adjective ἀγήρω has preserved its ancient Ionian flection. This means that the word must have been used in this same form by Anaximander himself and that Hippolytus' mention of it is a literal quotation. As ἀγήραος or ἀγήρως must have been a traditional epithet of the ancient Time-deity, as we can still see in the Orphic texts, we must conclude that Anaximander designated his ἄπειρον by the attribute that used to be distinctive for the ancient Time-deity. From this it is not a far cry to assuming that the ἄπειρον may have been nothing different from the all-embracing Χρόνος itself.

The divine character of the ἄπειρον is confirmed by what Aristotle says about Anaximander in *Phys.* III 4, 203 b 6 - 15: the ἄπειρον is unborn and imperishable (ἀγένητον καὶ ἄφθαρτον); it is immortal and indestructable (ἀθάνατον καὶ ἀνώλεθρον); it embraces and rules all things (περιέχειν ἅπαντα καὶ πάντα κυβερνᾶν); therefore it is τὸ θεῖον: the supreme divine power.

The very short lines that have been transmitted to us as the only surviving fragment of Anaximander's writings (DK 12 B 1), may be interpreted in the light of what we have found. The ἄπειρον is the basic principle and the root of all things, for all things rise out of it, and into it they return. This taking-up and losing of independent existence is for all things as the working of an ordeal: they must do penance for coming into independence by perishing and returning to their first origin, thus making room for others to come into existence. This way of doing justice has been ordered by the supreme ruling deity of Time; it is, in the words given by Simplicius: κατὰ τὴν τοῦ χρόνου τάξιν. Though it would be easy to explain this as meaning 'in the sequence of time', in the light of the mythical parallels we have seen above it seems better to take it as meaning 'by order of Time'. It was the all-embracing Time-deity who ordered that this should be ordeal and expiation: things coming into independent existence had to perish out of it, thus passing judgement on one another.

There is every reason to assume that Simplicius, who gives us the words of Anaximander, did not see the mythical symbols in the words he quoted. Simplicius did not intend us to understand τὸ ἄπειρον as having the attributes of an ancient Time-deity. He interpreted the terms used by Anaximander as more poetical expressions conveying a meaning that could as well be put in more abstract and Aristotelean words. This may be seen from the explanations he adds to his account of Anaximander's theories. In spite of the Aristotelean interpretations given by Simplicius, the original meaning of Anaximander's words has survived thanks to Simplicius' literal quoting of them.

Summing up we may say that in very ancient mythical images a supreme divine power is found described as Χρόνος, embracing and ruling the whole universe. This divinity is all-embracing in both its temporal and spatial aspects; it has power over the process of coming-to-be and passing-away, and it keeps hold of the boundaries of the universe. In both aspects it may be said to rule from beginning to end. For this reason it is identified with the outmost boundary of the heavens. This boundary is unlimited because it is outermost, and at the same time because it is a sphere, which, going round, makes all things return to their beginnings.

In the descriptions of the ancient Time-deity both the spatial and the temporal elements are found. The Unbounded has unlimited extension or spatial infinity, and at the same time temporal infinity, seen as an unending series of succeeding events. These succeeding events form the life-cycle of the universe. In this life-cycle not only birth and dying of plants and animals are comprehended but also the life of minerals and mountains, of seas and stars, in a word, all that moves. The sum total of all these moving things was considered to be a whole, moving in a cyclical rhythm, under the sway of Time.

This mythical description of cyclical Time may be regarded as an early attempt at explaining cosmic life. It was, as such, a forerunner of later theories about the evolution of life. This evolution was explained, in the mythical vision, as developing by order of a deity called Χρόνος or Time, ruling the cycle of events and 'finding out all things', i.e. bringing them into existence. Χρόνος or Time is described as spatially and temporally infinite. It is the forerunner of Anaximander's ἄπειρον.

Returning now to the ἀποφθέγματα ascribed to Thales of Miletus it is not difficult to see that the seven ἀποφθέγματα as a whole contain a description of this eternal and unbounded Time-deity. This Time-deity is a God uncreated, living immanently in the universe and in all its life-processes, and at the same time embracing it outwardly. The universe is created by this God. Outside the universe unbounded space is found, filled by the presence of omnipotent Time only. All Nature's processes are under the rule of a blind necessity, ἀνάγκη, which nevertheless must submit to the cyclical order of Time who rules all things with wisdom and justice. Time is present everywhere; this is expressed by the words: intelligence (Νοῦς) moves fastest for it penetrates all things. The assertion of the second line that the cosmos has been created by God, is repeated in a more specific way in the sixth line by the words: Time is wisest, for it brings into existence all things. At the end, the description of God with which the verses started, is amplified in the expression: God is that which has neither beginning nor end.

Most important in this description are the spatial aspects of this divinity. Time is the creator and ruler of a cosmos which is pervaded by an omnipresent intelligence or Νοῦς. Afterwards, in the Pythagorean school, even cyclical Time was described in spatial terms as an all-embracing σφαῖρα.

The attributes of the ancient Time-deity make it seem very probable that behind Anaximander's ἄπειρον may be hidden the ancient Χρόνος, God of the heavens. The ἄπειρον, at any rate, has the qualities of Χρόνος: ἀγήραος, ἀίδιος, ἀθάνατος, ἀνώλεθρος, never-aging, eternal, immortal, and indestructable. In an expression which in current Greek means 'infinite' or 'infinity' in the spatial sense the addition of temporal qualities might ask for an explanation. The key to this seemingly incongruous way of adding adjectives to a name is given by the fact that, at bottom, the ancient Time-deity is described by these qualities. The ἄπειρον even has the same function, for it is said to be the root or principle (ἀρχή) of the cycle of events. These descriptions are found in Aristotle as well as in the doxographic tradition (see DK 12 A 9 - 15). In these statements we must distinguish carefully between explanations from the standpoint of later philosophies, and descriptions which may give a more or less literal account of Anaximander's ideas. When for instance, τὸ ἄπειρον is said to be quite the same thing as ὕλη, the statement (DK 12 A 14, from Aëtius) is Aristotelean in character. When, on the contrary, the ἄπειρον is described as 'never-aging' and 'eternal', we recognize the authentic mythological attributes. In the case of ἀγήραος even the grammatical form reveals the authenticity of the statement. In the same way we must recognize as authentic the statement by Aristotle *(Phys.* 203 b

7

6 - 13), that the ἄπειρον 'embraces and rules all things' (περιέχειν ἅπαντα καὶ πάντα κυβερνᾶν), and that it was, to Anaximander, τὸ θεῖον. The description is that of the old divinity of Time disguised in philosophical garments by Anaximander.

Pointing out the early history of the concept of ἄπειρον may have its importance even as an explanation of the background of certain Neoplatonic theories. It is true that we cannot say of the Neoplatonic theories that they are founded on mythical connotations, but they do betray a way of thinking, which must have been familiar with mythical structures. The relation between myth and philosophy has, in Plotinus, a double aspect. In the first place it is historical, because Plotinus often gives his ideas, e.g. on infinity and emanation, in the form of comments on Platonic and Presocratic thought. Secondly it is systematic, because even in Plotinus' own way of systematic thinking, a direct influence of mythical symbols can be observed. It must not be deemed impossible that some of the old mythical images should have lived on well into the times of Neoplatonism. As to the ἄπειρον, there is in a certain sense an interruption in its history in the centuries that follow Aristotle. Due to the influence of Aristotle the concept of ἄπειρον in these centuries has a predominantly negative ring, because infinity is taken as indeterminedness and identified with matter and unfulfilled potency. The later Platonic schools more and more insist on the idea of positive infinity as a source for all things that emanate from it, in the same way in which, for Anaximander, the ἄπειρον was the source from which all things came into existence and into which they returned. This last element, the returning of all things into their unbounded and eternal source also offers a remarkable parallel between neoplatonic thought and the theories of Anaximander.

The interpretation of Anaximander's philosophy in modern literature has generally moved on the level of speculative thinking. This had the disadvantage of explaining Anaximander in terms of later philosophical systems (see e.g. Kahn 1960, Seligmann 1962). It was Cornford who for the first time offered a consistent historical interpretation (1912, 1936, 1952 II). Cornford noticed that in the very first attempts at a philosophical theory about the universe we can trace "the persistence in philosophy of the primitive circularity of time" (1952 II, 169). About Anaximander's apeiron he says (ib. 171): "The Boundless is the source (ἀρχή) from which the world arose, and it remains outside the world as the 'eternal' background of the cycle of change and becoming."

Once we have seen the mythical background of the ἄπειρον, it is difficult to tell where the myth ends and where philosophy comes in. The two go together a long way. It is not easy to draw a sharp line, but at any rate the development is from a mythical symbol to a metaphysical concept. Later theories make it clear that, in the long run, the concept of ἄπειρον left the field of mythical symbols and was taken as expressing a cosmic theory, the elements of which could be reasoned out mostly by means of mathematical descriptions. The question remains if it was Anaximander who made the decisive step.

The only text that has come down to us in Anaximander's own words contains a short account of his cosmic ἀδικία -doctrine: there is eternal Justice in this universe under the reign of Time. This theory, at least, is not likely to have been the result of philosophical speculation. Cyclical Time, doing justice to all particular things, too strongly resembles the old all-embracing Time-deity to make it probable that this theory was an invention of Anaximander's. Apart from this fragment we have only the statements by later philosophical authors on Anaximander's theories, all of which have a recognizable element of later philosophies in them. Both Simplicius and Hippolytus say that Anaximander was the first to use the term ἀρχή and that, by this term, he meant the ὑποκείμενον. The second part of this statement has the ring of Aristotle's method, who declares every forerunner to have invented part of his own theory. The first part, however, must be claimed as authentic. It is not at all improbable that the first Milesians should have put themselves the question of the first origin of all things, and given it a philosophic form. Maybe, by doing so, they were the first de-mythologizers. They left the myth for what it was and tried to replace its symbols by abstract terms. It is a very common trait in the Milesian school to ask for the first source or the first principle of things; according to Simplicius (*Gr. Ph.* 11 a), Anaximander was the first who called it ἀρχή (cf. Lumpe 1955). There is good reason for assuming that Anaximander and his teacher Thales were the first to formulate this question about a first principle for all things. By doing so they probably were the beginners of Greek philosophy.

It is not very clear if we are to consider Anaximander at the same time as the very first metaphysician. If we were to interpret his theories in that sense, the ἄπειρον would have to be considered an abstract concept, not indicating in the first place the starting-point of the evolution of things, but rather the root or principle of their existence. This principle then would be a half transcendent, half immanent

9

root or ground of all things. As Anaximander is known to have used the term ἀρχή, the scanty lines which have survived have opened a wide field for metaphysical speculations. Nietzsche and Rohde (see *Gr. Ph.* 11 a) elaborated, on the authority of Anaximander, a complex doctrine, which, however, was founded on a text in which a word (ἀλλήλοις) was missing. The text on which they worked can be found in Mullach's *Philosophorum Graecorum Fragmenta* (Parisiis 1857, vol. I, 240). In their interpretation the concept of ἄπειρον was the core of a metaphysical theory, having a well-elaborated formula on absolute and relative being. On the absolute being infringement is made by particular beings with their fragmented existence. For this infringement they suffer punishment by losing their independent existence, which passes on to others while they themselves pass away into the Boundless from which they emerged. Thus, in terms of vital drama, the opposition was described between eternal being, which supports its own existence and the being of individuals who committed their most reckless crime by coming into existence. This crime or ἀδικία is a crime against the majesty of the ἄπειρον. The punishment supposes an order of time, for it needs an unending series of new beings superseding former beings. Over them all, the ἄπειρον reigns supremely as their transcendent principle.

Maybe this interpretation was all the more attractive, because it was philosophical and mythical at once. It is doubtful whether the theory was elaborated by Anaximander in this explicit way, because this interpretation supposes a well-developed system of abstract thought, which is not likely to have existed at the very beginning of philosophical speculation.

A fairer chance must be reserved for another interpretation of the concept of ἄπειρον. Just as a too metaphysical interpretation of Anaximander's theory is unhistorical, in the same way an interpretation in which Anaximander's ἄπειρον becomes the equivalent of the infinite space of the atomists must be considered an anachronism. The idea of an infinite space as the atomists took it could, only rise in a time when a rectilinear conception of space had come to dominate. Though we cannot trace in particulars the development which led to this conception, we see from Aristotle's discussion of infinite space in *De caelo* that by Aristotle's time mathematics, in this respect, had developed into the system that later-on, due to Euclid, was to become sacred. What is most striking in Aristotle's discussions is the incongruity between rectilinear infinity and sphericity of the universe.

When we compare Plato's descriptions of the universe in the Timaeus with those of Aristotle, we see that to Plato there was no problem of rectilinear infinity. Plato's universe is spherical. Going further back we see that before Plato a practically uniform tradition is found about the sphericity of the universe. The well-rounded sphere of being of Parmenides is its best-known example. Pursuing this line further back to Anaximander, we are entitled to suppose that to Anaximander as well the universe must have had a spherical shape. As we have seen, he probably identified his all-embracing Time with the sphere of the outermost heaven, as also the Pythagoreans did. The supposition is further confirmed by the fact that Anaximander described the earth as being in the centre, at an equal distance in all directions from this outermost heaven (DK 12 A 11): τὴν δὲ γῆν μένουσαν διὰ τὴν ὁμοίαν πάντων ἀπόστασιν. In Anaximander's view this explained the stability of our earth.

If, then, Anaximander declared the heavens to be unbounded, his infinity must be thought of as the infinity of a sphere which, out-wardly, is not bounded by anything different from itself. It seemed impossible that the universe, as something undetermined, should float in an empty space. Inwardly the sphere is determined as to balance and as to distances. It must have been the sort of universe as was described by Parmenides (28 B 8, vs. 44): from the centre in all directions well in balance. Because the universe is taken as that which contains all things, and because there is an infinity of things in un-bounded time, there is no problem as to the question how the universe may be well determined and unbounded at the same time. This question is simply not asked. Nor is there any need for breaking out from this spherical universe into an infinite rectilinear empty space.

Though it is tempting to explain all this in modern mathematical terms, this would probably mean asking questions that were not asked by Anaximander. The infinity of a spherical universe can be ex-plained by the example of a traveller who covers infinite distances by going straight on all the time on the surface of a globe; nevertheless the globe itself is a finite globe. Only a theory that brings out the difference between three- and four-dimensional spaces can eliminate incongruities in the theory of a boundless and yet spherical universe. It is not probable that these post-Euclidean concepts were alive in the pre-Euclidean period to which Anaximander belongs. However, it is not too much to suppose that, for Anaximander, the theory of a spherical universe was not affected by difficulties coming from rectilinear mathematics. Though it is putting it too strongly to say that Anaximander had an implicit intuition of the curvature of space, and that, in this respect, pre-Euclidean and post-Euclidean mathematics coincide, there may be some point in the remarks made by Cornford on this subject ('*The Invention of Space*', 1936). If we cannot define Anaximander's space as non-Euclidean in the modern, technical sense, it is, at all events, not Euclidean in the sense that it is not to be explained by rectilinear mathematics. Cornford is right in comparing it with the descriptions given by Parmenides (28 B 8, verses 46-49) and Plato (*Theaet*. 180 E).

As we have only some four lines by Anaximander in the original version, there is a peculiar problem in stating what exactly his doctrines were. With the exception of these four lines all our information is indirect and formulated in terms of later philosophy. Aristotle, e.g., (DK 12 A 15) thinks he may regard Anaximander as his own forerunner by interpreting the ἄπειρον as a first vague notion of the concept of ὕλη. Simplicius, following Theophrastus, gives analogous comments: the ἄπειρον, he says, is the substrate, ὑποκείμενον, of all things, clearly meaning Aristotelean matter (DK 12 A 9, 9a). Aëtius declares without hesitation: the ἄπειρον is no other thing than matter (DK 12 A 14). Least influenced by later thought are the statements by Plutarch and by Hippolytus (DK 12 A 10 and 11).

Having eliminated from all these statements the technical terms belonging to later thought we are left with a small number of reliable conclusions. Mostly those conclusions affirm only in a general way that certain theories and certain patterns of thought are present in Anaximander. One conclusion is about the principle of all things or ἀρχή. Anaximander did put to himself the question of a general first principle. As has been said above, we must be careful not to explain this in the sense of Aristotelean hylemorphism. A second reliable conclusion was that this general principle of all things was stated by Anaximander to be an ἄπειρον. In this case, too, there is no justification for explaining Anaximander's principle in logical or ontological terms, in the way Melissos and Aristotle built up their reasonings about the concept of infinity; nor are we justified in representing the ἄπειρον as constructed along Euclidean lines.

The statements by Plutarch and by Hippolytus, which may be considered more authentic, contain a description of the ἄπειρον in which both its temporal and spatial aspects are adequately commented upon. Plutarch (following Theophrastus) says that the ἄπειρον is the ultimate and complete cause of all coming-to-be and passing-away. All the heavens and all the innumerable worlds have come forth from this first cause. The term given for this coming forth is ἀποκεκρίσθαι as if it were a splitting-off. Now this splitting-off is subject to a cyclical return: all things are reduced to their first cause ἐξ ἀπείρου αἰῶνος, 'from boundless eternity'. The expression unites spatial infinity with boundless time, as was the case with the ancient Time-deity. In an analogous way the statement by Hippolytus has the two aspects. Hippolytus says, that the ἄπειρον 'embraces all heavens' (spatial aspect); and: "he (Anaximander) calls it χρόνος, time, as he wants to make clear that coming-to-be, being and passing-away are fixed and determined".

There is a remarkable similarity between Anaximander's theories and more or less extensive passages in Plato's *Timaeus*. In *Tim.* 52 A Plato speaks about the causes of material being. There are three of them: the eternal ideas, their imitations and a third element that must be classified as a secondary cause in the Platonic sense of necessary condition. This third element is described by Plato predominantly in spatial terms.

He calls it χώρα, space, and further on he gives it the names of τιθήνη, nursing mother (52 D), δεξαμένη, receiving mould (53 A), and ὑποδοχή, receptacle (51 A). Plato intends it to be a kind of spatial substrate, with the strict reserve, however, that it does not itself enter into the things that come into existence as a constitutive part of them. This strict reserve made by Plato is probably an indication of the Eleatic origin of χώρα as a kind of μὴ ὄν, as we shall see later (ch. 8). Nevertheless, many of the elements in the description of this χώρα have a markedly Ionian character, e.g. when Plato describes it as the cause of the chaotic movements in the original mixture of the elements (53 A). The spatial connotations in the description strongly remind us of Anaximander's theories.

The ἄπειρον of Anaximander and the ὑποδοχή of Plato are treated in the same way by Aristotle. Aristotle is very apt to see the theories of his predecessors as foreshadowing his own philosophy, and he is ready to neglect the differences. As was explained above, there is no justification for explaining the ἄπειρον of Anaximander as a kind of ὕλη. It means modelling Anaximander's visions on an Aristotelean pattern when we say that Anaximander had a theory, in which a kind of undetermined spatiality was related to things becoming as an eternal principle to temporal things, subject to passing-away. The difference

13

is that Anaximander's vision was cosmic, whereas Aristotle's theory is intended as a theoretical ontology. More important still, the ἄπειρον of Anaximander is highest in the scale of beings, whereas Aristotle's matter is lowest.

When mythical symbols come to be explained in philosophical terms, the process must be called a rationalisation. That we may suppose this way of thinking fully present in Anaximander, may be illustrated by a fortuitous notice in Plutarch's *Symposion* (DK 12 A 30).

Plutarch mentions a tradition, according to which the veneration of Poseidon as ancestor had sprung from the conviction that man had been born from the waters of the sea. In the dialogue the speaker then says, this means that man and fish had their origin side by side and not the one from the other. Now this, as is explained in the dialogue, was changed by Anaximander into a theory, according to which man had developed from fishes. This means, that Anaximander transposed the mythical story into a theory of evolution. This may be considered a typical example of the rationalisation to which the myths were being subjected by the first philosophers. The presence in the first generation of philosophers of this way of thinking confirms our explanations as to the ἄπειρον of Anaximander. This concept must have been inherited by the Milesians from a mythical tradition and have been rationalized by Anaximander into a philosophical principle.

BIBLIOGRAPHY
(in chronological order)

Schulz 1907
Eisler 1910
Cornford 1912
Dörfler 1912, 1916
Brendel 1936
Cornford 1936
Tumarkin 1943
Croissant 1944
Kraus 1949
Frankfort 1949
Solmsen 1950, II
Cornford 1952, II
Hölscher 1953
Ballauff 1953

Gigon 1954
Loenen 1954
Kirk 1955
Lumpe 1955
de Corte 1958
Kahn 1958, 1960
Seligmann 1962
Stokes 1962
Classen 1962
West 1963
Burkert 1963
Boeder 1964
Schwabl 1964
Gottschalk 1965

CHAPTER II

XENOPHANES AND PARMENIDES

The oldest myths dealt with the problem of the origin of things, long before any form of philosophical abstraction had been attempted. In the myths that are concerned with this problem generally two characteristics can be observed: (1) the connection of causal sequences is explained in temporal form; (2) there is no sharp distinction between temporal and spatial concepts. The first characteristic mainly consists in that, in the myths, what is first is considered as cause. What is oldest is, by that same fact, also the first cause. Probably the first of Thales' sayings, that 'God is oldest of all things' must be explained on this line. In the development of myths, a certain phase must have occurred, in which symbolic figures were introduced into them, or, at least, in which the symbolic meanings of the myth were getting more pronounced. This was probably so with the old Time-deity, when he was described as generating all things and embracing the universe.

Although, as a result of this development, a more pronounced way of symbolic expression is found, yet this Time-deity may in no way be considered as a philosophical abstraction. On the contrary, he is identified very literally with the outermost heavens, whose revolution determines the fate of things, as well as birth and death to all beings. The adjective 'all-embracing' must be taken as having, in a very literal sense, a spatial meaning. The second of the characteristics mentioned above consists of the connection of these spatial attributes with the temporal ones. They are more or less melted together in one complex description.

The dividing-line between myth and philosophy is reached when, for the first time, rational distinctions are brought into play, and when attempts are made to coordinate the data of the myth in a coherent system. These attempts are recognizable by the preference for one of the many qualities that together make up the complex description of the mythical being. Anaximander fixes his preference upon the quality of being 'Unbounded' or ἄπειρον. The crossing of the borderline between myth and philosophy is, in the case of the Greek thinkers, marked by a very strong process of rationalisation. By this process the data of the myth are transformed into abstract principles. From these abstract principles, or from one of them, all the rest is derived by a line of reasoning which explains how, from a first cause, a process of evolution led up to the world as we know it.

As we saw above, at least two characteristics may be said to have been inherent in Anaximander's picture of the universe. His description of it implied a kind of geometrical description of space. The world-space, according to Anaximander, was infinite, and at the same time Anaximander said the earth was at equal distance from the boundaries of the cosmos. This implies, more or less, a spherical pattern in the description of the cosmos. This spherical description of the universe has persisted up to Plato, but it is contrasted by the rectilinear unending universe of Democritus. As we shall see, this probably corresponds to a change in mathematical thought, started by the problems of Zeno on the concept of infinity. After Plato a rectilinear infinity has come to replace definitely the old spherical descriptions of the cosmos.

The second characteristic of Anaximander's thought was his search for a first principle or ἀρχή. Though his ἄπειρον palpably has all the inherited attributes of the old Time-Deity, nevertheless Anaximander interprets it as, in a philosophical sense, the first principle of all things. This principle is present both temporally and spatially in all things. Every phase in the evolution of the cosmos and in birth and death of all living beings, is under the rule of this omnipresent ἄπειρον.

The two characteristics mentioned persist in the philosophies following on Anaximander's: mythical symbols are rationalized into abstractions, and the description of space implies a latent mathematical way of thinking.

A. XENOPHANES

Just as Anaximander had been the first to mark out the concept of ἀρχή for philosophical use, so Xenophanes was the first to introduce the concept of 'Unity' or 'the One', 'τὸ Ἕν'. Both Plato and Aristotle testify that Xenophanes originated the philosophical problem of how to combine unity and plurality in the description of being.

16

In the *Sophist* (242 D), Plato gives a short summary of the then existing theories that were intended as statements concerning the whole of things. Plato classifies them according to the number of their first principles. Some theories have three first principles, some two, and the Eleatics assume that all things are one:

τὸ δὲ παρ' ἡμῖν 'Ελεατικὸν ἔθνος, ἀπὸ Ξενοφάνους τε καὶ ἔτι πρόσθεν ἀρξάμενον ὡς ἑνὸς ὄντος τῶν πάντων καλουμένων οὕτω διεξέρχεται τοῖς μύθοις.

(The Eleatic Stranger is speaking:) "From Xenophanes onwards – and even before him – the Eleatic folks in my country have explained the myths in the sense that the so-called whole of all being is One."

Auguste Diès, in his translation of the Sophist, takes this as meaning: "la gent Eleatique, issue de Xenophane et de plus haut encore" etc., as if the participle ἀρξάμενον was intended to say that the Eleatic School had been started by Xenophanes. Grammatically, it is more correct to take it as an illustration of the action of the principal verb, which is διεξέρχεται, rather than as attributive to ἔθνος, as it is a participle of the aorist. As to the meaning of the sentence, there is another argument for our translation. It seems doubtful whether, even before Xenophanes, thinkers of the Eleatic caste can be found, whereas it is not so very impossible to trace some preparations of Eleatic doctrines in earlier thinkers. It is e.g. not a very long way from the all-embracing ἄπειρον of Anaximander to the Eleatic picture of a unified cosmos. In this sense, Anaximander might have been considered by Plato as a forerunner of the Eleatic theories, though Anaximander himself had nothing to do with the Eleatic school as such. It seems better, therefore, to translate the lines quoted in the sense that 'the Eleatic theories go back to Xenophanes and even to earlier thinkers'.

The difference is not a great one, and, as far as we know, Xenophanes must at all events be considered the first thinker who formulated a theory starting from the concept of 'the One' as a first principle (cf. Jaeger, *Theol.* 215).

It is not only Plato who speaks in this sense about Xenophanes. Aristotle (*Met.* A 5, 986 b 21 - 25 = *Gr. Ph.* 70 b) has the same statement:

Ξενοφάνης δὲ πρῶτος τούτων ἑνίσας . . . οὐθὲν διεσαφήνισεν, οὐδὲ τῆς φύσεως τούτων οὐδετέρας ἔοικε θιγεῖν, ἀλλ' εἰς τὸν ὅλον οὐρανὸν ἀποβλέψας τὸ ἓν εἶναί φησι τὸν θεόν.

"Now Xenophanes was the first of these thinkers to unify all things, but nevertheless he explained nothing by it, and he touched on neither principle [i.e. ὕλη and/or λόγος as a basic pattern for the explanation of unity]; he only says with a view to the whole of heavens, that its unity is constituted by the Godhead."

The lines quoted form more or less the starting-point for Aristotle's account of the thinkers who assumed the first principle of things to be one. They follow after an account of thinkers who took the principles to be two or more. In general, assuming two ultimate principles is more to the taste of Aristotle, as it seems to confirm his own views. For the same reason, Aristotle has little sympathy with the Eleatics.

Only Parmenides is shown some appreciation, because as Aristotle states it, he was constrained by the evidence of the senses to posit a duality of first causes, as e.g. the hot and the cold, taken as fire and earth. For this reason, Aristotle says, it seems as if Parmenides "spoke somewhat more like a person who keeps his eyes open (μᾶλλον βλέπων)." It is open to question whether Aristotle was right on all points in explaining Parmenides' intentions as he does, but at any rate he saw the difference between the two layers of thinking described by Parmenides: the metaphysical, where true Being is discussed, and the field of the senses where mortal insight in vain tries to establish certainty. Coming to Xenophanes and Melissos, however, there is only a sneer in Aristotle's words: "When setting out for the present investigation, we shall have to put aside the Eleatics, as has been said, and most of all those two of them, Xenophanes and Melissos, who take too primitive a course". (*Met.* A 5, 986 b 25 - 34).

This way of speaking occurs very frequently in Aristotle's treatment of doctrines of other philosophers. Aristotle thinks of himself as a discoverer of an ultimate truth, or at least of a decisive theory. From this standpoint he judges his predecessors. In a critical sense it is very important to recognize this self-assured way of speaking in the texts of Aristotle. We must pay attention to this to our taste somewhat arrogant tone, because it enables us to distinguish historically reliable from unreliable information. We can feel sure about the information, whenever Aristotle's text displays some irritation. In cases where he bestows praise on theories of other philosophers, we must suspect him of falsifying them, for Aristotle is in the habit of supposing all other people to have thought in Aristotelean patterns, that is to say, if they had a sound way of thinking.

The fact that Aristotle does not recognize Xenophanes and Melissos as true philosophers, and, accordingly, deals with them contemptuously, is significant. It enhances our chance of finding authentic statements on these early Presocratics because it means that Aristotle did not feel able to interpret their theories in terms of his own philosophy. In Xenophanes' case there is another reason for the possibility of interpreting Aristotle's statement as authentic. The account given by Aristotle betrays in its wording the old mythical way of representing the cosmic first principle:

ἀλλ' εἰς τὸν ὅλον κόσμον ἀποβλέψας τὸ ἓν εἶναί φησι τὸν θεόν.

"but, with a view to the whole cosmos, he says that the Godhead is its unity."

This reminds us of the mythical description of a first cause of all things, a divine being embracing all heavens. It is the same mythical figure that formed the background from which Anaximander's philosophy emerged.

There is, furthermore, a certain parallelism between Aristotle's statements on Anaximander and on Xenophanes. In both cases Aristotle's statement is about a first principle that had divine attributes. About Anaximander he says: καὶ τοῦτ' εἶναι τὸ θεῖον, 'and, according to him, this was God'. *(Phys.* 203 b 13), and about Xenophanes: τὸ ἓν εἶναί φησι τὸν θεόν (*Met.* 986 b 24) 'the One, he said, was God'.

By a process of rationalization, Anaximander transformed the inherited mythical deity into a cosmic principle. He made the spatial aspects of this principle, the ἄπειρον, prevail more or less over the temporal aspects. We find this same process in Xenophanes. Starting from the same pre-philosophic presuppositions, both philosophers develop their system into a rationalising view of the universe. Compared with Anaximander, Xenophanes goes a step further. As far as sources go, he must have been the first to formulate the concept of τὸ ἕν. In principle, what is described by this term must have been the same as what Anaximander meant by τὸ ἄπειρον. Xenophanes, however, emphasizes a new aspect when he calls his first principle 'the One', τὸ Ἕν.

The term possibly betrays influence of number-speculations. In that case Xenophanes' theory is the signal of a growing influence of the very early mathematical thinking of the Greeks. At all events it was a step further on the way to abstract thinking. From now on, the concept of τὸ ἕν has a growing importance in metaphysical speculation.

The parallelism between Anaximander and Xenophanes is further supported by the fact that both came from Ionia. Xenophanes had to

fly from his native town Colophon, when it came under Persian rule
(± 540 B.C.). From that moment his was a wandering life 'through
the land of Hellas', as he expressed it in a distich (DK 21 B 8). This
same fragment proves that his thought remained rooted in his native
soil. This is also clear from the verses in which he describes how he is
sitting by the fire one winter asking a stranger: "how old were you,
when the Persians came?" (21 B 22). With Anaximander he shares
a great respect for a highest Godhead. Anaximander described this
Godhead as providence doing justice to all beings within the cycle of
time. Xenophanes says about it:

οὖλος ὁρᾶι, οὖλος δὲ νοεῖ, οὖλος δέ τ' ἀκούει.

"With all of himself he sees, with all of himself he thinks, with all
of himself he hears" (DK 21 B 24).

The term οὖλος indicates the all-embracing character of the *one*
Godhead. Accepting the account by Aristotle quoted above as authentic, we may suppose the inherited identification with the outermost
heaven to be present in this verse as a background. This corresponds
well with the term οὖλος, and the same applies to the description of
B 23:

εἷς θεός, ἔν τε θεοῖσι καὶ ἀνθρώποισι μέγιστος,
οὔτι δέμας θνητοῖσι ὁμοίιος οὐδὲ νόημα.

"One is the Godhead, greatest among gods and men,
not like mortals, neither in shape nor in thought."

The two lines of B 26 even go a step further. Xenophanes here
insists on the immutability of this supreme Godhead. By doing so
he definitely abandons the figure of a Time-deity who rules the cycle
of things and is its embodiment:

αἰεὶ δ'ἐν ταὐτῶι μίμνει κινούμενος οὐδέν
οὐδὲ μετέρχεσθαί μιν ἐπιπρέπει ἄλλοτε ἄλληι.

"Eternally he remains in the same place, unmoved, and it does
not befit him to go now here then there." In these lines we find the
earliest formula for the immutability of the divine first principle of
things. This conception of Xenophanes must have been the preparation
of the doctrine, proclaimed so emphatically by Parmenides.

Immutability may be regarded as the temporal aspect of the
unity of the first principle. Anaximander described this unity mostly
in spatial terms. Even the term τὸ ἄπειρον has a spatial sense. The
cycle of time had, as to its unity, a foundation in this spatial first
principle. In Xenophanes we see the first attempt to reduce the divine
first principle of things to a unity, even in its temporal aspect.

20

Up to this point our exposition of Xenophanes' theories rests on the accounts given by Plato and Aristotle, and on the fragments that have been preserved in the original form. We took Aristotle's account at its literal value, because the depreciatory attitude of Aristotle towards Xenophanes makes it very probable that he did not undertake to interpret Xenophanes' theories on the patterns of his own way of thinking. We should all the more be prepared for finding this un-historical way of interpreting in all sources of later date. Among these later sources there is the pseudo-Aristotelean treatise *On Melissus, Xenophanes and Gorgias*.

This treatise gives short summaries of the various theories by Melissus, Xenophanes and Gorgias, but throughout in an unmistak-ably Aristotelean version. For this reason it is generally considered source-material that is to be handled very cautiously (cf. Loenen 1959, 179 - 180). It has left its traces in certain later doxographic traditions, notably in Simplicius, as was reasoned out by Werner Jaeger for one very striking example (*Theol.* 214, note 64).

Alongside this tradition, influenced by MXG, other and more reliable accounts have come down to us in works by later doxo-graphers. We found an example of this more reliable tradition in our first chapter, where an account by Hippolytus on Anaximander was analysed (DK 12 A 11). Our analysis showed it to be authentic. Diels, in his *Doxographi*, tried to show that the more reliable infor-mation must derive from Theophrastus, but it is difficult to distinguish reliable texts from unreliable ones by this criterion only. It is necessary to analyse the texts for each separate case.

Hippolytus gives this account on Xenophanes (DK 21 A 33 = *Gr. Ph.* 70 d):

Λέγει δὲ ὅτι οὐδὲν γίνεται οὐδὲ φθείρεται οὐδὲ κινεῖται, καὶ ὅτι ἓν τὸ πᾶν ἐστιν ἔξω μεταβολῆς. Φησὶ δὲ καὶ τὸν θεὸν εἶναι ἀΐδιον καὶ ἕνα, καὶ ὅμοιον πάντηι, καὶ πεπερασμένον, καὶ σφαιροειδῆ, καὶ πᾶσι τοῖς μορίοις αἰσθητικόν.

On the whole we may consider this account as authentic, because it agrees with the information we can gather from the texts by Plato and Aristotle. It is not difficult to see then that there was a consider-able parallelism between the doctrines of Anaximander and Xeno-phanes. Both had assumed the universe to be One, and to this One as a first principle they had attributed the characteristics of the highest divinity. The difference is that Xenophanes preferred the concept of being One to all other characteristics.

21

The parallelism can be brought out by an analysis of the two statements by Hippolytus on Anaximander and Xenophanes.

The divine first principle

according to ANAXIMANDER: (DK 12 A 11)	according to XENOPHANES: (DK 21 A 33)
(1) is eternal and never-aging ἀΐδιον εἶναι καὶ ἀγήρω he also calls it Time λέγει δὲ χρόνον	(1) is eternal ἀΐδιον
(2) it embraces all worlds πάντας περιέχειν τοὺς κόσμους	(2) is One (ἕνα) (when compared with 21 B 24: οὖλος, this may also bear on the One as a unifying function)
(3) it is unbounded, ἄπειρον This term 'ἄπειρον' has an im- plicit notion of mathematical space: the earth is the centre: τὴν γῆν ... μένουσαν διὰ τὴν ὁμοίαν πάντων ἀπόστασιν	(3) it is equal in all directions and spherical: ὅμοιον πάντηι σφαιροειδῆ

The first point deals with the temporal aspect, the second with the spatial aspect, the third with the mathematical notion of space implicit in it. There is another point of parallelism but only to a certain extent, for at the same time there is a remarkable difference: the first principle of Xenophanes may have been not only ἄπειρον, but also πεπερασμένον. It is true that in this crude form the statement is not found in Hippolytus. Hippolytus only says that to Xenophanes the divine first principle was πεπερασμένον, well-determined. But we can say with considerable certainty that Xenophanes attributed both characteristics to his first principle, as we shall see below, from a comparison with the statements by Aristotle and Simplicius (21 A 30 and 31).

As to the earliest thinkers, it is not quite sure that the two concepts are to be thought of as contrary to one another in an ontological sense. This contrast has an Aristotelean structure. Historically it could not be formulated until the Pythagoreans and Plato had set up the whole problem of unity and multiplicity, and tried to solve it by assuming one unchanging form for the many different material beings, character-ized by it. In this philosophy, form is eternal and well-determined, in

22

contrast to matter, which is ἄπειρον or wholly undetermined. In
the development that led up to this doctrine we can follow the various
stages of a struggle for maintaining the old sacrosanct unity of all
things. Its last champion was Parmenides. Probably in contrast to the
Pythagorean school, Parmenides defended the unity of all things in an
all-embracing Being, and he did so in terms that betray a religious
veneration for this highest principle. The Pythagoreans were the first to
introduce a cleavage in the up to then homogeneous universe. They were
dualists and set the One against the Two as a principle of manifoldness.

Bearing this historical development in mind, we are no longer
authorized to put the opposition form-indeterminateness as early as
Xenophanes. Moreover, it is not impossible to explain how, to Xenophanes, the divine unity of things could have at the same time the
predicate ἄπειρον, unbounded (or undetermined, as later philosophers
took it), and πεπερασμένον, well-determined. The most ancient symbol
of perfection is the sphere (cf. Brendel, 1936). A sphere is, from its
centre, well-determined in every direction. Notwithstanding, its outer
circumference may be infinite, if the sphere is identical with cosmic
space. The two suppositions are incompatible, because, if the radius
of a sphere is actually infinite, there is no longer a centre, and the
structure of the sphere as such is lost. But, if this be forgotten, or if
we fail to ask the question, as the Presocratics may have done, the
outer surface of the sphere may be considered as boundary and none
the less as infinite, or, put another way, the sphere itself may be
considered as having a centre (the earth) and a fixed radius, and being
infinite in dimension. At the same time, as it remains a sphere, it will
be perfectly determined without admitting even the slightest anomaly.
Thus, in cosmology, a conception is arrived at in which infinity goes
together with being well determined. The universe is spherical and
has a centre, the earth. Its spherical shape, as in all spheres, is determined from the centre in all directions. The surface of this sphere is
the divine outermost heaven. It is a remarkable fact that in Aristotle's
work 'On the heavens' (De caelo), the universe is described as having,
in the outward direction, an increasing degree of perfection, until we
come to what Ross calls 'the soul of the first heaven', encompassing
and imparting movement to all the heavens (De caelo 279 a 18 - b 3.
Cf. Ross Physics 97 - 102; Guthrie, Introd. De caelo, p. XIX - XX).
On the other hand, Aristotle has banished from the particular things
any divine presence by declaring that the determining form is in things
and need not be explained by any similarity to divine ideas.

It appears that the problem of unity and multiplicity (ἓν καὶ πᾶν), even in its earliest stage, was mixed up with a religious problem. The passion with which Parmenides champions the unity of all being cannot be sufficiently explained by logical motives only. The historical perspective does not even end with Parmenides or Aristotle, for the cosmic image of the sphere still survives in the theories of Plotinus. Plotinus exemplifies the emanation of the many things from their first origin, the One, by the image of a spherical space, in which a continuous stream of being is sent forth from the centre, just as light from the sun. It is true that the picture has changed. To Plotinus it is not the outermost sphere which is divine, but its centre, the ineffable One. The problem, however, of how to combine a multiplicity of things and a One as their first principle into a consistent theory, is still exemplified by a cosmic spherical figure, and bound up with a religious vision.

In view of all this it must not be deemed impossible that Xenophanes might have applied both the attribute of ἄπειρον and that of πεπερασμένον to the divine first principle.

When we compare Hippolytus' statement (DK 21 A 33) with Simplicius' (DK 21 A 31) we see a remarkable difference as to the concepts of infinity and well-determinateness. According to Hippolytus, Xenophanes attributed to his godhead the characteristic of being πεπερασμένον. According to Simplicius, there is no certainty about this point. On the authority of Theophrastus he says that Xenophanes called his first principle neither πεπερασμένον nor ἄπειρον. As Jaeger has shown (*Theol.* 214, note 64), this must be due to a misunderstanding of a statement, borrowed by Theophrastus from Aristotle. Theophrastus may be supposed to have reproduced what Aristotle said about Xenophanes in the first book of the *Metaphysics* (A 5, 986 b 22 - 24). This is the well-known passage in which Aristotle shows his irritation with the too primitive level of thinking of Xenophanes and Melissus. About Xenophanes he says: "As it appears, Xenophanes, though unifying all things, did not explain anything about them, nor did he come near either to the concept of πεπερασμένον or to that of ἄπειρον." The upshot of this is that Xenophanes did not use either concept. This is what Theophrastus must have copied from Aristotle. The unknown author of MXG, however, understood it in the sense that Xenophanes had said that the godhead could neither be said to be πεπερασμένον nor ἄπειρον. This leads to the formula (DK 21 A 28 = MXG 977 a 36 - b 3): "the Godhead, being to Xenophanes one (a 36: ἕνα) and spherical (a 37: ὅμοιον πάντηι, b 1: σφαιροειδῆ), is neither

24

unbounded nor determined (b 3: οὔτε ἄπειρον οὔτε πεπεράνθαι)".
Simplicius reproduces this misunderstanding of MXG, and even wraps
it up in a number of Aristotelean explanations. As Jaeger states,
Simplicius did not see that the account by Theophrastus, which is
quoted by him immediately before, has a completely different meaning.
He understands Theophrastus in the sense of the author of MXG, thus
canonizing the wrong interpretation. It is worth noticing that the
misunderstanding, once introduced, is integrated into a system of
Aristotelean theories. This has often been so in the history of philosophy: a misinterpretation of a text is justified by a doctrinal construction.*

We may conclude from Jaeger's critical remarks that the lines
on Xenophanes found in Aristotle's *Metaphysics* were the starting-
point of the doxographic tradition as regards Xenophanes. This does
not mean that, having found the oldest account, we may feel sure of
having found the most reliable information. If we think so, we are
probably going one step too far. It does not seem altogether justified
to consider Aristotle the most matter-of-fact informant. As the
distinction between infinity and determinateness had not yet acquired
in Xenophanes' days the Aristotelean status of strict contrariety,
the possibility remains that it was not the unknown author of MXG
who started the misunderstanding about Xenophanes, but Aristotle
himself. One does not need too much imagination to suppose that
Aristotle himself may have found both attributes, unbounded and
well-determined, in Xenophanes' description of the One, and that he
did not feel able to integrate this into his own no-nonsense philosophy.
It is true that we cannot support our suggestion by any precise texts.
The texts that have come down to us, however, allow us to see that
the general trend of Xenophanes' theories did not exclude it. There is,
moreover, one argument that gives some support to our hypothesis.
As we shall see in the next chapter, we can trace the presence of both
qualifications, unbounded and well-determined, in the descriptions
by Parmenides of the one Being, though, as we shall see at the same
time, Parmenides avoids using terms that have a too perceptible
contradiction in their linguistic form.

There is a general reason why this excursus had to be inserted,

* The problem of the doxographic tradition as regards Xenophanes was discussed as early as 1887 by the 'Directeur des Tabacs de Lot-et-Garonne', M. Paul
Tannery (Tannery 1887, 134-138).

though it was already sufficiently clear, from Plato and Aristotle themselves, i.e. from sources anterior to the doxographic tradition, what Xenophanes had said. The example adduced makes it clear how all accounts about the Presocratics given by Aristotle and later authors may have suffered from Aristotelean corruption, as we shall term it. Putting it into Latin we get a better idea of the two senses in which this corruption may occur. 'Corruptio Aristotelis' taken as 'a distortion practised on Aristotle', may mean a distortion of Aristotle's words in the sense that later authors introduced a mis-interpretation of certain information given by Aristotle. In this case the possibility still remains that Aristotle himself has been the author of the confusion, as we saw in the example discussed above. Secondly, 'corruptio Aristotelis' taken as 'a distortion practised by Aristotle', may mean a distortion by Aristotle himself of the theories of his predecessors. In this sense the corruption is very frequent in the works of Aristotle, as we shall have ample opportunity to see. Aristotle is in the habit of evaluating the theories of his predecessors according to the contribution they made to the development of coherent and acceptable theories. As such, Aristotle generally considers his own views. Led by this criterion, Aristotle has two ways of treating other people's views. If he does not see his way to bring them into line with his own theories, he dismisses them scornfully. This often enables us to find out the authentic contents of the rejected theories, because in such cases Aristotle is not interested in misrepresenting them. Things go worse when he follows the second course. In this case he considers his predecessors as his own forerunners, and to show this he makes their theories mean, in a more primitive form, the same things which have much better been worked out and formulated in Aristotle's own system. The result is that in Aristotle's account the theories of the Presocratics lay generally hidden behind a dense vegetation of Aristotelean interpretation. The highway on which Aristotle imagines himself going is marked by this vegetation on places where he did violence to other people's philosophies. The accounts by Aristotle must therefore be analysed separately to see what historical truth may be found behind Aristotle's way of expressing himself. Putting it in terms which avoid accusing him, we may say that Aristotle preferred systematic philosophy to historical treatment.

A more special reason for inserting these remarks on historical method lies in the history of the concept of ἄπειρον itself. As we saw, Aëtius misrepresented Anaximander's theories by declaring his ἄπειρον to be no other thing than the Aristotelean ὕλη (DK 12 A 14). In this way, the historical description of the concept of ἄπειρον has suffered from a wrong method of reporting. Not only external factors, however, have contributed to misunderstandings. The concept itself absorbed two contradictory senses on its way through the first centuries of Greek philosophy. In the Pythagorean school it acquired, instead of the old lofty sense of divine infinity, the sense of Indeterminateness or 'undetermined principle'. The last philosopher to maintain the old venerable unbounded first Being was Parmenides, but from the terms he uses and from the terms he avoids, we can already see the growing importance of the Pythagorean ideas. After Parmenides the term ἄπειρον definitely becomes ambiguous, because it preserves traces of both conceptions, divine unboundedness in positive sense, and undetermined principle in the negative sense of being devoid of all qualities. In the problems discussed by Zeno the concept loses what is left of its credit, because these discussions show how ambiguous the terms of 'many' aud 'actual infinity' were. This leads to a distrust of the concept of actual infinity, a distrust that keeps working through some centuries, mostly owing to Aristotle's influence. The later Platonism and Neoplatonism restore it to its positive meaning.

In the negative sense of undeterminedness the evolution of the concept of ἄπειρον led to the theory of matter as undetermined principle in contrast to the determining principle of form. The question may be asked if, ultimately, there may not be a trace of a historical inheritance in the way in which materialistic philosophies declare matter to be the creative principle of all things.

Putting aside the later confusion as to ἄπειρον and πεπερασμένον, we may say with reasonable certainty, that in Xenophanes' One the old representation of an all-embracing and omnipresent godhead is still present, the same that survived in Anaximander's philosophy by the name of τὸ ἄπειρον. Perhaps we must prefer saying, in Xenophanes' case, that his godhead fills the universe, because his philosophy is about τὸ ἓν καὶ πᾶν, rather than saying that it embraces the universe. This latter description fits better into Anaximander's philosophy, in which the ἄπειρον represented the Time-deity who was identified with the outermost heaven. Anaximander's godhead as well as Xenophanes's are described in spatial images. In the account by Hippolytus (DK 21 A 33) the godhead of Xenophanes is said to be ὅμοιον πάντηι, equal in all directions, and σφαιροειδής, spherical. The account by Sextus Empiricus has a similar description (DK 21 A 35):

τὸν θεὸν συμφυῆ τοῖς πᾶσιν, εἶναι δὲ σφαιροειδῆ

"the godhead is grown together with all things, and spherical".
Even in an account by Cicero (*Acad.* II 118) the spherical shape comes through: "Xenophanes proclaimed all things to be One, and he said that this One was the Godhead, unborn, eternal and in a spherical shape, *conglobata figura*". This last information sounds, in the text of Cicero, as if it were a senseless and useless addition. Its meaning was certainly not understood by Cicero himself.

Summing up, we have the following results.

(1) Xenophanes was the first philosopher who developed a theory in which the principle of all things was the One, and who described this principle by the name of τὸ Ἕν. Without speaking of an organized school, Plato considered Xenophanes as the beginner of the Eleatic way of thinking (τὸ Ἐλεατικὸν γένος, *Soph.* 242 D).

(2) In the same passage of Plato's *Sophistes* we find the concepts of 'one' and 'many' put together in one formula (ὡς ἑνὸς ὄντος τῶν πάντων). This formula is repeated four lines further on in the standard form πολλά τε καὶ ἕν. Plato says that Xenophanes' theory implied that "all things are one". In the account by Aristotle (*Met.* A 5, 986 b 21) the word πάντα is not found, but the verb ἑνίσας (which, in Aristotle, is a hapax legomenon) indicates clearly enough, that Aristotle means to say: 'to reduce all things to unity'.

(3) The background of Xenophanes' theories is the same as Anaximander's. That which constitutes the unity of all things is at the same time the principle of all things. This principle is divine and eternal and embraces all things (c.q. is present in all things). It is described in spatial images.

(4) Both Anaximander and Xenophanes try to develop rational ideas from the old mythical images by way of abstraction.
Anaximander develops the theory of the ἄπειρον, Xenophanes that of the One.

(5) It is not improbable that Xenophanes ascribed to his first principle the qualities of ἄπειρον as well as of πεπερασμένον at the same time.

Xenophanes must have combined a deep sense of respect for the gods with a great gift of rational thinking. We can see this in the advice he gave to the citizens of Elea. They had asked him if they were to bring offerings to Leukothea, goddess of the sea, and execute the ritual lamentations for her (DK 21 A 13). The cult of Leukothea must have been the cult of a vegetation goddess, dying in autumn and coming to life in spring. Xenophanes answered that they should not bewail her, if they considered her a goddess, but should not bring offerings, if they thought her mortal.

B. PARMENIDES

As regards Parmenides a somewhat remarkable problem has been raised by Mario Untersteiner (1955, I), who argued that the Being of Parmenides should be characterized as οὖλον, 'a whole', rather than as ἕν, 'the One'.

This question is primarily one of textual criticism. In Diels' standardwork *The Fragments of the Presocratics* the reading οὖλον μουνογενές in 28 B 8, verse 4, has been replaced from the fifth edition onwards by ἔστι γὰρ οὐλομελές. For both readings evidence is found in ancient sources. The history of the textual criticism about this verse was given by Diels-Kranz in a note in the sixth edition.

Untersteiner makes a fresh start with a thorough treatment of verse 4. Next he proposes a correction in vs. 5 and 6, the issue of which is the accepted reading of verse 6: ἕν, συνεχές. Untersteiner adduces a quotation from Asclepius, which, he thinks, authorizes him to change these two words into the expression οὐλοφυές. That which annoys him most of all is the term ἕν.

Plato's testimony (ἓν φὴς εἶναι τὸ πᾶν *Parm.* 128 A) is put aside by Untersteiner, because it is possible that here Plato is opposing the Eleatic views in the form they took with the Megarians and Melissus. As Plato was well acquainted with the Megarians, it may, as Untersteiner sees it, well be supposed that, in the dialogue, Parmenides speaks for this school and its theories, and not as the historical Parmenides. Aristotle's testimony (*Met.* A 5, 986 b 28 - 30) is also put aside. Aristotle says that to Parmenides the unity of all being implies the rejection of not-being:

παρὰ γὰρ τὸ ὂν τὸ μὴ ὂν οὐθὲν ἀξιῶν εἶναι, ἐξ ἀνάγκης ἓν οἴεται εἶναι τὸ ὄν, καὶ ἄλλο οὐθέν.

"because he assesses not-being as a non-entity over against Being, he necessarily thinks that Being is One, and that besides Being there is nothing."

Untersteiner with good reason points out the fact that this way of reasoning is absent in Parmenides. This means that we have to do with an 'interpretatio Aristotelis', which is often synonymous with 'corruptio Aristotelis'. The logic of the demonstration is somewhat too strict and too closely adapted to the Aristotelean ontological theory. The reasoning of Aristotle became traditional in doxographic literature, as so many of Aristotle's at first sight historical accounts did. There is, however, one point that can hardly be attributed to the explanation given by Aristotle. Parmenides, at all events, must have spoken about the concept of unity. Being right in rejecting Aristotle's reasoning, Untersteiner might have saved from the Aristotelean account at least so much that Parmenides did indeed evolve "a theory about the 'One'". The corruption brought about by Aristotle must be located in the logical form he gives to the subject in question. The subject itself, on which Aristotle reasons, must have been found by him in the sources he read. The subject, in this case, was the ἕν.

In order to avoid this conclusion and give further support to his theory, Untersteiner avails himself of two arguments. The first of these is based on Alexander and Simplicius. It is not necessary here to discuss in detail the texts of these commentators of Aristotle, which Untersteiner adduces because they are even in a higher degree impaired by Aristotelean distortion. The second argument is a variation of a hypothesis we saw Untersteiner already availing himself of. According to this hypothesis it was not Parmenides' own theories which were being put to the test by Plato in the *Sophist*, but those of the 'reformed Eleaticism' ascribed to the Megarians and to Melissus. Untersteiner thinks the theory of the One may have been originated by Melissus, though before him Zeno had dealt with the problem of the One, but only by the way and in the context of an unsolved aporia. Parmenides, as Untersteiner interprets him, had a philosophy in which, as in Zeno's, only Being, τὸ ὄν was the object of thinking.

The texts adduced by Untersteiner prove that in Melissus' and Zeno's theories the One was object of thinking. For Melissus it was even the foundation his philosophy was built on. For Zeno it was the starting-point of the problem how to reconcile being many with being one. All this, however, does not prove that Parmenides avoided the problem or banished it from his thought. No texts are put forward by Untersteiner to make this even probable. When it comes to drawing conclusions Untersteiner (p. 17) writes that "as to the One, only in Melissus' case we have been able to give sufficient proof". He means by this that no texts can be found by which the existence of the concept of the One can be proved beyond doubt for Parmenides and for Zeno. We must remark that the absence of a proof for the

30

existence of a thing does not mean the existence of a proof for the absence of it.

So far, Untersteiner has tried to prove the unacceptableness of the reading ἕν, συνεχές, on the ground that the theory did not exist. As it appears, his arguments are not strong enough to come inevitably to the conclusion, that the term ἕν should be rejected from the text of Parmenides. What remains are arguments of a philological character.

Asclepius (in *Metaph.* 42, 30 - 31) has a different reading of the verses 5 and 6:

οὐ γὰρ ἔην, οὐκ ἔσται ὁμοῦ πᾶν, ἔστι δὲ μοῦνον
οὐλοφυές·

Untersteiner thinks this reading entails fewer inner contradictions than the accepted reading:

οὐδέ ποτ' ἦν οὐδ' ἔσται, ἐπεὶ νῦν ἔστιν ὁμοῦ πᾶν
ἕν, συνεχές·

The contradictions pointed out by Untersteiner are between ὁμοῦ πᾶν and συνεχές on the one hand, and ἕν on the other. The expressions συνεχές, οὐλοφυές, οὐλομελές (p. 21) may be considered synonyms, but the intrusion of ἕν forms a stumbling-block. As Untersteiner says: ἕν is in complete contradiction to νῦν ἔστιν ὁμοῦ πᾶν (p. 21).

It must be said that this last statement is not self-evident. Why should ἕν be considered impossible as a synonym for οὖλον? In the first part of this chapter we saw that both words were found in the descriptions of the divine first principle by Xenophanes. This means that it is at least not impossible that to Parmenides the two concepts were not yet separated by very sharp logical distinctions.

As a second point the translation given by Untersteiner (p. 20) gives rise to critical remarks. Untersteiner thinks we should read:

5 οὐ γὰρ ἔην, οὐκ ἔσται ὁμοῦ πᾶν, ἔστι δὲ μοῦνον
6 οὐλοφυές

and translates as follows: "for neither it was, nor it will be a complex unity of all things, but it is only οὐλοφυές." The last word is not translated by Untersteiner but, at any rate, it is clear that the translation given brings the expression ὁμοῦ πᾶν in contrast with the expression οὐλοφυές: "Being must not be considered as a ὁμοῦ πᾶν, but, on the contrary, as οὐλοφυές." If this must be contradiction, it is a curious example of contradiction, as the terms would rather suggest that ὁμοῦ πᾶν and οὐλοφυές are synonyms.

As a third point we may ask if Untersteiner is right in thinking

Plato's discussion in the *Parmenides* referring exclusively to Melissus and the Megarians. The text in *Parm.* 128 A reads:

Σὺ μὲν γὰρ ἐν τοῖς ποιήμασιν ἓν φὴς εἶναι τὸ πᾶν

"for you say in your poems that the whole of things is one." Because of the expression "in your poems" it would seem strange if this did not refer to the theories of Parmenides himself. Moreover, a number of direct quotations from Parmenides' poem is found in the works of Plato, e.g. *Tim.* 37 E, where we read one of the verses questioned by Untersteiner (fr. 8 verse 5). We may feel justified in supposing that Plato did not read texts by Megarians only.

As an argument against the way in which Untersteiner builds up the problem, it must be said that the term ἕν is too generally used in Presocratic literature to make a special case out of it for Parmenides. Its current meaning is that of a unified whole, as may be seen from the following quotations:

Heraclitus (DK 22 B 10) says that "all things together constitute a One, and from the One all things arise",

ἐκ πάντων ἓν καὶ ἐξ ἑνὸς πάντα·

Empedocles (DK 31 B 17, verses 1 and 2) says: "I must say two things; alternately, from the many it grows into being only One, and from the One it is dispersed into being many",

δίπλ' ἐρέω· τοτὲ μὲν γὰρ ἓν ηὐξήθη μόνον εἶναι
ἐκ πλεόνων, τοτὲ δ' αὖ διέφυ πλέον' 'εξ ἑνὸς εἶναι.

The problem stated in these lines by Empedocles is amply developed by Plato in strictly logical reasonings in *Soph.* 245 a: ἀμερὲς δήπου δεῖ παντελῶς τό γε ἀληθῶς ἓν κατὰ τὸν ὀρθὸν λόγον εἰρῆσθαι, "if a thing must be really one it must be absolutely without parts according to the right use of reason." In the same dialogue Plato epitomizes Empedocles' theories in the words (242 E): ὡς τὸ ὂν πολλά τε καὶ ἕν ἐστιν, ἔχθρᾳ δὲ καὶ φιλίᾳ συνέχεται, "that Being is many and one, and is bound together by hate and love".

Aristotle also uses the term ἕν in the sense of 'a unified whole', for instance in *Phys.* A 3, 186 a 20: οὕτως δὲ ἓν καὶ τῶν φυσικῶν τινες λέγουσιν, "in this sense the φυσικοί also talk about the one."

In describing Parmenides' system we shall stick to the view that the ἕν of fr. 8, verse 6 is synonymous with οὖλον. In that case the opposite of ἕν is πολλά, the many. This latter term implies the view that being is discontinuous, which means that properly speaking there is not one being, but there are many individual beings. If, while

32

preserving the traditional text, we take ἕν to mean what Untersteiner thinks it to mean, we should have to suppose that ἕν in verse 6 is intended to be the opposite of ἄλλο. In this case the expression would mean that there is no other complete and wellrounded being besides the Being discussed by Parmenides, i.e., the expression ἕν would have to be taken numerically and would imply that there cannot be a plurality of worlds (cf. on this question Cornford 1934). In the text the word ἄλλο does not occur. The attributes by which the word ἕν in verse 6 is surrounded make the impression of being synonyms, added by Parmenides in order to emphasize the concept he wants to explain: οὐλομελές, ὁμοῦ πᾶν, συνεχές. This makes it improbable that ἕν should have the meaning Untersteiner wants it to have, an improbability which is even strengthened when we consider the structure of Parmenides' poem.

The 49 verses of fr. 8 can be divided, from verse 6 onwards, into four well distinguished parts. In each of these parts Parmenides explains one of the main characteristics of Being which he has indicated in the introductory verses 1-6. These verses contain a kind of short program of the instruction to be given by the philosopher. The subjects to be treated are indicated in the introduction by one or more names, which Parmenides imagines to be written on sign-posts alongside the road on which the horses of the goddess are to carry him.

Accordingly he speaks of σήματα, sign-posts. Following these sign-posts, we can write out the structure of the poem as follows.

	ΣΗΜΑΤΑ	*which are explained by Parmenides in:*
A. terms of Anaximander	ἔστιν (vs 2) { ἀγένητον (vs 3) (ἀνώλεθρον (vs 3)	vs. 6-21: Being has not come into existence and *for this reason* is imperishable. The reason: there is no alternative with not-Being.
B. terms of Xenophanes	{ οὐλομελές (vs 4) (ὁμοῦ πᾶν (vs 5) ἕν, συνεχές (vs 6)	vs. 22-25: Negation of the discontinuous: 'being closes in upon being', ἐὸν γὰρ ἐόντι πελάζει.
C. the very essence of Parmenides' own theory of being	ἀτρεμές (vs 4) = not subject to change	vs. 26-42: all movement must be denied to Being, for Being is perfectly determined (πεῖρας, οὐκ ἀτελεύτητον). The reason: the concept of Being itself implies immutability; our thinking represents reality or else it could not be called thinking.

D.

the cosmology of Anaximander	ἀτέλεστον (vs 4) (= spatially unbounded, see the discussion below)	vs. 42-49: Being reaches out homogeneously in all directions. It is represented spatially ⎮as a sphere which (a) is perfectly in balance within, μεσσόθεν ἰσοπαλὲς πάντηι, and (b) whose outward boundary is not a boundary against something different from it: οὐκ ἐὸν ἔστι τό κεν παύοι μιν ἱκνεῖσθαι εἰς ὁμόν, there is no other Being which could prevent it from continuing its own homogeneity in all directions.

The term ἀτέλεστον is found in verse 4 as a sign-post pointing to the cosmology of verses 42-49. The history of this term from antiquity to the present day has been rich in vicissitudes, because many variants in the text have been attempted as well as many interpretations. The difficulty is in the contradiction, at first sight insuperable, to the expressions of verse 32: οὐκ ἀτελεύτητον and verse 42: τετελεσμένον ἐστί. In these verses the context confirms the literal meaning of these terms. Therefore, there can be no doubt as to the correctness of the reading. This means that solving the contradiction depends on finding a satisfactory explanation for verse 4.

It may be surmised that in antiquity already this difficulty gave rise to the numerous variants we find in the quotations of this verse by ancient authors. In the nineteenth century a solution was found by Brandis, which has the advantage of making the whole problem disappear. Brandis proposed to read: οὐδ' ἀτέλεστον = not without bounds, instead of: ἠδ' ἀτέλεστον = and without bounds. From the standpoint of textual criticism an objection to the reading Brandis proposed can be found only in the fact that not a single line or word from antiquity confirms it. It is a mere conjecture, which has to confirm itself by its own internal evidence. This means that the reading proposed must be rejected the moment a coherent explanation is found for the *textus receptus*.

Diels (1897, 75) maintains the traditional reading, explaining it by declaring ἀτέλεστον to be a synonym of ἀνώλεθρον, not-perishing, and ἄπαυστον, never-ceasing. Maybe this explanation was not very satisfactory to Diels himself. He writes: "Man wird sich bei der von Simplicius gegebenen Erklärung beruhigen müssen ... Man hat also zu lernen, dass der Dichter die verwandten Ausdrücke ἀτέλεστον und ἀτελεύτητον willkürlich, wie es scheint, nach ganz verschiedenen Sinne hin ausgeprägt hat." On p. 83-84 he once more affirms his preference for taking 'temporally infinite' as the translation of the term ἀτέλεστον.

In the year when Diels' work came from the press, another work on Parmenides by Patin was in preparation. It appeared in 1899 as an extensive contribution to the *Jahrbücher für classische Philologie*. Patin proposes a theory according to which, wherever there is a polemic tone in Parmenides' verses, the polemics are directed against Heraclitus. The words ἠδ' ἀτέλεστον, Patin thinks, must mean that Being is not a flux without permanence or an evolution toward a more perfect state. For this reason Patin translates it as 'non perfectibile' (1899, 539). If, for a moment, we put aside the question whether indeed the polemics are directed against Heraclitus, Patin's explanation has an advantage over Diels's because it avoids inner contradictions. The explanation is in perfect harmony with the expression found in verse 32: ἔστι γὰρ οὐκ ἐπιδευές, Being is not deficient. The difficulty, however, is that, grammatically, it is rather unusual to form the compound ἀ-τέλεστον, to express the idea of 'non perfectibile', and that no parallels for this meaning can be found in Greek.

In 1916, Kranz, who, starting with the fifth edition, was to be the editor of Diels' *Fragmente der Vorsokratiker*, tried to rehabilitate Brandis' reading οὐδ' ἀτέλεστον (Kranz 1916, 1175 note 1). Kranz supposed that, if Parmenides really wrote οὐδ' ἀτέλεστον, it must have been a conscious variation on a verse-formula of Homer which reads ἠδ' ἀτέλεστον (e.g. *Iliad* IV 26). If this should be true, it makes the impression as if Brandis' hypothesis was in no way original, for then it was already Parmenides who replaced the Homeric ἠδέ by his own οὐδέ. At all events, it is a fact that Parmenides has some word-plays on Homeric expressions, e.g. in fr. 14, a verse on the moon, wandering around the earth with its 'borrowed light' ἀλλότριον φῶς. This may be a variation on the Homeric expression (e.g. *Od.* 5, 214) ἀλλότριος φώς 'a strange fellow'. In DK sixth edition, however, Kranz maintained the current version ἠδ' ἀτέλεστον. He translates this as 'ohne Ziel', adding the remark that it is a variation on a Homeric clause, that it means 'ohne Ziel in der Zeit' and that Brandis' reading is not right. We see that, to escape difficulties, Kranz prefers a translation in a temporal sense.

Once the reading ἠδ' ἀτέλεστον was accepted, various translations were attempted. H. Gomperz (1924, 10 note 31), following Patin, translates: 'der Erschütterung unfähig wie der Vollendung', at

35

bottom the same interpretation as Patin's 'non perfectibile'. The temporal interpretation, as given by Kranz, was followed by Cornford (1939) and Raven (1948). Kirk-Raven (1962, 273), however, translated 'without end' and so did Burnet (EGP 174). Gigon gives a somewhat divergent interpretation (1945, 261): 'ziellos', adding the remark that he thinks the passage is very difficult. Loenen (1959, 100) writes: "More in particular, the predicate imperishable seems to be implied in ἀτέλεστον", which is not very clear and seems to have been taken over from Diels. Verdenius (1942, 43) has no special discussion of the passage, but he is probably on the right track when writing: "Parmenides' Being has a far more universal and fundamental character, *which does not permit of limitation in space.*" In the same way Cornford (1933, 103) points to the spatial image, which he says is predominant: "the essential point is that all the attributes possessed by this Being belong to the categories of *extension and quantity, the mathematical categories.*" On the same page, nevertheless, he translates ἀτέλεστον as 'endless (in time)'.

The only author who decidedly opposes a temporal interpretation of Parmenides' ideas has been Fränkel (1930, 149), but his remarks have no direct bearing on the ἀτέλεστον of verse 4. Commenting on the πείρατα of verse 32 he says: "An unserer Stelle schliesst der Text eine Missdeutung ins Zeitliche dadurch aus, dass er gleich anschliessend die Anfangs- und Endlosigkeit des Seins ausdrücklich feststellt."

It seems reasonable to conclude that the interpretation of ἀτέλεστον in a temporal sense has been followed mostly for want of something better. The real problem of ἀτέλεστον remains the same, and it seems that there is no way out of it so long as one sticks to a systematic interpretation. An expression, however, which, taken in its systematic meaning, produces contradictions, may often be found to be perfectly explicable when taken historically.

In the survey given on p. 33-34 we saw that in the sections A end D an unmistakable affinity was found between Parmenides' theories and the cosmic theories of Anaximander. The Being of Parmenides, unborn and imperishable, may be regarded as the offspring of the eternal and divine power, which was characterized as ἀΐδιον and ἀγήρως by Anaximander. Parmenides speaks about his Being with the same religious awe with which the original cosmic divinity must have been venerated. To this religious inspiration the whole poem of Parmenides bears witness. The poem is, as it were, full of gods. It is a 'goddess of just decisions' who keeps Being within the limits of its determinations. Though Parmenides is building on the foundation of religious convictions, he tries to give a philosophical description of this cosmic Being as he experienced it. The characteristics of Being are reasoned out in the poem by logical means. Jaeger (*Theol.* 100) specifies this as "a carry-over of religious symbolism into the intellectual processes of philosophy".

It is true that the concept of 'eternity' is found in Parmenides' verses. It is formulated in the same terms that were used by Anaximander: ἀγένητον and ἀνώλεθρον. But, though the concept itself is marked by these very characteristic and traditional attributes, the marks do not serve as signposts, for the concept is not further developed. This is in line with the whole trend of Parmenides' thought. In his system there are no views on the problem of time and this may be characteristic of his static way of thinking. Parmenides tries hard to develop a system of logical expressions in order to build up abstract metaphysical speculation. Nevertheless, the images lying at the bottom can be discerned easily, and it is not difficult to see that they all have a spatial ground-pattern. We may convince ourselves of this by looking over the list of significant themes as drafted on p. 33-34. The way Parmenides develops his initial themes hardly anywhere implies a temporal view. This is a first argument against the interpretation of ἀτέλεστον as 'without end in time'. (It is taken in this sense by DK 28 B 8, verse 4 note; Cornford 1939, 36; Raven 1948, 27).

A second argument against the temporal interpretation lies in its history. It was, indeed, in order to escape from the difficulty that Brandis took resort to the explanation of ἀτέλεστον as 'without end in time'. This way out was chosen, as it were, for want of a better explanation. It may seem there was not sufficient evidence for the interpretation itself.

Another argument may be added to this. In the sense of 'without end in time' the term ἀτέλεστον would be a *hapax legomenon*. In Euripides, ἀτέλεστος means 'not initiated into the mysteries'. In Homer it means: 'idle, without result'. As a synonym of ἀτελής it has the meaning 'tax-free', and, in philosophic use, 'unfinished' or 'undetermined'. Plato and Aristotle use ἀτελής as, more or less, synonymous with ἄπειρος, e.g. *Philebus* 24 B: ἀτελῆ δ' ὄντε δήπου παντάπασιν ἀπείρω γίγνεσθον, *de gen. anim.* A 1, 715 b 14: ἡ δὲ φύσις φεύγει τὸ ἄπειρον· τὸ μὲν γὰρ ἄπειρον ἀτελές, ἡ δὲ φύσις ἀεὶ ζητεῖ τέλος, *Phys.* III 6, 207 a 14: τέλειον δ' οὐδὲν μὴ ἔχον τέλος· τὸ δὲ τέλος πέρας. The only passage adduced by Liddell-Scott to illustrate the meaning 'endless or eternal' is the verse in question itself, Parm. fr. 8, verse 4.

The most conclusive argument lies in the structure of Parmenides' poem. As we can see when consulting the survey on p. 33-34, the verses 42-49 are a development of the characteristic of ἀτέλεστον, marked on a signpost in verse 4. In the verses 42-49 we can observe as a background the cosmic views of Anaximander and Xenophanes: Being is well-balanced from the centre in all directions and its form is spherical. The representation lying at the bottom is spatial and possibly implies a certain mathematical view of space, as was argued by Cornford (1936). Parmenides' verses have more in them than this underlying representation only. The distinguishing characteristic of Parmenides' thought lies in the strength of his logical abstractions. Without deciding the question whether the Eleatics had developed already a more or less explicit system of logic, we can see their logic at work in their struggle to build up the first abstract ontology. As abstract terms had, for the most part, not yet been developed, Parmenides was forced to use the traditional terms and images. With these the old cosmic views survived, as we have ample opportunity to observe. The mythological structure of the universe, as it was described by the ancient Ionians, manifests itself in Parmenides even in the presence of such deities as Δίχη, goddess of Justice. Just as the ancient Χρόνος administered justice to all beings and made them do penance for any violation of the eternal laws, so this Goddess of Justice pronounces her unshakable sentences as to the laws of Being: χέχριται δ' οὖν (verse 16) and χρίσις (verse 15) are juridical formulas: 'sentence has been pronounced'.

All this makes it clear why the description of Being, as we find it in Parmenides, should have been bound up to such a high degree with spatial images. At the same time we shall not be able to escape the conclusion that in Parmenides ἀτέλεστον represents Anaximander's ἄπειρον. This will hold true, even if we shall have to recognize in Parmenides' theories a considerable change concerning the idea conveyed by this term.

With great strictness Parmenides formulates his theories. More than once, moreover, he contrasts them with the 'opinions of mortal men' as he calls them. There is no exact indication against whom he is maintaining his positions. The great emphasis with which he begs his readers (or hearers) to reject these false ways of thinking makes us wonder to which philosophers the criticism may refer. To this problem a solution has been attempted in two different ways. Either Heraclitus or the Pythagoreans have been regarded as Parmenides' opponents. It is fascinating to see the considerable variety of opinions on this point.

German scholars have a tradition of considering Heraclitus as the philosopher against whom Parmenides' criticisms are directed. This opinion is found in Baeumker (1890, 54), Patin (1899), Kranz (1916, 1174), and even in the Gifford lectures, given by Werner Jaeger in 1936 and published many years afterwards as *Theology of the Early Greek Philosophers*. In this work Jaeger does not even mention the name of F. M. Cornford, who had, as early as 1922 and 1923, developed his views on the discussion, which, he thinks, had been going on between Parmenides and the Pythagoreans. It is not far-fetched to raise this question, because we have two accounts, by ancient authors, according to which Parmenides was a disciple of the Pythagoreans (DK 28 A 1 from Diogenes Laertius, and DK 28 A 12 from Strabo). Diogenes Laertius says Parmenides was 'converted to the silence' by a Pythagorean named Ameinias. If this is a reliable account, Parmenides must have partaken more than superficially of the way of life of the Pythagorean sect and must have been thoroughly acquainted with Pythagorean thought. Cornford developed a very subtle method of criticism of the texts, a method which was even brought to a higher degree of perfection by Raven (1948). Cornford aimed at defining the different stages of the discussion between Parmenides and the Pythagoreans. He was not the first to identify Pythagorean elements in Parmenides. As early as 1887 Tannery had called attention to the fact, and so did Covotti in 1897.

The adherents of either interpretation appear to be divided according to the geographical division of Europe. The followers of the Heraclitean theory are found on the continent and write mainly in German, whereas the Pythagorean theory is found in English-speaking countries. The two theories live on, as it were, side by side. The champions of either theory do not even mention the opinions of the other side. Few historians mention both views. In the sixth edition of Zeller, Nestle has added a survey of the two divergent opinions (707, 4), and a very objective account of the question is given by Burnet (EGP 179). One author, Reinhardt (1916), turned the question upside down: it was not Parmenides who attacked Heraclitus, but, on the contrary, Heraclitus who criticized Parmenides. Reinhardt is alone in this view, which avoids the difficulty of having to choose between the two former theories. As it is important to the present investigation to find out how the views on the apeiron were divided between the Eleatic and the Pythagorean schools, we shall try to identify the traces of Pythagorean elements that may lie hidden between the lines in Parmenides' verses. In doing so we shall leave aside Reinhardt's theory and follow in the main line the method developed by Cornford and Raven. From the results we shall have to judge if an interaction between the Eleatic and the Pythagorean schools may be assumed to have existed.

First of all we must state that both the theories of Heraclitus and those of the Pythagoreans betray their presence in the work of Parmenides. To Heraclitus may be referred the symbolism of light and darkness (fr. 8, verses 56-59); the way of cyclical return, παλίντροπος κέλευθος (fr. 6, verse 9), reminding of the ὁδὸς ἄνω κάτω; and, possibly, word-plays such as fr. 6 verse 6: φοροῦνται (cf. Plato *Theaet*. 179 e: φοροῦνται, and 181 a: ῥέοντες, where Plato has Heraclitus in mind) as well as fr. 8 verse 21:

τὼς γένεσις μὲν ἀπέσβεσται καὶ ἄπυστος ὄλεθρος

"so becoming is quenched as well as perishing without leaving a trace." Becoming and perishing and the allusion to quenching a fire may be taken as referring to Heraclitus' primordial fire. The verse quoted gives the impression as if Parmenides felt he had definitely quenched this whole theory.

On a par with this evidence, pointing to Heraclitus, lies the evidence relating to the Pythagoreans. Parmenides is very strict when affirming the homogeneity and continuity of Being (vs 4: οὐλομελές, vs. 6: συνεχές, vs. 25: ἐὸν γὰρ ἐόντι πελάζει). This means, among other things, that there is no void (κενόν) between the individual beings, as was taught by the Pythagoreans. On the other side, the whole of Being is determined by its own boundaries, and may, therefore, not be thought of as being surrounded by a large empty space or void, from which it then should draw breath, as was also asserted by the Pythagoreans. Parmenides takes the utmost care not to leave any void neither between the individual beings nor outside the whole of Being.

It is true that the term κενόν does not occur in Parmenides' verses. From Plato onwards it was, however, the established view that the Parmenidean μὴ ὄν, not-being, was equivalent to the κενόν or empty space. This is not so strange, because we can observe in some accounts of the Presocratics a survival of a very early view of air as being emp-

40

tiness. The first who undertook to show that air was a substance was Empedocles, who speaks of ἀέρος ὄγκος. He describes an experiment which showed that air offered resistance (DK 31 B 100, cf. *Gr. Ph.* 115). Aristotle attributes the same kind of experiments to Anaxagoras (*Phys.* IV 5, 213 a 23 - 31). According to a primitive view, to make a vessel or wine-skin empty was to fill it with air. When air is considered as being nothing, it is self-evident that empty space, too, must be defined as not-being, and this is what we must expect in a period during which every abstract concept had still to be laboriously detached from its connection with space.

An explicit identification of κενόν with not-being is found for the first time in Aristotle's accounts of certain Presocratic theories. Most clearly he states this in the case of the atomists: they identified, he says, the Full and the Void with Being and not-Being (*Met.* A 4, 985 b 4). In the case of the Eleatics his statements are less accurate. He says that "some of the Ancients held that Being was of necessity one and without motion; for, they said, the void was a not-being, and Being could not be moved unless there should be a separate void, nor could there be a many unless there should be a separating factor" (*De gen. corr.* 325 a 2 - 5). The reasoning in this account seems to betray a certain Aristotelean way of interpreting, but it is not necessary to suppose that the account is unreliable. The reason for regarding it as true to fact is principally that the whole texture of Parmenides' thought implies a spatial way of representing concepts. The problem, moreover, is a general one in the Presocratic tradition. It is intrinsically bound up with the problem of ἓν καὶ πολλά, which is so clearly a dominating problem with the Pythagoreans and with Zeno. Even in Plato's *Parmenides* we can see in the treatment of the problems that, up to then, hardly any ontological concept had been completely made free from its connection with space. Lastly, there is a direct testimony by Plato as regards the fact that the Eleatics identified not-being with empty space. It is found in a passage where Plato explains that, to the Eleatics, Being was not subject to motion because motion presupposes the void. The reasoning is the same as the one given by Aristotle and it has the same connection with space implied in it. This gives us a reasonable certainty that the Eleatics and Parmenides really understood the concept of not-being as a spatial void. Plato's account runs as follows (*Theait.* 180 E): Μέλισσοί τε καὶ Παρμενίδαι . . . διισχυρίζονται ὡς ἕν τε πάντα ἐστὶ καὶ ἕστηκεν αὐτὸ ἐν αὑτῷ οὐκ ἔχον χώραν ἐν ᾗ κινεῖται,

"People like Melissus and Parmenides assert with great emphasis that all things form one whole, and that this whole stands unmoved by itself as there is no room for it to move within." The fact that Being has no space to move in is used here as an argument to prove that all beings are One. This means that no place can be found in which Being is not found. Thus, the reasoning implies that, if Being should be absent, empty space would be left. For 'empty space' Plato uses the term χώρα, which here stands for the concept of κενόν.

With a view to all this it is not unreasonable to suppose that, though the term κενόν does not occur in what we have left of Parmenides, it was this same concept of κενόν which he attacked so insistently in his criticism of the μὴ ὄν. We know it was the Pythagoreans who admitted the void as a first principle in the development of being. Therefore it seems plausible to think the Pythagoreans were the target of Parmenides' attacks. If we accept this view, we may remark that the incriminated theory is indicated by Parmenides in formulas in which the term κενόν itself is altogether avoided.

There is a further point in which, though the contrast must be reconstructed, we may reasonably suppose Parmenides to have been criticising Pythagorean theories. It is, in our opinion, the Pythagorean opposition of πέρας and ἄπειρον which Parmenides is trying to eliminate at all costs, when he defends his view that the universe of Being is well-determined within its own boundaries. The insistence with which Parmenides defends his view on this point gives the impression that his discussion is directed at unnamed opponents. Just as in the case of the non-existence of the void, the suspicion that there were opponents leads us to think of the Pythagoreans as the philosophers with whom the dialogue was going on.

There is no agreement about the question who these Pythagoreans were, or what their doctrines were.

What interests us here is the so-called table of oppositions, mentioned by Aristotle (*Met*. A 5, 986 a 22 - 26). The Pythagoreans had a number of principles, divided into pairs of opposites. By interaction of the opposite principles they explained the character of things and the processes of becoming. There is no reason to suspect Aristotle of not giving matter-of-fact information on this point, as the matter offered no opportunity to Aristotle to use it for the construction of his own philosophy by changing things somewhat. Only the question has been asked, if the Pythagoreans Aristotle knew of had the same doctrines as the Pythagoreans who were contemporaries of Parmenides.

Cornford was convinced that the first Pythagoreans had a monistic system. This view is not generally accepted, and for all we know the Pythagorean system implied a dualistic method of explaining the universe. The discussion on this subject was summarized by Guthrie (I 249 - 251). Guthrie thinks that Cornford's view that the earliest Pythagoreans were monists can be reconciled with the dualistic view. If their first principle was the One as opposed to multiplicity (ἔν-πλῆθος), it was only too natural that they should consider the One as first and highest principle, and should give it preference over the principle of multiplicity. Unity was revered as highest and most divine. This, however, may not have excluded that in the explanation of the universe the Pythagoreans had recourse to the interaction of two opposite principles, first of all those of the One and the Many. If it may be doubted that all of the ten pairs of opposites mentioned by Aristotle from the beginning formed part of the Pythagorean theories, at all events the logic of their system, and, we may add, the historical context in which their theories appear postulate a dualistic way of thinking for the earliest Pythagoreans. De Vogel (1966, 4) says on this dualism of the ancient Pythagoreans: "We must undoubtedly look upon this as a reaction to the Milesians and also as the doctrine which, a little later in the sixth century, was strongly opposed by Parmenides." We may confidently maintain the view that, if not the whole table of ten pairs of opposites, at any rate the two pairs of ἔν-πλῆθος and πέρας-ἄπειρον are of an early date. These principles determined Pythagorean thinking to such a degree that we can only deny them to the first Pythagoreans if we are disposed to ascribe to them a philosophy which is completely different from any later Pythagorean tradition.

It is the Pythagorean theory of πέρας and ἄπειρον which probably determined a change in the attitude towards the concept of ἄπειρον. We can trace this change in the verses in which Parmenides gives his doctrine on the well-determinedness of Being (vs. 29 - 33):

ταὐτόν τ' ἐν ταὐτῶι τε μένον καθ' ἑαυτό τε κεῖται
χοὕτως ἔμπεδον αὖθι μένει· κρατερὴ γὰρ 'Ανάγκη
πείρατος ἐν δεσμοῖσιν ἔχει, τό μιν ἀμφὶς ἐέργει,
οὕνεκεν οὐκ ἀτελεύτητον τὸ ἐὸν θέμις εἶναι·
ἔστι γὰρ οὐκ ἐπιδευές·

"remaining the same and in one place it rests in itself, and so unshakable it stays there; for mighty Ananke keeps it within the bounds of determination (πεῖρας), and this (πεῖρας) embraces it all round, because it is against the divine law that it should be undetermined; for it is not wanting anything."

Clearly the verses imply for πεῖρας the sense of 'determinedness'. It is true that there is a certain notion of space lingering in the background, especially in the expressions 'in one place' and 'embraces it'. This last expression reminds us of the ancient Time-deity, who had the fate of things in his arms, embracing the universe. The characteristics of this Time-deity survived, as we have seen in the first chapter, in Anaximander's theory of the ἄπειρον, in which at the same time the connection with time more or less lost its importance, to the benefit of a predominantly spatial one. As we saw earlier in this chapter, the cosmic vision of Anaximander lives on in the descriptions by Parmenides, with the difference that Parmenides tries hard to develop the spatial concepts of Anaximander into abstract ontological principles. In the verses quoted we see, as it were, Parmenides at work. Though in the background certain spatial images linger on, it is evident that Parmenides means to say, without spatial implications, that Being is perfectly determined. Being is kept within the bounds of well-determinedness, πείρατος ἐν δεσμοῖσιν, and it is impossible that it should be undetermined, ἀτελεύτητον, for it is not in want of anything. This means that it is perfect. Divinities such as 'Ανάγκη (vs. 30) and Θέμις (vs. 32) have disposed that no perfection should be wanting in it.

The tendency of the verses leaves no other meaning for πεῖρας than that of 'well-determinedness'. However, when we realize that even in these verses the old notion of space still survives, we might expect πεῖρας to be the opposite of ἄπειρον. In that case the use of the term πεῖρας implies the rejection of the opposite concept ἄπειρον, in the sense in which this term had been in use before Parmenides: that of 'spatially unbounded'. Now, as in the case of the κενόν, it may be remarked that Parmenides does not use the incriminated term, probably in order not to leave any doubt as to the rejection of it. There can be no misunderstanding as to Parmenides' intention to banish the ἄπειρον. We have, however, to read this in a text in which the ἄπειρον is not even mentioned, but only its opposite πεῖρας is all the stronger and exclusively affirmed.

This gives us a clue to the meaning of the so much debated expression of verse 4: ἠδ' ἀτέλεστον. This, in our opinion, must be taken as an expression intended to convey the same meaning as had been formulated by Anaximander in the term ἄπειρον. Parmenides could not use this term because it reminded him too much of the

44

undeterminedness, which he so completely wanted to banish from his concept of Being. By doing so he rejected one of the opposites of the Pythagorean pair of πέρας-ἄπειρον. At the same time, however, he wanted to maintain the loftiness of a highest infinite Divinity, which he had experienced as absolute Being, revealed to him by the Goddess. Leaving aside the term ἄπειρον, which, due to the influence of the Pythagoreans, had acquired as a second meaning that of 'undeterminedness', Parmenides avoided the difficulty by expressing himself in the term 'ἀτέλεστον'. This is completely in line with Parmenides' description of the universe being spherical, well-determined and, because of that, absolutely perfect.

The acceptance of πεῖρας as determination and of ἄπειρον as indetermination, and, accordingly, the rejection of ἄπειρον as a characteristic of universal Being, can only satisfactorily be explained if we admit that this change in the meaning of the terms was caused by the influence of the Pythagoreans, or resulted from Parmenides' discussions with them. In contrast to the Ionian tradition, which made all things develop from one primordial being, the Pythagoreans posited a contrast of two principles as the starting-point for evolution. This entailed two essential differences in their cosmic theories in comparison with the theories of the Ionians. There was not any longer one primeval entity out of which all things grew, but from the very beginning a division and an interaction between opposing forces. The most important conclusion to be drawn from this is that the Pythagorean theory allowed the many beings to have a more outspoken individuality by contrasting them with and separating them from one another. The Pythagoreans were the first to give a philosophical explanation of the existence of a multitude of separate beings. Secondly, to the Pythagoreans the universe was no longer a great but closed society, in which all things had a definite status and only changed position according to the cycle of Time. On the contrary, it was in a process of evolution, which had started when in the primordial chaos the first nucleus sprang to life. From this primordial seed the cosmos had developed by breathing the surrounding void (cf. Ar. *Phys.* 203 a 5 and 213 b 23, *Met.* 1091 a 15 - 18). Thus, the limited and well-determined principle of a very first living germ, together with the unlimited and undetermined principle of primordial empty space, had generated the universe.

If we accept the theory that Parmenides started his philosophical career as a Pythagorean, we must suppose that, later on, he marked out his own theories. A revelation had come to him, as it were, by divine inspiration opening his eyes to the unity and well-determined perfection of Being. The horse-carriage of the goddess had taken him through all the realms of Being. On his way, goddesses had opened the gates, and a goddess welcomed him in the realm of Truth where Θέμις and Δίκη had led him (fr. 1). Parmenides' words betray the proud conviction of having captured a new truth on a way as yet untrodden. This truth is absolute, and guaranteed by a divine authority. All the same, from the absolute truth preached by Parmenides not every element of Pythagorean origin was eliminated. What Parmenides rejects are the negative poles of the Pythagorean pairs of opposites. With all the greater enthusiasm he accepts the positive terms. If there were masters who passed on the first elements of philosophical thought to Parmenides, we can think only of the Pythagoreans as the philosophers who made him aware of the fact that Being can only be perfect and self-sufficient owing to its well-determinedness (πεῖρας). By rejecting the negative pole of undeterminedness or ἄπειρον, Parmenides, paradoxically, remained true to Anaximander's all-embracing ἄπειρον. This is a paradox only in the terms, but it is important enough to identify the paradox. It explains why Parmenides, while admitting the cosmic views of Anaximander, at the same time avoided using his expression: ἄπειρον, for it. The one line in which Parmenides comes close to using it has ἀτέλεστον (vs. 4) instead.

The conclusion arrived at in this chapter is centered around the first appearance of Pythagorean influence in philosophical discussion. Parmenides tried to maintain the old vision of one universe, ruled and penetrated by a divine presence. To this he added his own intuitions about absolute Being, together with a relatively well-developed method of logical reasoning. The idea of absolute Being, however, was still connected with the notion of space, originating from ancient traditions about cosmic deities. Foremost in this connection was the idea that the universe extended indefinitely, i.e. was an apeiron. This term does not appear in the extant fragments of Parmenides, who conveys the idea of it by a synonym: ἀτέλεστον. The reason for this probably was, that the term ἄπειρον had acquired an ambiguous meaning, owing to Pythagorean influence.

The Pythagoreans may be regarded as the first school of thought which called attention to the individual being, as distinguished from other beings and from the whole of things. They had a dualistic way of looking at things, and tried to explain their characteristics by the

46

interplay of opposing principles. One of their pairs of opposites was that of πεῖρας and ἄπειρον. Of this pair, πεῖρας stood for the restrictions within which each being moved, that is to say for their very individual determinedness. In this sense, πεῖρας is fully adopted by Parmenides, and so probably was given its standard philosophical signification. This, however, had a consequence for the opposite term ἄπειρον. In the old sense it had indicated the unboundedness of the universe. It now acquired a new sense, not completely compatible with the old one: that of undeterminedness, as opposed to the determinedness of πεῖρας. The result was that from that time ἄπειρον was an ambiguous term. Two significations, representing, in their oldest form, two completely different world-views, lived on in one and the same term, like two souls in one word: (1) infinite in a positive sense, in the way the universe was infinite, and (2) in the negative sense: undetermined. From Zeno onward this latter meaning was even further divided, owing to the mathematical use of ἄπειρον: a line could be extended indefinitely by adding new lengths, without ever reaching a fixed point where it could be said to be actually infinite in length. This meaning is more or less a mathematical correlate to (1), with the difference that it has a stronger negative accent: the line never becomes actually infinite however many additions to its length may be made. In contrast to this way of describing an indefinite infinity stands the concept of infinity by division. If a given line is divided into two half-lengths, and the half-length is again divided into two equal parts, and so on, the division may indefinitely be continued without ever reaching the point of absolute zero. Both concepts, infinity by adding and infinity by dividing, were by Zeno's times the subject of mathematical problems. In both ways the concept of infinity is characterized in a negative sense, because an actual infinity is never reached. The problem of infinity by dividing gave rise to the theory of the atomists Leucippus and Democritus, if, at least, we are to believe Aristotle's explanations on this point.

As we shall see in the next two chapters, the problem of infinity soon grew out into an unsolvable problem. That is why Plato probably avoided to use the concept of ἄπειρον in the first sense. Plato only uses the concept in the context of the Pythagorean opposition of πέρας and ἄπειρον. Aristotle settled the question as to the actual infinite by declaring that it is simply non-existent. Infinity, according to Aristotle, is always potential, because to every quantity, however large or extended, new quantity can always be added. The only school that acknowledged a positive infinity was that of the Megarians, who declared infinity to coincide with perfection and the Good.

The Pythagoreans started in their philosophy from pairs of contrasting principles. In the process of evolution, the developing beings were separated from each other by the void, inhaled as a breath from the surrounding universe. Their theories left room for individual things to exist separately as distinguished from other things. This way of thinking was not shared by Parmenides. With all his energy he stresses the unity and homogeneity of Being: ἐὸν γὰρ ἐόντι πελάζει, being borders on being, there is no void to be inhaled. Seen historically, Parmenides is the last defender of the divine unity of all things. After him the universe, as it were, explodes into a multitude of individual things, even, in Democritus' theory, into atoms.

BIBLIOGRAPHY

A. *Xenophanes.*

von Fritz, RE
Tannery 1887
Deichgräber 1938
Lumpe 1952
Untersteiner 1955, I; 1956

Schwabl 1957
Guazzoni Foá 1961
Steinmetz 1966
Heitsch 1966

B. *Parmenides.*

Diels 1897
Patin 1899
Kranz 1916
Reinhardt 1916
Cornford 1922-1923
Gomperz 1924
Fränkel 1930
Cherniss 1932
Calogero 1932
Cornford 1933, 1939
Coxon 1934
Verdenius 1942
Gigon 1945
Raven 1948
Schwabl 1950, 1953

Vlastos 1953
Untersteiner 1955, II
Virieux-Reymond 1956
Untersteiner 1958
Loenen 1959
Owen 1960
Guazzoni Foá 1960, 1961, 1966
Kirk-Stokes 1960
Dolin 1962
Schwabl 1963
Long 1963
Bröcker 1964
Mansfeld 1964
Klowski 1967

CHAPTER III

PYTHAGORAS AND PYTHAGOREANISM

A. THE MYTH: CHAOS AND PRIMORDIAL GERM.

One of the central points in the so-called Orphic theologies was the myth of the world-egg. In an account by Damascius on the central themes of Orphic myth the story runs thus (Kern 54 = DK 1 B 13). In the beginning there was earth and water, or, according to a different reading, earth and slime. From these two came forth never aging Time (Χρόνος ἀγήραος), represented as a winged monster with three heads: a man's, a bull's and a lion's. Time, accordingly, had three names: Χρόνος, Ἡρακλῆς and Ἀνάγκη, i.e. Time, Heracles and Fate, obviously only loosely corresponding to the three heads. Time not only had three names and three heads, but was also flanked by the powers of Ἀνάγκη and Ἀδράστεια, Fate and Ineluctability. These powers serve as expressions of the qualities of the Time-deity himself. It is said that Adrasteia embraced the whole universe, keeping hold of its boundaries (διωργυιωμένην ἐν παντὶ τῷ κόσμῳ, τῶν περάτων αὐτοῦ ἐφαπτομένην). We recognize in this description the qualities of the ancient Time-deity, whose offspring in the history of philosophy was Anaximander's ἄπειρον.

Damascius next says that the Time-deity generated a new triad: moist air (Αἰθῆρ), endless chaos (Χάος ἄπειρον), and dark nether-world (Ἔρεβος ὀμιχλῶδες). In the middle of this Triad the world-egg comes into existence, generated by Χρόνος. This world-egg is herma-phrodite (ἀρρενόθηλυς). It contains the male and female germs of all things that were developed from the primeval Egg. The further generation of the universe, from the primeval Egg onwards, is again described as a triadic process. We are left with the impression that the account, as Damascius gives it, is to a high degree a mixture of mainly synonymous elements, arranged according to a triadic principle. The triad Ether, Chaos and Erebos e.g. is a triple variation on the same idea of yawning dark Void, filled with unformed matter. In

49

many other Orphic fragments Chaos and Erebos appear as synonyms, and Ether has a similar function: that of an indefinitely extended space, in which all things are developed. The name of Ether has been introduced, as is clear from other sources, in order to have the necessary scenery for explaining how light came into existence. At all events, the Orphic myth contains the idea of a widely extended cosmic space, in the middle of which a cosmic egg is generated, containing the germs of all future beings.

This idea of a cosmic egg, or variations of it in more philosophical language, is frequently found in our sources for the Orphic theology. The account by Damascius is followed, in Kern's collection, by a parallel passage from Apion (Kern 55). Here the texture of the story is less mythological, as there are no gods having symbolic forms. The formulas are those of a philosophical cosmology. There is an unformed primordial matter moving disorderly in the depths of a yawning abyss. The unformed mass of primordial matter already possesses the animated germs of the four elements (τετραγενὴς ὕλη). At a certain time the most fertile elements of the mixture were blown by a kind of whirlwind into a central region, where they condensed into a 'critical mixture' (κριτικὴ σύστασις), capable of generating life. When concentrating in this central region, the fertile seeds had drawn with them the surrounding wind (τὸ περικείμενον πνεῦμα), which encompassed it like a divine breath (θειώδης πνεῦμα). The rotating mixture developed a sort of skin (κύτος), and was made pregnant by the encompassing divine breath. The pregnant egg sprang open, and in the greatest light gave birth to a godhead called Phanes.

The divine breath as factor in Orphic cosmogony is also found in a remark of Aristotle in *De anima* (410 b 28 - 29; this passage is quoted by Philoponus and Iamblichus, see Kern 27). Possibly the wording of Aristotle's remark was influenced in some degree by what he knew about the Pythagorean theory, but there can be no doubt as to its contents: "this is also the case with the story told by the Orphic poetry; it says that the soul enters from the universe by a process of inhaling, borne by the winds."

The testimonies, quoted so far, differ in the way they represent the myth. The account by Damascius seems to be a late mixture, incorporating many superfluous elements. The terminology in which Apion presents the theory has been adapted to philosophical use. What Aristotle tells us is very short and essential. The image itself has an archaic character and must have been a current one because many sources repeat it. There can be no reasonable doubt about its authenticity.

The oldest text in which we hear of the myth of the world-egg is the well-known chorus in Aristophanes' *Birds* (vs. 693 - 702). Here, too, the story is about how the cosmos came into existence, starting from Chaos, Night, dark Hades and broad Abyss. In the endless bosom of dark Abyss, dark-winged Night generated the first pregnant germ, an egg, from which sprang Eros, life-giver:

Ἐρέβους δ'ἐν ἀπείροσι κόλποις
τίκτει πρώτιστον ὑπηνέμιον Νὺξ ἡ μελανόπτερος ᾠόν,
ἐξ οὗ ... ἔβλαστεν Ἔρως. (694 - 6)

The elements of the myth are the same: there is the unbounded primordial void, in which the first pregnant germ came into existence; there is the divine breath of life, represented by the adjective ὑπηνέμιον: the primordial egg is said to have been surrounded by wind. The wording of the verse seems to imply that Night generated this primordial egg by wrapping it up in a whirlwind. It is not impossible that Aristophanes added a second meaning, if ὑπηνέμιον ᾠόν is to be understood as 'wind-egg'. The expression existed in Greek as well as in English, as is proved by *Frogs* 186. In the *Clouds* Aristophanes makes fun of the whole theory by representing the whirlwind in the primordial chaos as a 'God Whirlwind', and playing upon the many vulgar connotations of this idea (*Clouds* 379 - 393). This need not exclude that the fun took its starting-point from expressions in use with the Orphics. In the same work even the orthodox Orphic term ἀὴρ ἀπέραντος 'unbounded air', is found. In the same way we can recognize an element of Orphic cosmogony in the adjective ὑπηνέμιον: the primeval germ was surrounded by divine breath and took its vital impulse from it. This is in line with the ancient idea that the soul, as the principle of life, consisted of breath. As has been remarked, no clear distinction existed between air and void.

It must be surmised that the Orphics themselves did not distinguish in their myths the principles which were to be considered essential in contrast to less important elements. This distinction is, in general, not peculiar to mythical thought. The exuberant way in which many synonymous powers and gods have been incorporated into the myths bears witness to this mythical rhetoric. In the course of centuries, moreover, a number of additions have been introduced, which, in our late sources, have been more or less brought into a system. From the standpoint of the more rationalized theories of Greek philosophy, we may focus our attention on three important elements of Orphic cosmogony: (1) a primordial chaos, in which an unformed mass of material elements moves disorderly; (2) a pregnant nucleus, having the shape of an egg, brought forth by a whirling blast of life-giving breath; (3) life inhaled from the outer void and filling the pregnant nucleus, which, bursting open, gives birth to a winged divinity, called Phanes (Kern 56, 58, 60, 61 and passim), and sometimes Mètis (Kern 56, p. 135) or Ericapaeus (Kern 60, 65), less often Eros (Kern 28, 74).

The pregnant nucleus or primeval egg draws its vitality from its begetter, who probably for this reason is called by the name of Heracles, the giant of vital power. The dynamism he had infused into his offspring was such as to cause the enormous egg to explode. Its two halves grew into heaven and earth. In Aristophanes' chorus, quoted above, (*Birds*, 690 - 702 = DK 1 A 12 = Kern 1) it is not heaven and earth, but winged Eros who is born from the egg, and who, by making a mixture of all things, brings forth living beings and man. In one of the Orphic hymns (Quandt 6 = Kern 87), the god, born from the egg, called Phanes here, is addressed as γένεσις μακάρων θνητῶν τ' ἀνθρώπων, 'begetter of the blissful and of mortal man'. All this means that Phanes or Eros concentrates in himself all generative power. The origin of this vital power is the breath inhaled from the universe. The same idea is hidden in a verse in Aristophanes' *Clouds* (627), where Socrates exclaims:

Μὰ τὴν 'Αναπνοήν, μὰ τὸ Χάος, μὰ τὸν 'Αέρα,
"by the Deep Breath, by Chaos, by the Airy Space."

The picture we gather from these Orphic sources is completely different from the myth which could be reconstructed from the proverbial sayings, discussed in our first chapter. This myth was the ancestor of the first apeiron-theory, and contained, in essence, a unifying cosmological theory. The evolution of all things and birth and death of all beings were ruled in this theory by one supreme divinity. The philosophical theories which are descended from this myth are all characterized by their tendency to maintain the unity of all things and to describe the unifying principle as supreme and divine. Anaximander declared it to be a law of cosmic and reciprocal justice that all things should return to that from which they originated. In Xenophanes, the ancient conception caused a strong emphasis to be laid on the unity and divinity of the universe, to such an extent that the description of it borders on pantheism. To Parmenides the unity

52

of Being is a sacrosanct truth, preached with divine authority, and venerated with religious awe.

The Orphic myth represents quite a different way of thinking. To the later rationalizing development the fact that, in Orphic myth, two or three different working powers are described, is of foremost importance. These primordial powers generate the cosmos by their interaction. They are called primordial chaos, pregnant germ, and divine vital power or Eros. It is interesting to find Eros described, in Plato's Symposium, as the godhead of poverty, that is as the vital desire for self-expansion, acting in the sphere between nothingness and fulfilment. Even in Aristotle's doctrine of form and matter there is a third principle called στέρησις or privation which suggests that ὕλη so to say "desires" for the εἶδος which is to give it the state of actual being.

Giving the name of primordial matter to the unordered mixture of the Orphic chaos may cause the impression of anticipating later philosophic development. In many late sources on Orphism this primeval chaos is interpreted as representing the ὕλη of the philosophers. Though there may be a historical connection, the identification of the two is an anachronism. When describing Presocratic theories, the term ὕλη or matter in the technical sense of Aristotelean philosophy must be avoided altogether. There is, however, in modern linguistic use a non-technical sense in which the word matter may be used to designate the substance of which things are made. In this sense the term 'matter' can be used without implicitly introducing Aristotelean metaphysics. It is, at the same time, the sense in which the concept had existed for many centuries before the dawn of Greek philosophy.

In Hesiod already we find chaos as the origin of men and gods. (*Theog.* 116, Cornford 1912, 66, 70; Cornford 1952, II, 194). The pedigree of Chaos, however, is much older, for it goes back to the Babylonian notion of the primeval ocean, called Tiamat, from which all beings originate. Akin to this Babylonian idea is the Biblical description of tehôm, the waters over which hovered the Spirit of God. The Ἔρεβος ὀμιχλῶδες of the Orphics, Hesiod's Chaos, water as the first principle of all things, as Thales took it –, all probably have a common origin with the Babylonian and Biblical myths. (See: Heidel 1942; Solmsen 1950, II; Cornford 1952, 248; Eisfeldt 1952; Hölscher 1953; Guthrie 1957, 17 - 18; Dornseiff 1937 and 1956; Laemmli 1962; Brandon 1963.)

An interesting parallel of these myths is found in certain Phoenician conceptions, an account of which is found in Eusebius (Eusebii Pamphyli *Evangelicae Praeparationis* libri XV, rec. E. H. Gifford, Oxonii 1903, I 33 c - d = ed. Mras, Berlin 1954, vol. I p. 42-43. The text also in Hölscher 1953, 394).

Τὴν τῶν ὅλων ἀρχὴν ὑποτίθεται ἀέρα ζοφώδη καὶ πνευματώδη, ἢ πνοὴν ἀέρος ζοφώδους, καὶ χάος θολερὸν ἐρεβῶδες. Ταῦτα δὲ εἶναι ἄπειρα, καὶ διὰ πολὺν αἰῶνα μὴ ἔχειν πέρας. Ὅτε δέ, φησίν, ἠράσθη τὸ πνεῦμα τῶν ἰδίων ἀρχῶν καὶ ἐγένετο σύγκρασις, ἡ πλοκὴ ἐκείνη ἐκλήθη πόθος. Αὕτη δὲ ἀρχὴ κτίσεως ἁπάντων. Αὐτὸ δὲ οὐκ ἐγίνωσκε τὴν αὐτοῦ κτίσιν· καὶ ἐκ τῆς αὐτοῦ συμπλοκῆς τοῦ πνεύματος ἐγένετο Μώτ. Τοῦτό τινές φασιν ἰλύν, οἱ δὲ ὑδατώδους μίξεως σῆψιν. Καὶ ἐκ ταύτης ἐγένετο πᾶσα σπορὰ κτίσεως, καὶ γένεσις τῶν ὅλων. Ἦν δέ τινα ζῷα οὐκ ἔχοντα αἴσθησιν, ἐξ ὧν ἐγένετο ζῷα νοερά, καὶ ἐκλήθη Ζωφασημίν, τοῦτ' ἔστιν οὐρανοῦ κατόπται. Καὶ ἀνεπλάσθη ὁμοίως ᾠοῦ σχήματι. Καὶ ἐξέλαμψε Μώτ, ἥλιός τε καὶ σελήνη, ἀστέρες τε καὶ ἄστρα μεγάλα.

"As the first principle of all things he posits a misty air moved by a breath, or also a breath of misty air, and chaos as a turbid and dark abyss. He says all this is unbounded and has no end throughout eternity. When this breath, as he says, fell in love with its own first principles and a mixture came about, the intertwinement received the name of love's desire. This was the starting-point for the building-up (or: the creation) of all things. It did not know its own building-up. From this intertwining of breath arose Moot. Some call this slime, some a fermentation in a watery mixture. From this fermentation originated every germ of the building-up of the universe, and the origin of the whole. There existed a number of living beings, without any perception, from which spiritual beings originated, and these were called Zophasemin, that is contemplators of the heavens. It was moulded just like the shape of an egg. Then from it emerged shining Moot, sun and moon, stars and great heavenly bodies."

As the source from which he got his information, Eusebius mentions a certain Philo of Byblos. Under the name of this author no other writings have been preserved, which means that it is extremely hard to assess his reliability. The account as quoted above seems somewhat muddled and mixed-up, as if it were a compilation from various sources. The Greek expressions Philo used have caused a considerable distrust of its authenticity. One of the earliest critical studies on the subject of this Phoenician mythology was published by Ernest Renan in 1858. It was not until the excavations at Ras Shamra that Eusebius' account regained a good deal of its reliability.

The Ugaritic texts, found at Ras Shamra proved the existence of very old mythological texts in this same style, and also their parallelism with the Phoenician mythology given by Eusebius. Due to these discoveries, an account given by Eudemus and preserved in a passage of Damascius (Eudemus ed. Wehrli fr. 150) has gained a background. In this text of Eudemus we find a comparison between the mythology of the Greeks, the Babylonians and the Phoenicians. In what Eudemus says about the 'mythology of the Sidonians' there are very close parallels with the extracts from Philo of Byblos given by Eusebius. Among other things we find here three principles of Being: Χρόνος, Πόϑος and 'Ομίχλη, Time, Desire and Mist. When Desire and Mist combined, airy Breath originated. To this account by Eudemus Damascius adds his own information, taken directly from Phoenician sources: from airy Breath new beings came forth, among which there was a heavenly egg. When this egg burst open, heaven and earth came into existence.

However confused and complicated these genealogies may be, this much is clear that many elements of the so-called Orphic theology are akin to elements of eastern, and more especially Babylonian, resp. Phoenician mythology. The most important are: the dark abyss of unbounded chaos, the egg as the first germ of vital power, the breath inhaled as a generating principle, and the part played by Eros in the development of the universe. It is worth noticing that in Eusebius' account the primeval mixture is indicated as a 'watery mixture' (ὑδατώδης μῖξις), or 'slime' (ἰλύς), probably the same kneadable material out of which, in the story of *Genesis*, man was moulded and called to life by the Spirit of God.

The Pythagorean theories are in many respects a duplicate of the Orphic traditions. Cornford (1912, 198) even regards Pythagoreanism as a reformation of Orphism. Their doctrines coincide practically on two points: the immortality of the soul, conceived as a rebirth after death, and the way they represent the cosmic evolution. Mathematics was probably a specially Pythagorean branch of activity.

As early as in antiquity the affinity of the Pythagorean to the Orphic doctrines has been noted. Herodotus mentions both of them, when describing an Egyptian taboo on clothing (II 81). The soul's migration, sacred to the Orphics, is one of the Pythagorean doctrines of which we have early evidence, viz. in Xenophanes' verses (DK 21 B 7) where the story is told of the wailing dog, in whose voice Pythagoras recognized the voice of a deceased friend. Plato fairly often quotes Orphic and Pythagorean theories, though the theories are not always indicated as Orphic or Pythagorean. He seldom says anything about Pythagoras himself. The name of Pythagoras occurs only once (*Rep.* 600 B). When talking about the Pythagorean doctrine, Plato generally says that the 'Pythagorean way of Life' (ὁ Πυθαγόρειος τρόπος τοῦ βίου) implied this or that consequence, or he indicates the adherents of this doctrine by the name of 'the Pythagoreans', οἱ Πυθαγόρειοι (e.g. *Rep.* 530 D). Sometimes he even restricts himself to the indication 'this is a theory handed down as a secret doctrine' (ὁ ἐν ἀπορρήτοις λεγόμενος λόγος), e.g. when Socrates in the *Phaedo*, describes the Pythagorean convictions of the Thebans Cebes and Simmias (62 B). From the way Plato quotes Pythagorean theories it is obvious that he is speaking about the Pythagoreans he knew in his own days, not about Pythagoras himself or the first school of his adepts. Nevertheless, we may safely assume that the theories mentioned, especially the theory of the soul's migration, and the purity-rites and taboo-precepts connected with it, were part of the early doctrine of Pythagoras' school. It is mainly their affinity with the Orphic doctrines which assures their being ancient.

Plato's statements on the Orphic doctrines can generally be identified more easily than his accounts on Pythagorean theories, because more often he mentions the Orphics by name. Plato does so, when he is quoting verses from Orphic sources, by saying that οἱ ἀμφὶ 'Ορφέα 'the adepts of Orpheus', or οἱ 'Ορφικοί, 'the Orphics', were the authors of the verses or the proverb (e.g. *Crat.* 400 C, *Laws* 782 C). Many times, however, the Orphics are also hinted at indirectly. In these cases Plato introduces his account with formulas such as 'according to an ancient theory' (παλαιὸς λόγος e.g. *Phaed.* 70 C, *Ep.* VII 335 A), or 'in the initiation-rites' (οἱ τὰς τελετὰς καταστήσαντες *Phaed.* 69 C). A passage such as *Crat.* 402 B shows that Plato had a fairly specified knowledge of these rites and doctrines. In the *Apology* Socrates professes his belief in immortality in formulas of the Orphic creed (cf. de Vogel 1936, 61). Of all the numerous passages in which Plato quotes Orphic doctrines, a good many are devoted to the belief in a life hereafter, and, in that connection, to the doctrine that the soul is to be purified by practices of abstinence and purificatory rites. It is this class of doctrines of which we have the most conclusive evidence that the very earliest Pythagoreans had also accepted them (cf. Guthrie 1962, 157-169).

There is a special problem which, for the moment, must be left out here; that is the problem of how far Plato's mathematical doctrines, and also some of his scientific views in the Timaios, were his own or had been borrowed by him from the Pythagoreans. This is a very important problem, because in Plato's later philosophy the mathematical method of thinking is to such a high degree interwoven with his cosmological theories and sometimes with his metaphysical theories as well. It is difficult to draw a line between the historical development leading up to Plato's theories, and Plato's own special way of making use of the material that was handed down to him by tradition. The most extreme hypotheses on this point have been worked out by Burnet (G.P.), Taylor (1928) and Frank (1923) (cf. de Vogel 1936, 23 - 31, 116 - 118, 213 - 216).

It is, however, the cosmological myth which interests us at this moment. The oldest forms of Pythagorean and Orphic cosmology are based on a small number of first principles which, in their later rationalized form, grew into the prinicples of a dualistic cosmology, in which form was opposed to matter. This dualistic theory stands in contrast to the monistic doctrines of the oldest Milesian tradition. The roots of the dualistic cosmology go back to Phoenician and Babylonian mythology.

The Pythagorean and Orphic movements must have been manifestations of a broad religious current spreading over the whole Mediterranean in the sixth century B.C. Evidence of the Orphic movement is found in almost every region where Greek was spoken. One of the more active centres of Orphism must have been South-Italy. This is suggested by the numerous allusions to Orphism in authors living there, such as Empedocles (cf. Jaeger *Theol.* 143 and Rostagni 1924, 183-247) and also by the fact that several times Plato makes allusion to Sicilian or Italian sources when talking about Orphic theories. The most eloquent evidence are small golden plates with Orphic inscriptions, found in towns of *Magna Graecia*, which is in the country where Pythagoras lived (DK 1 B 17 from Petelia, DK 1 B 18, 19, 20 from Thurii). As we have found convincing parallels between Pythagorean and Orphic myths, these findings by themselves confirm the view that both movements were branches of that large complex of religious convictions which emerged in so many Greek towns in the sixth century. Orphism provides us with the link between Pythagorean cosmology and Babylonian myth. A number of elements in the Orphic theology presents so striking a resemblance to these eastern myths that it is hard not to believe in an eastern origin. An example is the history of χάος discussed above, and also the many heterogeneous divinities, described in Orphic sources, and reminiscent of Babylonian monsters (e.g. DK 1 B 13).

The pedigree of this mythological cosmology is of special importance when we ask for the origin of certain cosmological theories, which are positively ascribed to the Pythagoreans by Aristotle. They most clearly show the old ground-pattern of a Chaos and a primordial vital nucleus. In terms of later date this nucleus is indicated by Aristotle as "the One, or the faces of the solids, or the Sperm, or principles even they themselves cannot account for". Aristotle's obvious irritation in his description of their wild theories once more guarantees the authenticity of the description (see Ross' commentary ad *Met.* 1091 a 13 - 18).

Οἱ μὲν οὖν Πυθαγόρειοι πότερον οὐ ποιοῦσιν ἢ ποιοῦσι γένεσιν οὐδὲν δεῖ διστάζειν· φανερῶς γὰρ λέγουσιν ὡς τοῦ ἑνὸς συσταθέντος, εἴτ᾽ ἐξ ἐπιπέδων εἴτ᾽ ἐκ χροιᾶς εἴτ᾽ ἐκ σπέρματος εἴτ᾽ ἐξ ὧν ἀποροῦσιν εἰπεῖν, εὐθὺς τὸ ἔγγιστα τοῦ ἀπείρου [ὅτι] εἵλκετο καὶ ἐπεραίνετο ὑπὸ τοῦ πέρατος (*Met.* N 3, 1091 a 13 - 18).

"Now there is no need to be ambiguous about the question whether the Pythagoreans did or did not introduce becoming; for, as everyone may convince himself, they say that when the One had been formed, whether from planes or surfaces or sperm or from principles even they themselves cannot account for, instantly the nearest parts of the Infinite were drawn in [as a breath] and defined by the definite."

Εἶναι δ᾽ ἔφασαν καὶ οἱ Πυθαγόρειοι κενόν, καὶ ἐπεισιέναι αὐτὸ τῷ οὐρανῷ ἐκ τοῦ ἀπείρου πνεύματος ὡς ἀναπνέοντι καὶ τὸ κενόν, ὃ διορίζει τὰς φύσεις, ὡς ὄντος τοῦ κενοῦ χωρισμοῦ τινὸς τῶν ἐφεξῆς καὶ διορίσεως (*Phys.* VI, 213 b 22 - 26).

"The Pythagoreans also said there was a void, and that it entered heaven from the unbounded breath, because the heaven inhaled this void, which sunders the several natures. In this they started from the supposition that the void is a kind of separation of and a boundary between things that come next to each other."

As always, Aristotle does not speak of Pythagoras, but of 'the Pythagoreans', and these must have been either the Pythagoreans that were his contemporaries or the Pythagoreans whose writings Aristotle had read. By itself, Aristotle's account gives us no clue as regards the antiquity of the doctrine. Once we know, however, the contents of the theory, we can see from a remark by Xenophanes that it goes back to the earliest generations of Pythagoreans. Diogenes Laertius (IX 19 = DK 21 A 1) states that, according to Xenophanes, "the Godhead is spherical and sees and perceives with all of itself, but that it does not inhale." The spherical figure belongs to the tradition of the all-embracing heavenly deity, which was discussed in our first two chapters. The addition 'that it did not inhale' calls for discussion. The best interpretation seems to be, that these words were a reaction of Xenophanes to the current Pythagorean cosmology. If this interpretation is sound, the words must be more or less authentic, because in later centuries they would have sounded superfluous. They only acquire their full sense if Xenophanes had opponents who held a theory of a breathing universe. This seemingly strange theory was found with the Pythagoreans only. It was a point that was likely to arouse the criticism of thinkers of the type of Xenophanes and Parmenides, who saw a divine unity in the universe and absolutely rejected the view that this divine world had developed from a first germ like a living being.

In this theory of the breathing universe three points are of importance. (1) The evolution of the cosmos starts with a primordial unity, which is opposed to an undetermined Void. (2) The first living nucleus in the Pythagorean theory developed by breathing. The breath it inhaled is called, in Aristotle's account, ἄπειρον πνεῦμα, 'boundless breath', or simply τὸ ἄπειρον, 'the Unbounded'. As we saw above in the discussion on Parmenides (p. 40-41), a very ancient conception implied that breath, air and void were identical. When speaking of Anaxagoras, Aristotle informs us of an experiment intended to prove that air was a thing. A wine-skin was filled with air and closed. The air in the skin then offered resistance (*Phys.* 213 a 26). Aristotle adds the remark that "people stick to the view that where no bodies can be perceived there is empty space; supposing all existing things to be bodies, they say that void is that in which there is absolutely nothing; this amounts to saying that what is full of air is empty." In two other places (*De anima* 419 b 34, *De part. an.* 656 b 15) Aristotle remarks that 'according to popular thinking' (δοκεῖ, τὸ καλούμενον) the air is a void (cf. Burnet EGP 74 n. 2, 109 n. 1).

(3) The air or void which is inhaled does not only serve as the principle of growth for the living being, but at the same time it has the function of separating individual things, thus making the universe discontinuous. This is expressed in the words διορίζει τὰς φύσεις (*Phys.* 213 b 24). In this expression the subject of the clause is τὸ κενόν: the

void brings separation between beings. This may give rise to the question whether the void is to be considered the delimiting, and, consequently, form-giving principle. Probably the early Pythagoreans did not make this sharp distinction, formulated in concepts of Aristotelean metaphysics. First of all, the fragment taken from the *Metaphysics* seems to convey the opposite meaning: the void inhaled was itself delimited by the πέρας. The quotation is not to be interpreted in terms of the Aristotelean distinctions. Burnet (EGP 108) pointed out that the question is unnecessary, because διορίζει simply means: 'keeps the units apart from each other'. This is also made clear by the expression χωρισμοῦ τινος: the void represents the interval between things. A further confirmation of this is found in a fragment from Aristotle's work on the Pythagorean philosophy (DK 58 B 30), where we read that "the void causes separation between the fields, occupied by things", διορίζει τὰς χώρας, more or less in the sense that the void is the principle of discontinuity. The term διόρισις must be understood in the sense that the void is the cause of the universe being discontinuous. The void is the principle by virtue of which the Pythagoreans, though in a somewhat primitive way, tried to ensure the well-delimited individuality of things.

Summing up, we must say that, as far as we can discern, the earliest Pythagoreans admitted two different kinds of oppositions in the construction of their cosmology: the opposition of Chaos and primordial germ, and the opposition of ἄπειρον and πέρας. The two oppositions have a certain parallelism, though a rather vague one. Chaos, identified with infinite space or void, surrounding the universe, is described as awakening the primordial germ to life. Thus infinite void or breath, or, in the Greek word, πνεῦμα = spirit, becomes the determining factor, inhaled by the developing germ. The parts of determining and determined factors are not as clearly distributed as might be desired. Though standing in contrast to the infinite void, the developing germ also has in itself a determining factor. As a germ it contains a principle of form which will work itself out into a developed constitution from the moment when the life-giving breath or spirit intervenes. It is as if, in terms of later philosophy, the germ bears within itself the innate idea, which is going to express itself in the special characteristics of the fully developed being. The distribution of the parts becomes more clearly marked when the opposition of ἄπειρον and πέρας is added as a parallelism. As we shall see in the eighth chapter, the theory of ἄπειρον and πέρας in Plato's *Philebus* was probably the nearest preparation to Aristotle's hylemorphism. In this dialogue, Plato uses the term ἄπειρον not in the Anaximandrean sense, but strictly as the opposite of πέρας, thereby introducing the Pythagorean pair of opposites as a starting-point for his ontological theory. The ἄπειρον is the indeterminate principle, πέρας is the delimiting factor. It seems not unlikely that, in the early Pythagorean theory, the two sets of opposites, on the one hand Chaos and primordial germ, and on the other hand ἄπειρον and πέρας, may have been viewed as embodying the same principle of explanation. The interaction of indeterminate void and living nucleus produced the evolution of the universe, just as the interaction of ἄπειρον and πέρας produced the special characteristics of every individual thing.

The great importance of Pythagorean philosophy to the history of Greek thought lies in the fact that it introduced dualistic principles in order to explain the qualities of things and the evolution of the cosmos. The starting-point of this philosophy is in direct opposition to the Ionian way of explaining the universe. In the Ionian view, an all-embracing godhead ruled all cosmic life. The Ionian tradition implies a monistic tendency, because the whole universe forms a unity of interplaying forces, in which the first principle of life and being is omnipresent and omnipotent. This unity of all things, therefore, was invested with divine majesty. The philosophers who followed this tradition have emphasized different aspects of this one principle of unity, but they all show the same religious veneration in describing and defending it. It is not saying too much that the introduction of an undetermined void as an antagonistic principle in the production of individual beings must have horrified the philosophers whose thoughts were penetrated by the consciousness of the divine unity of the cosmos. In the verses of Parmenides we are, as it were, eye-witnesses to Parmenides' reaction to this horror: the new theory is banished with all force as an impiety. Perhaps we may add: as a philosophic impiety, because the rejection has its ground in the argument of salvation for human reason, rather than in religious awe of a highest divinity: ἀλλὰ σὺ τῆσδ' ἀφ' ὁδοῦ διζήσιος εἶργε νόημα, "but thou, keep thy thought away from this course of investigation" (fr. 7, verse 2). Parmenides speaks as a philosopher, but nevertheless he preaches, and he does so with the fervour of an apostle. The old awareness of divine omnipresence and cosmic unity has maintained its sway over his thinking.

61

The dualism described here is a capital point in the history of the concept of ἄπειρον. From the moment the Pythagorean influence comes into play, this concept carries with it an inner contradiction. This contradiction can be traced to its historic origins. In the Ionian philosophy the ἄπειρον is the very positive infinity of an all-embracing divine power, uniting all beings, and principle of their existence and unity. Due to the Pythagorean influence the term acquired the negative meaning of cosmic void and indeterminate principle, cause of the discontinuity of things and of their being a multitude. It is this latter signification which develops widest in the following centuries. In a mathematical sense it is present in the concept of 'measurable field', in cosmology it appears as the empty space offering room (χώρα) for coming into existence to all things, metaphysically it is the undetermined substrate (ὑποδοχή) for all things, necessary to, though not participating in, their existence. These three significations can be observed in Plato's work. The measurable field plays its part in the construction of the groundpatterns of the elements as regular solids. Empty space and undetermined substrate are deeper and more general foundations for the theory by which Plato attempts to explain the nature and existence of matter.

As in the case of the development which led from the ancient Time-deity to the philosophical concept of ἄπειρον in its Ionian sense, so in the development of the Pythagorean ideas a certain stage was reached at which the concepts lost their mythical contents and grew into metaphysical theories. Aristotle describes the Pythagorean theories (*Met.* 986 b 2 - 3 and 987 a 13 - 19) as if from the very start the concepts of ἕν, ἄπειρον and πέρας had been conceived as ontological principles. This may have been influenced by Plato's theories on these points. In the case of the Pythagoreans, the actual border-line of the transition from myth to metaphysics cannot be identified with all clearness. It seems not impossible that it was Plato himself who rationalized the ground-patterns of Pythagorean thought for the first time to such a degree that they could form the starting-point of a coherent metaphysics.

The importance of the Pythagorean theories to our investigation is that they provide us with the missing link between the development leading up to the Aristotelean hylemorphism and its mythical ancestors. Aristotle's theory was prepared by Plato's theory on ἄπειρον and πέρας, and probably also the μὴ ὄν-theory of the *Sophistes*, as well as the theory of χώρα of the *Timaeus*, played their part in suggesting to

Aristotle his doctrine of hylemorphism. As it seems, the most direct preparation lay in the πέρας - ἄπειρον doctrine of the *Philebus*, which has its roots in Pythagoreanism. Thus, we may assume that, with a certain number of intermediary stages, the Aristotelean hylemorphism was a descendant of the Pythagorean doctrines. These, in their turn, go back to the Eastern myth, in which the infinite Void or Chaos was contrasted to the life-bearing primordial nucleus. In the pedigree of the theory the earliest ancestor of Aristotelean hylemorphism was Babylonian chaos.

B. MATHEMATICS: THE INFINITE AS THE INDETERMINATE

In the first volume of a recent work on the history of Greek philosophy Guthrie gives a comprehensive account of the history and the doctrines of the earliest Pythagoreans. He starts his discussions by noticing that the literature on this subject is 'a bottomless pit' (p. 146). The range of this literature is inversely proportional to the scarcity of our sources on the earliest form of Pythagoreanism, that is to say, the scarcity of sources antedating the year 400 B.C.

There are plenty of later authorities on early Pythagoreanism, because during the Hellenistic period there was an important revival of Pythagorean doctrines. Since Zeller, the tendency has been to reject these later sources as mainly pious legends devised by preachers of Pythagorean morals to meet the needs of the period. It was not until recent times that a new evaluation of the evidence has been attempted. In 1961 Thesleff published his investigation on *'the Pythagorean writings of the Hellenistic period'*. The traditional view persists in the works of Burkert (1962) and Philip (1966), who, in the wake of Frank (1923), tend to regard the tradition on the early Pythagorean theories as mainly an invention of later, 'pythagorizing' philosophers. As such they consider Plato's successors in the Academy, Speusippus and Xenocrates, and, of course, the writers of the Hellenistic period. An unprejudiced account of the evidence was given by Kurt von Fritz in RE ($\pm$ 1962). In 1966 a work was published by C. J. de Vogel, in which the evidence from the later sources is taken into full consideration.

The abundance of modern investigations makes the problem even more complex. The outlines of the earliest Pythagorean doctrines have to be built up from materials coming to us from widely dispersed sources. Each separate source often calls for a special critical treatment. Uniting the scattered evidence is in itself a complex task but sometimes it produces remarkable results. In such cases the modern investigations often come to have the status of source-material by their own standards. A highly ingenious method of criticism had to be developed in order to deduce a coherent picture of Pythagorean doctrine from this scattered material. It was F. M. Cornford and J. E. Raven who showed great intelligence as well as patience in performing this painstaking work of reconstruction. They built on the foundations laid by John Burnet (EGP and GP). Their work was continued by W. K. C. Guthrie.

One of the special problems concerning early Pythagoreanism is that of Pythagorean mathematics. Direct information on the mathematical doctrines of early Pythagoreanism must, for the greater part, be derived from Hellenistic sources. Certain theories are mentioned by Aristotle whose work on the Pythagoreans is unfortunately lost. It is mostly the archaic character of the theories which determines their being assigned to the early stages of Pythagoreanism. There are no contemporary sources for these early stages. Both Plato and Aristotle when speaking on the subject are, as a rule, discussing theories of the Pythagoreans who were their contemporaries. Nevertheless, the authority of the later sources may be relied on whenever the mathematical theorems they attribute to the earliest Pythagoreans confirm this attribution by their archaic character.

The decipherment of Babylonian texts has brought to light to what extent the earliest Greek geometers borrowed their techniques from Babylonian tradition (cf. van der Waerden 1948, 1966, Neugebauer 1936, 1952). It is no longer possible to think the Greeks were original in developing mathematics. The so-called theorem of Pythagoras had existed in Mesopotamia for more than a thousand years before Pythagoras. Not even the attempt at developing a general form for the demonstration of a theorem can be regarded as properly Greek. A mathematic tradition was transmitted to the Greeks from the East, probably along the same caravan-routes by which trade went east- and westward. The general direction in this migration of techniques and science was from Mesopotamia to Ionia. It seems very probable therefore that Thales in Miletus and Pythagoras on Samos acquired rather extensive mathematical and astronomical knowledge from this eastern tradition.

Little information about Pythagoras' life has come down to us from the first century after his death, but what we know is sufficient

64

to confirm the later, more detailed accounts. There are four lines by Xenophanes (DK 21 B 7), in which Pythagoras' doctrine of metempsychosis is ridiculed. Heraclitus criticizes his ambitious way of accumulating knowledge without making the proper use of it in two passages, transmitted to us by Diogenes Laertius. In one of these two passages (DK 22 B 129) he says that "Pythagoras, son of Mnesarchus, surpassed all people in collecting information, and by making a choice from these collections came into possession of wisdom, much learning, and evil practices." The other passage (DK 22 B 40) reads: "Much learning does not impart knowledge, for else Hesiod and Pythagoras would have learnt from it, as well as Xenophanes and Hecataeus."

Xenophanes and Heraclitus may have been late contemporaries of Pythagoras. Their remarks make it clear that Pythagoras advocated the doctrine of metempsychosis, and that he occupied himself very extensively with the then available science. The way he did so was vulgar in Heraclitus' eyes. There is a fragment of Empedocles (DK 31 B 129), probably referring to Pythagoras and showing the same tendency.

After Xenophanes and Heraclitus comes Herodotus (II 81, II 123, IV 95 - 96). Herodotus may have taken his information from sources contemporary to Pythagoras, but at the same time his way of telling the stories suggests that Pythagoras must have become the subject of myths soon after his death. Of the passages quoted II 123 does not mention the Pythagoreans. It contains, however, the same theory about the transmigration of souls which we know to have formed part of the Pythagorean doctrine, and even has the detail that there is a return of the soul in 3000 years' time, just as Plato has it in his myth (*Phaedrus* 249 a). Herodotus says he does know the names of those Greeks who are adherents of this doctrine, but he does not want to write them down. This may be due to the fact that, in his later years, Herodotus lived in South-Italy, where the Pythagorean sect was eager to keep its traditions secret. In II 81 Herodotus mentions a taboo on wearing woollen clothes, observed by the Egyptians, adding that "in this respect they have the same traditions as the followers of Orpheus and Dionysus, who, in fact, are Egyptians and Pythagoreans." Leaving aside the question whether some Pythagorean convictions really originated in Egypt, we may gather from this account by Herodotus that the Pythagoreans were known to Herodotus as a sect observing certain religious taboos. The story in IV 95-96

65

is about a slave of Pythagoras' named Salmoxis, who migrated from Samos to the barbarian country of the Thracians, taking with him the knowledge and the skill he had learnt from 'Pythagoras the sophist'. By playing tricks on the credulous Thracians he convinced them both of his immortality and of their own. Probably Salmoxis was a Thracian hero or divinity, wrongly associated in the myth with the great name of Pythagoras. The conclusion, if any, to be drawn from the account, is that to the Greeks the name of Pythagoras stood for something between a wisdom-monger playing sophisticated tricks and the founder of a religious sect with rather curious customs. This latter feature may have been the more dominant one in the current tradition about Pythagoras. The irritation of Heraclitus possibly had a real motive if Pythagoras used his knowledge in the manner of a self-confident preacher, head of a mysterious sect and guardian of a number of very exclusive theories. Xenophanes' story about the dog whose wailing voice reminded Pythagoras of a dead friend whose soul had become a dog's soul and now greeted him, may well give the impression that Pythagoras rather liked to show off his peculiar convictions. In later biographies Pythagoras is depicted as the leader of a closed group of initiates much devoted to their master. Outsiders may have gathered the impression that Pythagoras really enjoyed being revered as a master of wisdom.

When we come to Plato there is a special problem in interpreting his statements about Pythagoreans or Pythagorean doctrine. It is difficult to find statements in the texts of the dialogues, which may unequivocally be explained as matter-of-fact information in this respect. The reason for this is the large extent to which Plato found inspiration in Pythagorean doctrines. In general we may assume that they were the doctrines held by the Pythagoreans of Plato's own days. Plato incorporated these doctrines into his own views and, although the general tendencies can easily be identified, it is hardly possible to state where the borrowing from Pythagorean sources ended and Plato's own thinking comes in. Aristotle (*Met.* A 6, 987 b 10 - 26) tries to lay down a criterion for distinguishing Pythagorean from Platonic thinking. Its core is a misapprehension of Aristotle as to the principle of the ἄπειρον which Plato defined as a more-and-less. Though Aristotle did not rightly understand what Plato meant by it, it is beyond any doubt that the theory of ἄπειρον and πέρας of the *Philebus*, and also that of the ἄπειρον as a more-and-less, which is the later form of the same theory, were developed by Plato from Pythagorean principles.

66

This means, to the present problem, that there was a Pythagorean as well as a Platonic theory on the dualistic principles of ἄπειρον and πέρας. As far as our sources go, it is not possible to draw a clear dividing line between the two.

Plato once mentions Pythagoras' name (*Rep.* X, 600 B), in a passage where he says that Pythagoras, like Homer, showed others the way to culture (ἡγεμὼν παιδείας), and was the founder of a certain 'way of life' by which the Pythagoreans distinguished themselves. In *Rep.* VII, 530 D he expresses his sympathy to the view held by the Pythagoreans (οἱ Πυθαγόρειοι), that astronomy and music are sister-sciences because both are founded on the theory of numbers and proportions. This makes it clear that the Pythagoreans of Plato's days already had a well-developed arithmetical theory, on which they founded their speculations about astronomy as well as music. This, in turn, confirms the view that the Pythagoreans of the first days, and even Pythagoras himself must have occupied themselves with speculations of this order, though we have no contemporary sources to confirm this (cf. v. d. Waerden 1943).

A very important passage is *Philebus* 16 C. It is the page where Plato starts his exposition of the theory of πέρας and ἄπειρον. He does so by saying that this theory must have been 'handed down from the region of the gods through some Prometheus'. This has since antiquity been understood as pointing to Pythagoras. Burkert (1962, 76-81), who is very critical about attributing later theories to early Pythagoreans, has a penetrating discussion of this passage. He analyses the discussion of 16 C together with the one in 23 C where, after a digression, it is resumed with the words: "We said that it was the god who made us aware of the existence of ἄπειρον and πέρας." Burkert distinguishes this as Pythagorean from the two concepts which Plato, according to his view, added to the theory: the 'mixture' and the 'cause'. He then expounds the further development of the theory, marked by the change in terminology from ἄπειρον - πέρας, *via* μᾶλλον καὶ ἧττον to the ἀόριστος δυάς of the 'unwritten doctrine', an exposition which may by now be regarded as representing a *communis opinio* of Platonists. For the moment we may leave this further development aside, and notice that Burkert, critical as he is about early Pythagorean theories, must confess that πέρας and ἄπειρον were taken by Plato from Pythagorean sources. We may assume that they belonged to the common stock of Pythagorean doctrines, and that they went back to the first generations of Pythagoreans, probably to the founder of the school himself. Moreover, the Pythagorean character of the theory is confirmed by what Aristotle says about it. It is a curious fact that in the fragments of Aristotle's extensive work on the Pythagoreans the mythical and mystic features, not to say the mystifications, once more seem to dominate. (See the texts in Ross, *Fragmenta Selecta*, p. 129-143). There are, however, a number of passages in the extant works of Aristotle, which confirm beyond doubt that the Pythagoreans of Aristotle's days held certain well-defined mathematical and metaphysical theories. One of these is the theory of ἄπειρον and πέρας. The most remarkable characteristic of this theory is that it was exemplified in mathematical form. The theory of ἄπειρον and πέρας in its oldest form must, in fact, have been linked up intimately with the arithmetical theory of odd and even, περιττόν and ἄρτιον. With the aid of what we know about early Pythagoreanism from later sources (see Ross in his commentaries on the *Physics* and *Metaphysics*) we can fairly adequately reconstruct the Pythagorean reasonings as follows.

In *Metaphysics* A, 986 a 17 - 21 Aristotle says:

τοῦ δὲ ἀριθμοῦ στοιχεῖα τό τε ἄρτιον καὶ τὸ περιττόν, τούτων δὲ τὸ μὲν πεπερασμένον τὸ δὲ ἄπειρον, τὸ δ' ἓν ἐξ ἀμφοτέρων εἶναι τούτων (καὶ γὰρ ἄρτιον εἶναι καὶ περιττόν), τὸν δ' ἀριθμὸν ἐκ τοῦ ἑνός, ἀριθμοὺς δέ, καθάπερ εἴρηται, τὸν ὅλον οὐρανόν.

"The elements of number are the even and the odd, the latter of which is well-determined whereas the former is undetermined (ἄπειρον); the One consists of both these elements (for it is at the same time even and odd), and from the One proceeds number, just as the whole heaven is also numbers, as has been said."

This text is followed by the account of the well-known 'table of opposites'. Our second chapter (see p. 42-43) already called for a discussion of these ten pairs of opposites. The mere number ten arouses suspicion, because it was a sacred number to the Pythagoreans. Tradition in antiquity is not unanimous (see Ross a.h.l.). Simplicius has a list of seven pairs of opposites, Porphyry has six. Even Aristotle's own account implies that the number was not always ten, for he continues with the words ἕτεροι δὲ τῶν αὐτῶν τούτων "others of this same sect hold that the principles are ten, the so-called principles κατὰ συστοιχίαν, i.e. principles ordered in pairs." We may be justified in assuming that, at any rate, those opposites which formed the core of the Pythagorean doctrine must also have formed part of the earliest tradition. The problem of πέρας and ἄπειρον as well as the problem

68

of the one and many with its formulas of a primitive theory of numbers, were essential to any Pythagorean doctrine.

We may notice that Aristotle's remark on numbers proceeding from the One runs a serious risk of not being matter-of-fact information as to the earliest form of the theory. In later Platonic theory the One indeed was made the origin from which multiplicity emanated, and though this theory was intended metaphysically, it was modelled on number-theory. This may easily have given occasion to project it back to the early Pythagoreans. Not being subject to seeing perspectives, Aristotle may uncritically have adapted his expression to a Platonic way of formulating the doctrine. If the earliest Pythagoreans were dualists they may not have felt inclined to have all things (i.e. all numbers, constituting the universe) proceed from the One. We must ask then how this latter view came to be predominant over the original dualism. A plausible answer is that this was due to the influence of Parmenides, who took great pains to eliminate the element of dispersion and multiplicity, i.e. the Pythagorean ἄπειρον from his world-view. If things really took this course, a last question must remain obscure: were there Pythagorean thinkers who, preceding Plato, already adopted the criticism of Parmenides, or was it Plato himself who first integrated the Parmenidean vision into Pythagorean tradition?

The text quoted earlier from the *Physics* (our p. 58) is followed by the words (213 b 26 - 27):

καὶ τοῦτ' εἶναι πρῶτον ἐν τοῖς ἀριθμοῖς· τὸ γὰρ κενὸν διορίζειν τὴν φύσιν αὐτῶν.

"The void is the first among the numbers; for it separates their natures." This can only be understood if we keep in mind that, to the Pythagoreans, one was not a number. The first of the numbers was the number two. Aristotle's statement, then, means that the 'void' is the opposite of the 'one'. This is exactly what we read in Stobaeus' comment on these lines (quoted by Ross a.h.l.): "The heaven is one, and from the unbounded are introduced into heaven Time, Breath and the Void." – Time, Breath and Void must be seen as synonyms of cosmic empty space, because emptiness, air and breath were the same thing, and because the original Time-deity was identical with the outermost cosmic space. It may also be seen from other texts that the Pythagoreans took the heaven to be composed of numbers, e.g. *De caelo* 300 a 15 - 17 and *Metaphysics* 1080 b 18 - 21 where Aristotle says: "The Pythagoreans construct the whole heaven out of

69

numbers", adding in his peculiar sneering tone: "When asked how the first One came into being, they seem to be at a loss." This remark runs parallel to that in *Met*. 1091 a 12 - 16. Aristotle disposes of the Pythagorean doctrines as if they were some sort of silly mythology. He fails to notice the capital importance to philosophy of this doctrine of an invisible One as a principle of beings. It was Plato who 'had his eyes open', to use an expression of Aristotle's (*Met*. 986 b 28: μᾶλλον βλέπων).

There is another text of Aristotle which tells us how the Pythagoreans treated the concept of ἀπειρία which in this context clearly means 'indeterminateness.' The text is also important because it shows how the opposition πέρας - ἄπειρον and that of περιττόν - ἄρτιον were identified.

καὶ οἱ μὲν τὸ ἄπειρον εἶναι τὸ ἄρτιον· τοῦτο γὰρ ἐναπολαμβανόμενον καὶ ὑπὸ τοῦ περιττοῦ περαινόμενον παρέχειν τοῖς οὖσι τὴν ἀπειρίαν· σημεῖον δ' εἶναι τούτου τὸ συμβαῖνον ἐπὶ τῶν ἀριθμῶν· περιτιθεμένων γὰρ τῶν γνωμόνων περὶ τὸ ἓν καὶ χωρὶς ὁτὲ μὲν ἄλλο ἀεὶ γίγνεσθαι τὸ εἶδος, ὁτὲ δὲ ἕν (*Physics*, III 4, 203 a 10 - 15).

"The Pythagoreans identify the indeterminate and the even; for, they say, when this is taken up (ἐναπολαμβανόμενον) into things and is limited by the odd, it brings indeterminateness to the beings; a proof of this is what happens to numbers; for when the *gnomons* are being laid around the one, or in the other way (καὶ χωρίς), in the latter case the figure is constantly changing, in the former it remains the same."

In this text two expressions call for an explanation: γνώμονες, and καὶ χωρίς. The word γνώμων means any instrument by which something is marked or by the aid of which it can be recognized. In carpentry it means a carpenter's square. Etymologically the word is derived from γιγνώσκω; the original meaning is 'discerner' (Cf. Heath, *Euclid's Elements*, vol I, 370-372). In the explanation given below it is taken in the meaning of 'carpenter's square', but it has a much wider sense. The use of γνώμονες was a characteristic feature of Pythagorean mathematics. The Pythagoreans devoted much attention to geometric diagrams in which a certain characteristic pattern repeated itself. An example of this is the famous pentagram. When in a regular pentagon the diagonals are drawn, the pentagon repeats itself within the intersections of the diagonals.

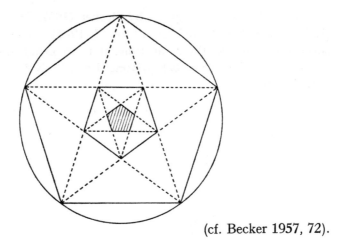

(cf. Becker 1957, 72).

In another way still, this figure offers an example how from a given figure, in this case the triangle with angles 72°, 72°, 36°, a new figure, similar to the original one, can be produced by always adding a similar figure, in this case the triangle 108°, 36°, 36°:

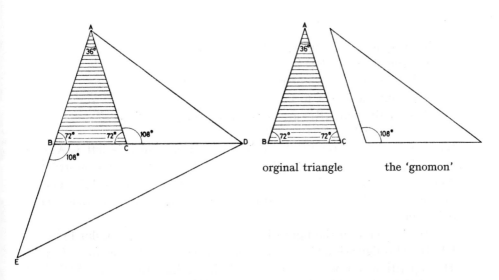

orginal triangle   the 'gnomon'

By adding first ACD as a gnomon to the original triangle, we obtain DAB; by adding DBE as a gnomon we obtain EAD. The triangles ABC, DBE and EDA are repetitions of the same ground-pattern. (Naber 1908). The process repeats itself *ad infinitum*.

71

A third example is given by Becker (1957, 73), and by Heath (1921, I, 208-209; *Transl. Euclid* vol. 3, 19-20). The example is important because, at the same time, it is an instance of the famous method of ἀνταναίρεσις or ἀνθυφαίρεσις (Eucl. *El.* X 2, cf. v. d. Waerden 1947/9, 689).

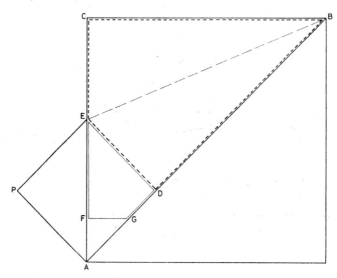

In a square the diagonal AB is drawn.
On this diagonal BD is equal to BC
In D a line is drawn at right angles to DB
This line meets CA in E
Then EBC and EBD are congruent, and ∠ AED = 45°
Therefore CE = ED = AD

If we measure AB by BC (= BD = CA), that which is left is AD. Measuring again BC (= CA) by AD, we find that we can subtract AD (= CE = EF) twice from AC. That which is left is AF. This measuring of the larger magnitude by the smaller repeats itself *ad infinitum.*

In the diagram the figure BCED is repeated in the similar figure EDGF. This figure is a kind of gnomon which repeats itself *ad infinitum.* The repetition can be seen more clearly if we draw the square ADEP.

Becker gives this diagram as a possible instance of the method by which the irrationality of $\sqrt{2}$ was proved in its earliest form. At any rate the recurrent figure may have a claim to Pythagorean origin. As regards the method of ἀνταναίρεσις, Becker himself seems to imply in an earlier publication (1936, 550) that this method belongs to a later stage of development, which he calls 'Theodorische Stufe', referring to Theodorus of Cyrene, the mathematician. There is another method, making use of the so-called 'side' and 'diagonal' numbers giving successive approximations to $\sqrt{2}$, which has a better claim to be of an early date (see Heath, *Euclid's Elements*, I 398 - 400, and Taylor in *Mind* 1926, 429-431). Possibly both methods, that of ἀνταναίρεσις and the one of the 'side' and 'diagonal' numbers, have had their origins in Pythagorean procedures, as is argued by Heller (1958). The fairest chance of being oldest has the apocryphal Euclidean demonstration of *El.* X 117, which will be discussed at the end of this chapter. Its essential feature is its being founded on the authentically Pythagorean doctrine of even and odd. Heath (*Euclid's Elements* vol. III, p. 2) says about it: "The actual method by which the Pythagoreans proved the incommensurability of $\sqrt{2}$ with unity was no doubt that referred to by Aristotle (*Anal. prior.* I, 23, 41 a 26 - 7), a *reductio ad absurdum* by which it is proved that, if the diagonal is commensurable with the side, it will follow that the same number is both odd and even."

The examples of recurrent figures or gnomons are inserted here because the mathematical method used in these examples is characteristic of the kind of problems with which the Pythagoreans occupied themselves. It is possible that the problem of incommensurability was in its earliest form tackled by the method of ἀνταναίρεσις. The fact that this ἀνταναίρεσις produced an infinite process in that case may have been taken as proof that the two lines in question were incommensurable. The infinite regressus was visualized in the diagram by the infinite repetition of the same gnomon. The problems caused by the discovery of the incommensurable could at first not be solved adequately, because the necessary theories had as yet not been developed (Heath, 1931, 105). This must have entailed a situation in which the concept of infinity came to be distrusted because problems involving the concept of infinity could not be mastered. The contradictions caused by infinite processes could not be solved by the mathematical methods in use early in the fifth century.

Having seen what the concept of gnomon stood for, we may return to the text quoted above (*Physics* III 4, 203 a 10 - 15). This text indicates two ways of putting gnomons round a given point or set of points. In the first case this method results in a figure which exactly reproduces itself, as should be the case with gnomons. This figure is a square. In the second case the method produces rectangles, but rectangles which at every new step show a changing proportion of the sides. Commentators have variant explanations of the method of the second case, but the fundamental idea seems to be the same. For a discussion of the various comments by Themistius and Simplicius see Ross ad *Phys.* 203 a 13 - 15. In substance the question of the two ways of applying gnomons, distinguished in the text by the indication καὶ χωρίς, amounts to the following arithmetical methods (Cf. Heidel, 1901; Heath, *Euclid's Elements*, vol I, 359; Burnet EGP 103; Raven 1948, 188-194; Michel 1950, 321; Becker 1957, 40; Kucharski 1959).

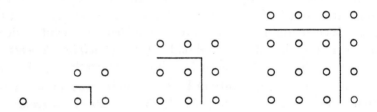

Starting from the number one and adding the next odd number 3, we obtain a square visualizing the first square number 4. Adding the next odd number 5, we obtain a square visualizing the number 9, and so on *ad infinitum*. This arithmetical method visualizes in geometrical diagrams the principle that every square number is the sum of an uninterrupted sequence of odd numbers starting with 1:

$$1 + 3 = 4$$
$$1 + 3 + 5 = 9$$
$$1 + 3 + 5 + 7 = 16 \text{ etc.}$$

In the diagram a new square is always produced by adding a gnomon representing the odd number following the odd number of the preceding gnomon. The diagrams visualize the mutual dependence of the sequences:

1	3	5	7	9	11	13
	4	9	16	25	36	49
	2^2	3^2	4^2	5^2	6^2	7^2

The important point is that by adding gnomons the square character of the number is maintained, however far the sequence is made to go on. That is why the Pythagoreans ascribed to the odd numbers the quality of maintaining a figure in its own character. The concepts of 'odd' and 'well-determined' went side by side.

If we take 'the other way' (καὶ χωρίς), starting not from one dot, but from a pair of two dots, we get a surprisingly different result:

```
                                              ○   ○   ○   ○   ○
                                              ─────────────────
                    ○   ○   ○   ○             ○   ○   ○   ○ │ ○
                    ─────────────             ─────────────
      ○   ○   ○     ○   ○   ○ │ ○             ○   ○   ○   ○ │ ○
      ─────────     ─────────                 ─────────────
○  ○  ○   ○ │ ○     ○   ○   ○ │ ○             ○   ○   ○   ○ │ ○
```

The sequence starts from the even number two, and the gnomons added likewise have even values. The diagrams visualize the mutual dependence of the sequences:

$$2 \quad 4 \quad 6 \quad 8 \quad 10 \quad 12 \quad 14 \quad 16$$
$$6 \quad 12 \quad 20 \quad 30 \quad 42 \quad 56 \quad 72$$
$$2 \times 3 \quad 3 \times 4 \quad 4 \times 5 \quad 5 \times 6 \quad 6 \times 7 \quad 7 \times 8 \quad 8 \times 9$$

In this latter form the sequence demonstrates most clearly that the rectangle more and more approximates the form of a square without ever coinciding with it. This observation may have given to the Pythagoreans the first inkling of the properties of infinite sequences. The important thing to them must have been the unstable proportion of the sides of the rectangle. When applying even gnomons to the even number two, the result was an ever-changing diagram, and the changing even went on *ad infinitum*. Infinite processes were evidently linked up with instability, because in their geometrical visualization none of the rectangles was similar to the others. The use of gnomons in this case did not simply lead to infinite repetitions, but to infinite changes of form. The Pythagoreans formulated this by saying that even was in the category of instability, and because this instability went side by side with infinite progression, the result was that evenness, infinity and instability were included in the same category. This is what Aristotle hints at when saying that 'the figure is constantly changing', ἄλλο ἀεὶ γίγνεσθαι τὸ εἶδος (*Phys.* 203 a 15, cf. Simpl. *phys.* 456, 16 - 458, 16). Simplicius is more explicit: ἡ δὲ τῶν ἀρτίων περίθεσις οὐ ποιεῖ τὸ σχῆμα ὡρισμένον, "The adding of even gnomons makes the figure unstable" (457, 22). Cf. Taylor 1926.

If our interpretation is right, there can be no doubt that the Pythagoreans occupied themselves with finding methods by which, if one started from one dot or a small number of dots and applied certain mathematical operations, numbers could be developed which had certain characteristics in common. The statements about this arithmetic come from later sources, but they are confirmed by incidental hints of Aristotle. Moreover, the tradition is practically unanimous on this point. This means that the Pythagorean mathematicians knew the idea of ordering numbers in a sequence obeying to a certain law.

This is an important conclusion to keep in mind when we shall come to Zeno. It is clear that to Zeno the problem of a sequence being continued to infinity and never coming to its end existed. It is present e.g. in the problem of Achilles and the tortoise. Achilles cannot overtake the tortoise unless he first traverses half the distance separating him from the animal, then half the remaining distance and so on, that is, unless he reaches the end of an infinite sequence of halves. Experience showed that this limit was actually reached and even crossed. It is highly probable that these problems were misunderstood by the sophists and later by Aristotle, as if they were meant to show how little our senses can be relied on. In our next chapter we shall discuss in what sense Zeno's paradoxes are to be understood within the context of Zeno's work itself. For the moment we must state that even as early as the Pythagorean arithmetic of the 5th century the existence can be traced of problems about sequences of numbers. These problems demonstrated, among other things, the connection between the concepts of infinity and indeterminateness. In the historical development of philosophy, Pythagorean arithmetic is a junction at which the concept of ἄπειρον inextricably becomes mixed up with the concept of instability and indeterminateness. For several generations this latter quality was to dominate every treatment of the concept of infinity. The concept of ἄπειρον acquired, metaphysically, a negative ring, only to be replaced by a more positive content when later Platonic thought began speculating about positive infinity.

Our last argument on the Pythagorean treatment of the concept of ἄπειρον will start from a discussion of the apocryphal Euclidean theorem of *El.* X 117. It seems possible to show that this theorem can be put in a form in which the *reductio ad absurdum* on which it is based runs parallel to a *reductio ad infinitum*. Before starting on this discussion, we must say something about the date of the first discovery of incommensurability.

It seems that this problem found its origin in the work by Erich

Frank on *"Plato and the so-called Pythagoreans"* (1923). Frank supposed that the whole tradition about early Pythagoreanism had resulted from an endeavour to make the Pythagorean theories seem old in order to confer on them the venerable aura of antiquity. According to Frank, this led to a general tendency of projecting the Pythagorean doctrines back to Presocratic times, a tendency starting with Plato's immediate successors in the Academy. Frank's vision was too rigorous, and now it has practically become an established view that the discovery of irrationality must be put about the middle of the 5th century B.C. Heath thinks that the discovery was made "with reference to the length of the diagonal of a square" (*Euclid's Elements* III 1), which means that the discovery of the irrationality of the division in extreme and mean ratio (which is found in the 'pentagram') did not precede the discovery of the irrationality of $\sqrt{2}$. He decidedly attributes the discovery to the Pythagoreans (*Euclid's Elements* I 351 and 411-414), and thinks that it was made "at a date appreciably earlier than that of Democritus" (1921, I 157). Von Fritz (1945) takes the same line. In *Gnomon* 1958, p. 82 he writes: "Die Entdeckung des Irrationalen wird von Becker ebenso wie von Van der Waerden und anderen mit Recht wieder in die Mitte des 5. Jahrh. gesetzt." The references in this quotation are to the study published by Becker in 1957, of which the article in Gnomon was a review, and to Van der Waerden 1948, 153. Van der Waerden thinks that the demonstration of the irrationality of $\sqrt{2}$ must have been found about 450 BC, or at least at a date before 420 BC by a method founded on the Pythagorean theory of odd and even. Burkert, who, at times, is perhaps somewhat hypercritical, thinks it is not certain that the discovery was made by Pythagoreans, and he is of the opinion that the discovery was made gradually and not by way of a shock, as is often supposed (1962, 439). He thinks, however, that the irrationality of $\sqrt{2}$ must have been known before Theodorus of Cyrene proved the irrationality of $\sqrt{3}$ upwards to $\sqrt{17}$, which means not later than about the middle of the 5th century.

An interesting summary of reliable conclusions that can be drawn from the various investigations into this matter is given by Szabó 1956, 136. Szabó mentions several theories which must have existed in full form about the middle of the 5th century. Szabó's discussion takes an unexpected turn when he tries to prove that to the development of abstract mathematical demonstrations the previous development of an explicit logic was necessary. Szabó points to the rather frequent use in mathematical demonstrations of the *reductio ad absurdum*. He thinks the Eleatics were the first to develop this way of reasoning, and that a fully abstract method for mathematical proofs could not be developed until the Eleatic philosophers had set the example. We are of the opinion that it is not necessary to assume that the mathematicians had to wait for the Eleatics to receive their first training in explicit reasoning (cf. Timpanaro Cardini 1964, 27-36). This is the more unlikely because in Babylonian mathematics already such fine examples of exact reasoning are found (see V. d. Waerden 1966). Moreover, the theories which Szabó himself thinks to be of an early date show a fairly advanced level in the construction of the proofs. This at least leaves us in doubt as regards the supposed Eleatic monopoly of logical thinking.

We shall keep to the view that the principle of incommensurability must have been found in the course of the 5th century BC, probably by mathematicians of the generation contemporary to or preceding Socrates. It is possible that the discovery was made by Pythagoreans. If the ascription to the Pythagoreans should seriously be doubted (as Burkert does), then at any rate the Pythagoreans must have taken a keen interest in the discovery. The method of proving the incommensurability of $\sqrt{2}$, as we find it in the addition to Euclid's *Elements* X 117, must, in that case, be regarded as an adaptation to the Pythagorean geometry of numbers. Leaving aside the discussion as to the authorship of the discovery itself, we have, at any rate, a text in which we can see Pythagorean thinking at work. The proof of the theorem seems to presuppose the existence of incommensurable lengths as an established fact. Our point is that the method of demonstration involves a *reductio ad absurdum* in such a form that it coincides with a *reductio ad infinitum*. The text as given by Heiberg is as follows (*Euclidis Elementa* X 117 = ed. Heiberg vol. III p. 408-410, appendix 27). A full translation of it is given by Maria Timpanaro Cardini (1964, 382-387). The proof is summarized in shorter form by Heath, *Euclid's Elements* vol. 3, p. 2, by Ross ad *Anal. Priora* 41 a 26 - 7, and by Becker, 1936, 544 - 5.

Προκείσθω ἡμῖν δεῖξαι, ὅτι ἐπὶ τῶν τετραγώνων σχημάτων ἀσύμμετρός ἐστιν ἡ διάμετρος τῇ πλευρᾷ μήκει.

Ἔστω τετράγωνον τὸ ΑΒΓΔ, διάμετρος δὲ αὐτοῦ ἡ ΑΓ· λέγω, ὅτι ἡ ΓΑ ἀσύμμετρός ἐστι τῇ ΑΒ μήκει.

Εἰ γὰρ δυνατόν, ἔστω σύμμετρος· λέγω, ὅτι συμβήσεται τὸν αὐτὸν ἀριθμὸν ἄρτιον εἶναι καὶ περισσόν. φανερὸν μὲν οὖν, ὅτι τὸ ἀπὸ τῆς ΑΓ διπλάσιον τοῦ ἀπὸ τῆς ΑΒ. καὶ ἐπεὶ σύμμετρός ἐστιν ἡ ΓΑ τῇ ΑΒ, ἡ ΓΑ ἄρα πρὸς τὴν ΑΒ λόγον ἔχει, ὃν ἀριθμὸς πρὸς ἀριθμόν. ἐχέτω, ὃν ὁ ΕΖ πρὸς Η, καὶ ἔστωσαν οἱ ΕΖ, Η ἐλάχιστοι τῶν τὸν αὐτὸν λόγον ἐχόντων αὐτοῖς· οὐκ ἄρα μονάς ἐστιν ὁ ΕΖ. εἰ γὰρ ἔσται μονὰς ὁ ΕΖ, ἔχει δὲ λόγον πρὸς τὸν Η, ὃν ἔχει ἡ ΑΓ πρὸς τὴν ΑΒ, καὶ μείζων ἡ ΑΓ τῆς ΑΒ, μείζων ἄρα καὶ ἡ ΕΖ τοῦ Η ἀριθμοῦ· ὅπερ ἄτοπον. οὐκ ἄρα μονάς ἐστιν ὁ ΕΖ· ἀριθμὸς ἄρα. καὶ ἐπεί ἐστιν ὡς ἡ ΓΑ πρὸς τὴν ΑΒ, οὕτως ὁ ΕΖ πρὸς τὸν Η, καὶ ὡς ἄρα τὸ ἀπὸ τῆς ΓΑ πρὸς τὸ ἀπὸ τῆς ΑΒ, οὕτως ὁ ἀπὸ τοῦ ΕΖ πρὸς τὸν ἀπὸ τοῦ Η. διπλάσιον δὲ τὸ ἀπὸ τῆς ΓΑ τοῦ ἀπὸ τῆς ΑΒ· διπλασίων ἄρα καὶ ὁ ἀπὸ τοῦ ΕΖ τοῦ ἀπὸ τοῦ Η· ἄρτιος ἄρα ἐστὶν ὁ ἀπὸ τοῦ ΕΖ· ὥστε καὶ αὐτὸς ὁ ΕΖ ἄρτιός ἐστιν. εἰ γὰρ ἦν περισσός, καὶ ὁ ἀπ᾽ αὐτοῦ τετράγωνος περισσὸς ἦν, ἐπειδήπερ, ἐὰν περισσοὶ ἀριθμοὶ ὁποσοιοῦν συντεθῶσιν, τὸ δὲ πλῆθος αὐτῶν περισσὸν ᾖ, ὁ ὅλος περισσός ἐστιν· ὁ ΕΖ ἄρα ἄρτιός ἐστιν. τετμήσθω δίχα κατὰ τὸ Θ. καὶ ἐπεὶ οἱ ΕΖ, Η ἐλάχιστοί εἰσι τῶν τὸν αὐτὸν λόγον ἐχόντων [αὐτοῖς], πρῶτοι πρὸς ἀλλήλους εἰσίν. καὶ ὁ ΕΖ ἄρτιος· περισσὸς ἄρα ἐστὶν ὁ Η. εἰ γὰρ ἦν ἄρτιος, τοὺς ΕΖ, Η δυὰς ἐμέτρει· πᾶς γὰρ ἄρτιος ἔχει μέρος ἥμισυ· πρώτους ὄντας πρὸς ἀλλήλους· ὅπερ ἐστὶν ἀδύνατον. οὐκ ἄρα ἄρτιός ἐστιν ὁ Η· περισσὸς ἄρα. καὶ ἐπεὶ διπλάσιος ὁ ΕΖ τοῦ ΕΘ, τετραπλάσιος ἄρα ὁ ἀπὸ ΕΖ τοῦ ἀπὸ ΕΘ. διπλάσιος δὲ ὁ ἀπὸ τοῦ ΕΖ τοῦ ἀπὸ τοῦ Η· διπλάσιος ἄρα ὁ ἀπὸ τοῦ Η τοῦ ἀπὸ ΕΘ· ἄρτιος ἄρα ἐστὶν ὁ ἀπὸ τοῦ Η. ἄρτιος ἄρα διὰ τὰ εἰρημένα ὁ Η· ἀλλὰ καὶ περισσός· ὅπερ ἐστὶν ἀδύνατον. οὐκ ἄρα σύμμετρός ἐστιν ἡ ΓΑ τῇ ΑΒ μήκει· ὅπερ ἔδει δεῖξαι.

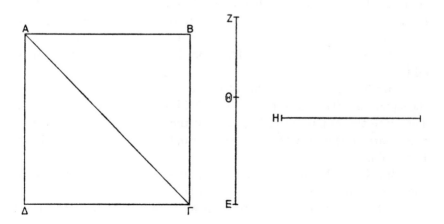

"Let it be required to show that in squares the diagonal is incommensurable in length to the side.

Let a square ABΓΔ be given, the diagonal being A.

I say that ΓA is incommensurable in length to AB.

For suppose them, if possible, to be commensurable. I say that, then, the consequence is that one and the same number will be even and odd at the same time. Now it is clear that the square on AΓ is double of the square on AB [I 47]. ΓA being commensurable to AB, ΓA has to AB the ratio which a number has to a number. Let it have the ratio which EZ has to H, and let EZ, H be the smallest of the lengths which have the same ratio to one another [VII 33]. In that case EZ is not the unit. For if EZ be the unit, and if it have to H the ratio which AΓ has to AB and if AΓ be greater than AB, then also EZ will be greater than H, [which is: the unit will be greater than] a number; which is impossible.

Therefore EZ is not the unit. Therefore it is a number.

Further, because EZ has to H the same ratio which ΓA has to AB, therefore also the square on EZ has to the square on H the same ratio which the square on ΓA has to the square on AB. But the square on ΓA is double of the square on AB. Therefore also the square on EZ is double of the square on H. Therefore the square on EZ is even; therefore also EZ itself is even. For if it were odd, then also the square on it would be odd, because, if odd numbers be added in whatever multitude and this multitude be odd, the whole is also odd [IX 23]. Therefore EZ is even.

Let it be bisected in Θ. Because EZ, H are the smallest numbers of those which have the same ratio, they are prime to one another [VII 22]. But EZ is even. Therefore H is odd. For if it were even, then the number two would measure EZ and H - for any even number is divisible into two parts – which are prime to one another [VII def. 6 and 12]. Which is impossible. Therefore H is not even. So it must be odd.

And because EZ is double of EΘ, the square on EZ is four times the square on EΘ. But the square on EZ is double of the square on H. Therefore the square on H is double of the square on EΘ. Therefore the square on H is even, and therefore also, for the reasons given above, H is even.

But H is also odd. Which is impossible. Therefore ΓA is incommensurable in length to AB. Q.E.D."

Following the proof step by step we obtain in modern notation:

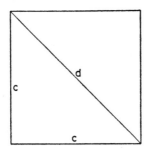

$d^2 = 2c^2$ . . . . (a)

d en c are commensurable in whole numbers . . . . (b)

From (a) and (b) together it follows that d^2 is even, therefore d is even . . . . (1)

If a square is even, it is divisible by 4

Therefore also the half of an even square is even

Therefore $\frac{1}{2} d^2$ is even . . . . (c)

From (a) follows that $\frac{1}{2} d^2 = c^2$

If $\frac{1}{2} d^2$ is even, then also c^2 is even, therefore c is even . . . . . . (2)

If c and d are measurable in whole numbers, their ratio to one another can be reduced to whole numbers which are prime to one another, e.g. $\frac{d}{c} = \frac{p}{q}$ in which p and q are prime to one another. This means that, if p be even, q will be odd and the reverse. The same then holds for $\frac{d}{c}$. Therefore, if we suppose that d is even, c will be odd . (3)

(2) and (3) cannot be true at the same time.

The text of this demonstration suggests that its form has been adapted to the structure of Euclid's work, from which several theorems are quoted almost literally (noted in our translation by square brackets). The substance of the proof, however, is clearly Pythagorean, and it must, in its general line, have existed for generations before it found its way as an apocryphal addition to the manuscripts of the *Elements*. Of its early existence we have a reliable testimony in a casual remark of Aristotle (*Anal. Priora* 41 a 26 - 27) who adduces it as an instance of the *reductio ad absurdum*:

Οἷον ὅτι ἀσύμμετρος ἡ διάμετρος διὰ τὸ γίνεσθαι τὰ περιττὰ ἴσα τοῖς ἀρτίοις συμμέτρου τεθείσης.

"E.g. that the diagonal is incommensurate for the reason that odd will be equal to even if it is supposed to be commensurate."

A parallel remark is found 50 a 37 - 38:

οἶον τεθείσης τῆς διαμέτρου συμμέτρου τὸ τὰ περιττὰ ἴσα εἶναι τοῖς ἀρτίοις,

"e.g. the conclusion that, if the diagonal is supposed to be commensurable, odd numbers will be equal to even."

The reasoning in the proof starts from representing length as a certain amount of numbers. This way of representing has an archaic ring, and is completely in line with the way the theory of numbers is treated in *Elements* IX 21 - 34. In fact, Becker has shown these chapters to be authentically Pythagorean. In our text even a theorem is used, which in its explicit form is found in *Elements* IX 23. It is the theorem that numbers of the type $(2n + 1)(2p + 1)$ are always odd.

It is possible to put the proof into a form in which a recurrent figure illustrates the absurdity of the supposition.

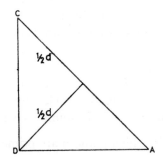

$d^2 = 2c^2$ therefore d^2 is even: d is even . . . . (1)

in CPD: $c^2 = 2\left(\dfrac{d}{2}\right)^2$ c^2 is even: c is even . . . . (2)

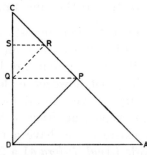

in PQC: $2\left(\dfrac{c}{2}\right)^2 = \left(\dfrac{d}{2}\right)^2$ $\left(\dfrac{2}{d}\right)^2$ is even $\dfrac{d}{2}$ is even . . (3)

in QRC: $2\left(\dfrac{d}{4}\right)^2 = \left(\dfrac{c}{2}\right)^2$ $\left(\dfrac{c}{2}\right)^2$ is even $\dfrac{c}{2}$ is even . . (4)

in RSC: $\dfrac{d}{4}$ is even . . (5)

etc.

This means that by drawing perpendiculars DP, PQ, QR, RS etc. not only d and c turn out to be even at the same time (which is another way of saying: c is even and odd at the same time), but also both d and c are subdivided into halves which will remain even *ad infinitum*. Put into this form the demonstration offers the same characteristics which could be observed in many other Pythagorean problems. By repeating a similar operation a similar figure is obtained. The repetition of the similar figure offers an inexplicable contradiction and this inexplicable contradiction repeats itself *ad infinitum*. It seems plausible to suppose that, if the Pythagoreans were not yet able to master the problem of these infinite repetitions satisfactorily, they may have felt a certain distrust of dealing with infinitesimal problems, and, generally, a distrust of any actual infinity. This distrust of actual infinity is not a supposition *ad hoc*, for we see it still at work in Aristotle's treatment of infinity in *De caelo* I. From the Pythagoreans onwards we observe a fairly uniform tradition in philosophical thinking as regards the concept of ἄπειρον. The old lofty conception of an actual divine Infinity is superseded by a way of thinking in which the ἄπειρον is seen as the opposite of πέρας. Accordingly, it is placed in a negative category, and the signification of indeterminateness prevails. This dyadic way of thinking originated with the Pythagoreans. It is present in Plato's theory of πέρας and ἄπειρον as expounded in the *Philebus*, and in Aristotle's doctrine of hylemorphism, in which ὕλη plays the part of the indeterminate principle.

BIBLIOGRAPHY

A. General

Heidel 1901
Schulz 1905
Boehm 1905
Gilbert 1909
Rostagni 1914
Méautis 1922
Delatte 1922
Cornford 1922-1923
Frank 1923
Rostagni 1924
Bollinger 1925
Lévy 1926
Cornford 1939
Festugière 1945
Raven 1948

Kerényi 1950
Vlastos 1953
Kucharski 1955
Morrison 1956
Rougier 1959
Kucharski 1959
Boussoulas 1959
Thesleff 1961
Burkert 1962
Ilting 1964
Timpanaro Cardini 1958-1962-1964
Philip 1966
de Vogel 1966
von Fritz RE

83

B. *Mythical and Eastern origins*

Renan 1858
Cornford 1912
Cornford 1926
Guthrie 1934
Nilsson 1935
Dornseiff 1937
Clemen 1939
Linforth 1941
Heidel 1942
Barnett 1945
Frankfort 1949
Solmsen 1950 II
Kerényi 1950

Eissfeldt 1952
Cornford 1952, II
Vlastos 1952
van der Waerden 1953
Prümm 1956
Dornseiff 1956
Guthrie 1957
Bianchi 1960
Stokes 1962
Laemmli 1962
West 1963
Brandon 1963
Ziegler RE

C. *History of Mathematics*

Tannery 1887
Cantor 1907
Milhaud 1900, 1906, 1911
Naber 1908
Vogt 1909, 1910, 1914
Zeuthen 1910, 1913, 1915
Loria 1914
Heath 1921
Taylor 1926
Hasse-Scholz 1928
Dijksterhuis 1930
Heath 1931
Rey 1930, 1933, 1939
Dijksterhuis 1935
Becker 1936
Heidel 1940

Brunschvicg 1947
Robin 1948
Reidemeister 1949
Michel 1950
Neugebauer 1952
Becker 1957, I and II
Heller 1958
Junge 1958
van Heemert 1963
von Fritz 1932, 1945, 1955, 1959, and
 RE
van der Waerden 1943, 1947-9, 1951,
 1966
Freudenthal 1957, 1966
Szabó 1956, 1958, 1960, 1964

D. *Special topic*:

a discussion on the scientific character
of Presocratic philosophy:

Popper 1958
Kirk 1960
Lloyd 1967

CHAPTER IV

ZENO

In his book on the *Theology of the Early Greek Philosophers* Werner Jaeger ends his chapter on Parmenides with a discussion of an internal discrepancy in Parmenides' ideas (*Theol.* 108). Jaeger states that Parmenides puts great emphasis on determinateness (πεῖρας) as a distinctive quality of being. He thinks Parmenides did so in order to dissociate himself from the Milesian theory of the ἄπειρον. Parmenides, Jaeger says, tries at all costs not to take the view of the Milesians who considered being as unbounded. Likewise he rejects the view of the Pythagoreans, who assumed the first principles to be twofold. The ancient religiously venerated unity of all things dominates his thinking to such an extent that Parmenides wants to defend it with all his might.

In our second chapter we have discussed the meaning of the terms ἀτέλεστον, οὐκ ἀτελεύτητον, τετελεσμένον ἐστί as used by Parmenides. The arguments developed in that chapter suggest that in Jaeger's description of Parmenides' philosophy the shades may be somewhat modified. The contrast to the Milesian theory of the ἄπειρον is not as absolute as Jaeger depicts it, mainly for the reason that as early as Anaximander we find the universe represented as a sphere of being, determined from within (see p. 11). It seems not even excluded that to the Ionians already the first intuition should have presented itself of a theory in which determinateness and infinity were combined (see p. 23-24). Xenophanes may have acted as the intermediary between the Ionian school and the Western, Eleatic tradition. The difference between Parmenidean and Milesian thinking must rather have centered on the word πεῖρας as indicating determinateness. Accordingly the terms οὐκ ἀτελεύτητον and τετελεσμένον are used by Parmenides with the emphasis on the signification of 'well-finished', 'brought to perfection', rather than on the spatial meaning of 'having an end in space'. This Parmenidean emphasis on determinateness must be due to Pythagorean influence.

As was argued in our chapter on Parmenides, the expression ἠδ'

85

ἀτέλεστον of fr. 8 verse 4 is probably to be taken as synonymous to Anaximander's term ἄπειρον. If Parmenides tried to avoid any expression of the idea of indeterminateness, his choice of the word ἠδ' ἀτέλεστον may have been a way out enabling him to retain the meaning of positive infinity. Parmenides may have avoided expressing this in Anaximander's term ἄπειρον for the reason that this term could too easily be taken as the opposite of πεῖρας in the Pythagorean sense. By πεῖρας Parmenides indicated that Being has the quality of well-determinedness and, for that reason, of perfection, as is made clear by the context of verses 29-33, and more especially by verse 33:

ἔστι γὰρ οὐκ ἐπιδευές,
"being is not in fault of anything."

If, however, it was Parmenides' aim to be clear and explicit, he must be said to have missed his purpose, because the verbal contrast comes out again when we compare the expressions ἠδ' ἀτέλεστον of verse 4 and τετελεσμένον of verse 42. The persistence of this terminological confusion may have been influenced to some extent by the fact that 'limit' in the spatial sense and 'determination' as an ontological concept had not yet come to mean different things. That may be seen from a comparison of verse 31 with 42. In verse 31 it is clear that the concept of determinateness is meant by the expression πείρατος ἐν δεσμοῖσιν, whereas the explanations given in the verses 43 and 44 put it beyond doubt that in verse 42 it is the spatial sense that dominates.

Though the terminology Parmenides makes use of may, only in this respect, be regarded as not yet completely accurate, it is fairly clear that Parmenides gives us two distinct descriptions of Being. The first of these is intended to be understood in a metaphysical sense: Being is determined in all respects (verses 26-42), the second is formulated in cosmological terms: Being is a spatial whole, kept in balance from within and not bordered upon by another Being (vs. 42-49). The two descriptions overlap each other to a certain extent, which means that most terms have at the same time a metaphysical and a spatial connotation.

In the cosmological description (42-49) the universe is described as filled with Being, expanding homogeneously and continuously. There is no reason to assume that at any point the continuity of Being should be interrupted by a kind of not-being, which would be powerful enough to cause interruption:

τό κεν παύοι μιν ἱκνεῖσθαι (46)
εἰς ὁμόν,

86

"something which would prevent it (i.e. Being) from being contiguous to itself."

Spatial Being, therefore, is continuous.

Nor can we assume that at any point a being could make its
appearance which would differ from Being as it had presented itself
up to that point. In that case Being as it had presented itself up to
that point would have been at fault:

οὔτ' ἐὸν ἔστιν ὅπως εἴη κεν ἐόντος (47)

τῆι μᾶλλον τῆι δ' ἧσσον, ἐπεὶ πᾶν ἐστιν ἄσυλον. (48)

"Nor is it possible that Being should be less than Being, or more
than Being, for the whole of Being is subject to no detriment."

This means that homogeneous Being, expanding in continuity
throughout the whole Sphere of Being admits of no intervals. This
is expressly stated in *frag.* 4:

οὐ γὰρ ἀποτμήξει τὸ ἐὸν τοῦ ἐόντος ἔχεσθαι, "for (the right way of
thinking) will not permit any separation to exist so that being
would be severed from being," and in *frag.* 8, verses 24 and 25:

πᾶν δ' ἔμπλεόν ἐστιν ἐόντος

τῶι ξυνεχὲς πᾶν ἐστιν· ἐὸν γὰρ ἐόντι πελάζει.

"The all is full of being, and therefore the all is continuous;
for being borders upon being."

It is here that we even find the term ξυνεχές indicating the concept of
continuity which from Zeno onwards was to give rise to so many
philosophical controversies. Its opposite, the concept of emptiness or
κενόν, does not occur in what we possess of Parmenides' work, but the
fragments that have been preserved make it perfectly clear that in
his philosophy there is no room for empty space. The existence of a
void would mean a break in the sacrosanct unity and continuity of
Being. Though the word κενόν itself is not found in Parmenides' verses,
the very idea of it is banished by the expressions which emphasize the
continuity of Being: οὐλομελές, ὁμοῦ πᾶν, ἕν, συνεχές (*frag.* 8, verses
4-6): "indivisible, homogeneous, one, continuous." In our second
chapter we saw that these terms were the sign-posts pointing to the
explicit treatment of the concept of continuity in the verses 22-25.
At the end of that chapter (p. 40-42) we saw that the Eleatic concept
of not-being was explained by both Plato and Aristotle as implying
the connotation of empty space, and also that this was in fact what
the Eleatics themselves had thought about it. In the description
Parmenides gives of Being the cosmological and the ontological aspects
constantly intermingle, and this is also the case with the concepts of

empty space and μὴ ὄν, not-being. In our seventh chapter, we shall discuss how far Democritus' conceptions presuppose an existing theory in which empty space and not-being were identical.

Leaving apart the very complex history of these two conceptions, we may for the moment focus our attention on the concept of continuity (τὸ συνεχές). As we have seen, continuity played an essential part in the Eleatic theory, because, in a cosmological sense, continuity was understood as a necessary condition of the perfection of Being. A break in this continuity was seen as an infraction of the autonomy of Being, and accordingly its existence could not be tolerated. Thus, the theory comes to rest on the metaphysical foundations of absolute argument. The same principle of continuity was, however, put to the test by Zeno on a quite different line of thought. It is very probable that this was done as early as Parmenides' lifetime. Zeno was his younger contemporary and, according to certain accounts, on very friendly terms with him. If Zeno was Parmenides' direct disciple, his paradoxes may confirm the view that the Eleatic theories were elaborated in a constant discussion with the then prevailing Pythagorean philosophy. Zeno's paradoxes are centred on the concept of continuity and on that of the ἄπειρον. In the paradoxes both concepts are put to the test, and the test takes the form of a mathematical demonstration. Both elements, the concept of ἄπειρον as well as the mathematical way of reasoning, most probably have their origin in the Pythagorean school.

In our third chapter we saw that to the Pythagoreans the problem of the concept 'infinite' had presented itself in two different mathematical demonstrations. If you started from an even number and continually added gnomons, the result was an oblong with an infinitely unstable proportion of the sides, because at every new step the sides acquired a new ratio to one another. The diagrams by which this process was visualized formed a sequence which only when prolonged into infinity approximated the form of a regular square (5×6, 6×7, 7×8 and so on). The other demonstration was that of the irrationality of $\sqrt{2}$. Here the difficulty centered on the distinction of odd and even. If, in the square, you suppose the diagonal d to be measurable to the side c, and if you continually bisect c and d, the operation produces *ad infinitum* magnitudes that can be denoted by even numbers, which is an absurd consequence. In both problems the result of the operation is a sequence; in the first case it is a sequence the terms of which are constituted by an uninterrupted process of adding, in the second case a sequence the terms of which are constituted by a constant process of bisecting. The two problems have one feature in common: an infinite process produces unstable proportions or absurd consequences, that is, the concept of infinity cannot be relied upon when it comes to arguing clearly, because it cannot be defined in an unambiguous way.

In Zeno's paradoxes a certain form of arithmetical sequences is recognizable. They serve Zeno to put the problem of infinity to the test. Very distinctly the form of a sequence can be discerned in the first and second of the four paradoxes of motion.

The first of these is known by the name of the 'dichotomy'. It is referred to by Aristotle in the words: "that which is in motion must first reach a point half-way before it will reach its goal."

The paradox must have been common knowledge if Aristotle could hint at it in this short form. When the quotation is compared with other passages in Aristotle's work and in the works of his commentators, it appears that an addition should be made in the sense that next that which is left of the trajectory must be traversed half-way, and so on *ad infinitum*. Zeno's paradox is based on two presuppositions which are taken for granted:
(1) that reality is discontinuous, (2) that there is no limit to this discontinuity, i.e. that the theoretically infinite divisibility of a mathematical magnitude is also applicable to spatial magnitudes. Starting from these presuppositions, Zeno builds up a demonstration *ad absurdum*. Any body in motion would, thus, have to traverse an infinity of infinitely small lenghts, counting them while traversing them, in order to cover a finite distance. Because counting an actually infinite quantity cannot be done in a finite time, the body in motion cannot finish its course.

The last step in the argument implies the transformation of a problem of spatial discontinuity into a problem of temporal discontinuity. The problem does not change much by this, only its formula is now an easier one, because the discontinuity of the sequence is more distinctly set before our eyes. Aristotle himself is aware that changing the spatial formula into a temporal one is not a solution of the problem. He next attempts a solution on the basis of a distinction between infinity by addition and infinity by division (*Phys.* Z 2, 233 a 24). If a sequence increases without having an end, it cannot be traversed in a finite time, but if the sequence is generated by division it can. This is only apparently a solution, because we are deceived by the evidence of our senses. We cannot survey the whole of the sequence if the sequence is an increasing one, whereas, in the other case, we seem to be able to survey the whole sequence, because it starts with a given length, which is only divided infinitely. Nevertheless the sequence is also in this case endless. The real difficulty lies in the problem how the terms 'continuous' and 'infinite' must be defined. In a passage which is of later date (*Phys.* H 8, 263 a 11 - b 9) Aristotle reverts to the solution he first propounded. He says that, in the pragmatic sense, this solution may be an answer to the question, but as regards reality it does not solve the problem. He then proposes another solution, which at any rate seems coherent, though perhaps it would have been more to the point to start from a mathematical definition of continuity rather than from an appeal to the general doctrine of actuality and potentiality. In substance, however, the solution Aristotle proposes centres on the essential point. A line which is continuous (γραμμὴ συνεχής) does have an infinity of bisected parts, but, so long as the line is continuous, only potentially. Accidentally, a point moving on a continuous line traverses an infinite number of points, but not in reality (ἁπλῶς δ' οὔ). Accidentally the line has an infinite number of points, but in its own way of being the line is something different from the infinite set of its points.

To all appearance this last distinction is in principle the solution of the paradox. A line is not so much a set of points as the track left behind by a moving point. The co-ordinates which direct the line in its field determine the track along which the line moves. The direction of this motion constitutes the line in its essence. This means that the motion has to be included in the definition of the line in so far as it is an expression of its continuity. So long as this is not done, and so long as the infinite set of points is taken to be discontinuous, it is not possible to make a body move along that line.

It must be noticed that Zeno's method of demonstration clearly shows that he is aware of using presuppositions. Starting from these presuppositions he draws his conclusions with mathematical strictness. To the logical structure of the paradox it is of no importance whether we suppose Zeno to have been convinced of the truth of his presupposition, or only to have aimed at demonstrating the consequences of certain axioms. The structure of the demonstrations is not dependent on whether we choose the first or the second of these alternatives. What does depend on this choice is the answer to the question in what historical situation we are to place Zeno's dilemmas. If we assume

Zeno to have been convinced of the truth of his starting-point, then we must also assume that he wanted to give a valid demonstration of some other truth, e.g. that he intended to prove that sense perception does not bring us into contact with reality. If we think that a certain point can be in motion towards a certain goal, we are deceived by our senses, for the demonstration proves that no motion can exist. The reality of Being lies hidden behind what our senses tell us about it. Interpreting the paradoxes on this line we come to look upon Zeno as a faithful follower of his master, Parmenides, whose doctrine he defended with new arguments

This interpretation of the paradoxes was already in antiquity more or less canonic, and we must probably say that it has become so on the authority of Aristotle. If, however, we give due attention to the fact that Zeno's paradoxes are constructed as reasonings *per hypothesin*, not only a number of obscure points will be clarified, but, what is more, the conception of the paradoxes comes to fit perfectly into the historical development of both philosophy and mathematics.

In a series of publications, the Hungarian scholar Szabó has tried to identify the oldest explicit form of logical demonstration. He thinks this oldest form was that of a *'reductio ad absurdum'*, and, moreover, he defends the view that it must have been the Eleatics who first made this method of demonstration explicit (Szabó 1955, 1956). He says e.g. (1967, 1 - 2): "My problem is to explain the change in the criterion of truth in mathematics from justification by experience to justification by theoretical reasons. My solution is that this change was due to the impact of philosophy, and more precisely of Eleatic dialectic, upon mathematics." As has been said above (see ch. III p. 78) it does not seem necessary to assume that Eleatic dialectic preceded mathematical deduction. As Szabó himself states, a method of strictly mathematical deduction must have existed very early in the fifth century. To our purpose, at all events, it is sufficient to know that by the time of Parmenides and Zeno a strict form of mathematical demonstration existed, be it developed by the mathematicians on the example of Eleatic philosophy or borrowed by the Eleatics from an existing mathematical practice. This justifies us in assuming that Zeno very consciously made use of a determined form of demonstration.

The form of his proofs resembled that of the *reductio ad absurdum*, which in this case even took on the more refined form of an axiomatic test in the sense that an axiom used in the demonstration was put to the test by seeing what consequences were developed from it. It is not necessary to know whether this method had first been developed on philosophical or on mathematical foundations, for we can easily convince ourselves that in fact Zeno's paradoxes are constructed on the lines of a mathematical problem. To avoid misunderstandings we must emphasize that we are not trying to prove that Zeno was or was not the author of a certain mathematical method, or to describe Zeno's place in the history of mathematics. What we intend to describe is the philosophical conclusions to which his paradoxes led him.

It is not very probable that the paradoxes were intended to prove that sense perception is unreliable. Demonstrations to that end would rather fit in with the Sophists. If we suppose, however, that they were aimed at testing a supposition, as is the case in every *reductio ad absurdum*, we can see that in two respects the paradoxes fit in remarkably well with the historical situation. As regards the demonstration, we see that Zeno used the method that was new in his days. As regards the problems, these are (1) the problem of continuity, which is a more special form of the question whether things are one or many, and (2) the then current problem of infinity. The very concept of infinity had become problematical as a consequence of Pythagorean arithmetical theories and of the discovery of irrational lengths, as we saw above. Zeno did not undertake to solve these problems in a mathematical way. He was rather a philosopher who was well-informed about the latest developments in the field of mathematics, and who first of all tried to make explicit what was implicit in the presuppositions, in order to obtain a better definition of the concepts used in them. Zeno cannot have applied this method if he was not aware himself of the logical form of his demonstrations (Cf. Mansfeld 1964, 114-121).

By supposing that Zeno consciously made use of a certain explicit form of logical reasoning we not only gain a much more coherent explanation of what his paradoxes were intended to be. There is also direct evidence that Zeno used a method which was aimed at testing the presupposition from which the reasoning started. This evidence is found in Plato's *Parmenides*. In this dialogue a meeting is described of Socrates with Parmenides and Zeno. In the first part Socrates has a conversation with Zeno in which he tries to find a new solution for the problem proposed by Zeno: that of the one and the many. In the second part, where the nine hypotheses are developed, Parmenides wants to give a systematic example of the way in which a problem must be tackled. This second part of the dialogue is introduced by the question: Τίς οὖν ὁ τρόπος τῆς γυμνασίας; Οὗτος ὅνπερ ἤκουσας Ζήνωνος (135 d). "What method shall we have to follow in our exercises? This very method you heard Zeno make use of." The method of reasoning must be the method developed by Zeno. Now the paradoxes which follow in Plato's dialogue are all aimed at testing the presuppositions by seeing what consequences are derived from them. We must conclude from this that in the same way Zeno's paradoxes had been meant as experiments, in which the soundness of the starting-point was to be judged by the consequences following from it. This means that Zeno's paradoxes were intended as axiomatic tests in the sense given above.

The ground-plan of Plato's dialogue *Parmenides* at the same time makes it clear that Plato wanted it to be understood that his metaphysical dialectic as developed in this dialogue was to be regarded as a continuation and elaboration of Eleatic philosophy.

If our remarks hold good, Zeno, in the paradoxes known to us, aimed at testing one or two fundamental concepts, one of which was the concept of ἄπειρον. The results of applying this concept to the problems dealt with had to determine whether or not this concept could be used in philosophy. In antiquity the first of the four paradoxes of motion is usually quoted as the 'dichotomy'. Possibly this name has caused Aristotle to take it as fundamentally the same as the second paradox. The first paradox is centred on the question (1) whether in fact a given length can be infinitely bisected, and (2) whether a body traversing this distance must actually count out the infinite series of these bisections. If, as Cornford supposed, a Pythagorean number-atomism existed, this first paradox might, among other things, be regarded as a discussion of this topic. The substance of the paradox, however, is the problem of how to reconcile the infinity of mathematical bisections with the finiteness of the given length.*

* In our first chapters we saw that the investigation of the mythical origins of philosophy received in many points its first impulse from the School of Vienna. The same must probably be said about the historical appreciation of Zeno's paradoxes. In the work of Theodor Gomperz already we find it stated that the paradoxes have a mathematical structure, and that, historically, their real significance lies in the problem of the relation between the infinity of the sequence and the finite distance. In *Griechische Denker* I 160 Gomperz says: 'Die Schwierigkeit gilt in Wirklichkeit dem Verhältnis einer unendlichen Reihe zu einer en-

Compared with the second paradox, the 'Achilles', the first paradox is a more direct approach to the philosophical aspect of the problem of how to reconcile infinity with being determined. The second paradox rather belongs to the problem of algebraical sequences.

Aristotle formulates the second paradox as follows (*Phys.* Z 9, 239 b 14 - 18 = DK 29 A 26).

δεύτερος δ' ὁ καλούμενος Ἀχιλλεύς· ἔστι δ' οὗτος ὅτι τὸ βραδύτατον οὐδέποτε καταληφθήσεται θέον ὑπὸ τοῦ ταχίστου· ἔμπροσθεν γὰρ ἀναγκαῖον ἐλθεῖν τὸ διῶκον ὅθεν ὥρμησε τὸ φεῦγον, ὥστ' ἀεί τι προέχειν ἀναγκαῖον τὸ βραδύτερον.

"The second paradox is the so-called Achilles. The argument is that even the slowest runner, when he is going, can never be overtaken by even the fastest, for inevitably the pursuer must first reach the point from which the pursued started, which means that the slower runner will always keep ahead."

This paradox is also mentioned as that of "Achilles and the tortoise." It seems that it was Simplicius who took the slower runner to be a tortoise. At first sight the argument seems to be a variation of that of the first paradox. A magnitude which is being continually divided according to a determined ratio decreases continually but can never actually decrease to zero. There will always be a last remainder of the decreasing distance which will have to be divided into a distance covered while overtaking the slower runner and a very short remaining distance, covered by the slower runner. It is as if thinking it out means putting oneself behind bars which get closer and closer to one another without ever coinciding or even overleaping. This is only so in so far as we stick to our concepts, for experience shows us that the slower runner is really overtaken by the faster. It does not seem plausible that Zeno should have used this and other mathematical examples in order to annihilate the force of evidence through the force of argument. The very quality of the examples makes this unlikely: a flying arrow which, if we state things correctly

lichen Grösse.' Even if we should have to state that Zeno did not aim at discrediting the concept of infinity, historically speaking, it was this concept at which the arguments were pointed as at a target. The conclusion to be drawn from the paradoxes was, in Zeno's days, "dass es untunlich ist, mit dem Begriff der Unendlichkeit vollen Ernst zu machen. Gegen diesen, so meinen wir, nicht gegen den empirischen Begriff der Bewegung richten die soeben erörterten Aporieën, sehr gegen die Absicht ihres Urhebers, in Wahrheit ihre Spitze" (p. 161).

and philosophically, would actually be at rest, – or the swift Achilles who must be supposed never to have overtaken even a very slow runner. The most plausible inference is that Zeno wanted to work out an axiomatic test of certain principles by a very definite method of reasoning.

In modern historiography the view persists that Zeno, following in the wake of Parmenides, attempted a systematization of a methodical doubt as regards the validity of sense perception. This interpretation is an inheritance from Aristotle. In modern historiography it survived tenaciously, a survival which is probably due to the influence of idealistic philosophy. It made Zeno a precursor of the Sophists. This is all the more improbable because Plato makes Zeno's method the necessary starting-point for any sound dialectic and metaphysics. Moreover, the view mentioned only holds good as long as we fail to notice the very simple mathematical form it has. Translated in algebraical formulas it runs:

$$v = \text{velocity}$$
$$t = \text{time}$$
$$vt = d = \text{distance}$$

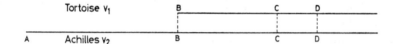

Every time Achilles reaches the point from where the tortoise started, the distances covered are compared. When Achilles arrives at point B, the tortoise arrives at C. AB and BC therefore are covered in the same time by Achilles and the tortoise respectively. The distances are in inverse proportion to the respective velocities. If we take this proportion as 10 : 1, then BC = 1/10 AB. In the same way CD = 1/10 BC and therefore = 1/100 AB. Because we have divided the total trajectory into these parts, Achilles will have to traverse an infinity of diminishing distances. These can be denoted as follows:

1, 1/10, 1/100, 1/1000 . . . . and so on.

When the number of terms of this series approximates infinity, the sum total of all terms is 1 1/9. Only if we assume that the infinite number of terms taken together produces a finite number, only then can we manage to reconcile the reasoning and reality; the fact is that Achilles actually overtakes the tortoise at a distance of 1 1/9 ×

AB from A. Probably Zeno recoiled before this conclusion because he was unable to bring finiteness and infinity together into one satisfactory formula (Cf. Whitrow 1961, 135 - 152).

The cause of Zeno's perplexity must be sought in the fact that Zeno considered infinity as an actual number that was to be reached by counting. The concepts of a counting number and that of an infinite number, however, do not fall within the same category. A satisfactory theory bringing out the difference between these two concepts was not developed in antiquity. For this reason actual infinity was considered a mathematical impossibility. Accordingly, infinity was defined in the negative sense of potential infinity. An infinite number was a number to which other numbers could infinitely be added. It was not until the nineteenth century that Bolzano and Cantor worked out a coherent theory of infinite numbers. In antiquity the problem could probably not be mastered mathematically because the algebra of sequences was insufficiently developed. Metaphysically, the problem resulted in an unsolved difficulty.

If the problem of the 'Achilles' did not give rise to an algebraical method of finding the sum of all the terms of the series, the possibility remains that the problem, in its mathematical form, served the purpose of studying the ratio between the individual terms. This is all the more plausible because the doctrine of proportions was a very central theme in ancient mathematics (cf. Heath 1921, I 84-90).

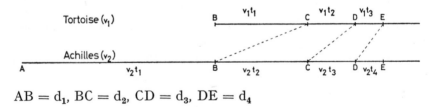

$AB = d_1$, $BC = d_2$, $CD = d_3$, $DE = d_4$

In the diagram $BC = v_1 t_1$. The time which the tortoise needs to cover BC is the same time which Achilles needs to cover $AB = v_2 t_1$. Next, the time Achilles needs to cover BC is the same time which multiplied by the velocity of the tortoise yields the distance CD. The distances BC, CD, DE are the same on either line.

The ratio of the first two distances is

$$\frac{BC}{AB} = \frac{v_1 t_1}{v_2 t_1} = \frac{v_1}{v_2}$$

and in the same way:

$$\frac{CD}{BC} = \frac{v_1 t_2}{v_2 t_2} = \frac{v_1}{v_2}$$

This means that between any two consecutive terms there is a constant ratio. This may be written as:

$$\frac{d_2}{d_1} = \frac{d_3}{d_2} = \frac{d_4}{d_3} = \frac{d_5}{d_4},$$

or also:

$$d_1 : d_2 = d_2 : d_3 \text{ and so on.}$$

If the series of diminishing distances is aggregated to a sum, the point where Achilles will overtake the tortoise can be calculated exactly. However, no algebraical operation to this effect existed in antiquity, and the theory of proportions was too static to provide a solution for the problem of motion. Heath (1921, I 279) distinguishes the question *when?* from the question *how?* The first is a question of algebraical calculation, the second is a matter of 'research into foundations'. This research into foundations was, in antiquity as well as in our days, influenced by philosophical points of view but the reverse is probably even more true: the methods of the mathematical demonstrations influenced to a high degree the development of logical methods. The very problems of Zeno bear testimony to this. They were the embodiment of axiomatic problems. One of the most problematical axioms was that about the concept of infinity. This axiom had the naïve form in which it survived up to the 19th century, according to which infinity is an undetermined concept of a magnitude or quantity which is in motion in the sense that it can always be added to.

The third paradox is that of the arrow. It says that an arrow cannot be in motion, because at any of the infinite number of moments in which it traverses its trajectory, it occupies a space equal to itself. At each individual moment it is not in motion, therefore it is neither in motion in the sum total of all the individual moments.

The kernel of this paradox lies in the question whether the points which are traversed by the arrow on its trajectory can indeed be regarded as disconnected from one another. If the demonstration starts from this premise, implicitly the axiom is introduced that space is discontinuous. The non-existence of motion is, therefore, not the conclusion of an argument, but was already presupposed in the given facts of the problem. The problem which is being put to the test in this argument, is the operational validity of the concept 'discontinuous' (cf. Croissant 1937).

Aristotle has a solution which is argued along the same lines (*Phys.* Z 9, 239 b 30). He says that time is not composed of moments. This remark must beyond doubt have originated from the discussions going on in Aristotle's days on the problem of continuity and discontinuity, a problem related to that of finiteness and infinity.

As regards the fourth paradox, we are probably justified in saying that from Aristotle onward it has been explained in the wrong sense. In general it can be said of all four of the paradoxes that the commentators in late antiquity only give more detailed explanations of the criticisms already formulated by Aristotle. A glance at the fragments from the doxographic tradition, given by Lee (1936), will suffice to see this.

The doxographic tradition explains Zeno's arguments as refutations of the concept of multiplicity, which means that Zeno's importance is reduced to that of a defender of Parmenides' cosmology according to which the universe is a homogeneous Being. This interpretation has no connection with the mathematical foundations of the arguments and, moreover, fails to appreciate the logical structure of Zeno's paradoxes. Here and there in the doxographic tradition it is also argued that Zeno, anticipating the Sophists, wanted to prove that sense perception is unreliable. According to this interpretation the paradoxes showed that to discursive reason the reality of motion is not tenable. In reality, Zeno is the brilliant renovator of a problem which for the first time had been formulated metaphysically by Parmenides.

Because it is highest and first, Being must be infinite, but at the same time it must be well-determined. In the theory the Pythagorean conception of indeterminateness had to be eliminated. Joining the two conceptions in one coherent theory caused insuperable difficulties as soon as the theory was applied to cosmology. Zeno was the first to introduce new methods in order to cope with these difficulties. Even more important, however, is the fact that his demonstrations mark a completely different outlook, as compared with the philosophy of Parmenides. The dogmatical way of thinking was turned into a critical approach, which was embodied in a well-developed new logical method. As a result of this Zeno's theories opened the way for a new philosophical method, which was to be critical, in the sense that it could test the validity of its own presuppositions by using them in argument. The historical importance of Zeno lies in the fact that he transferred this method from mathematics to philosophy. By doing so he became the 'father of dialectic'. We can measure the outcome of this historical development when reading such dialogues as Plato's *Parmenides*, in which metaphysical first principles are investigated by testing them in dialectical practice.

If we are justified in ascribing to Zeno this crucial importance in the history of philosophy, and in setting his demonstrations against the historical background here described, there is no doubt that the right explanation of the fourth paradox was given by Brochard (1888, 8-9).

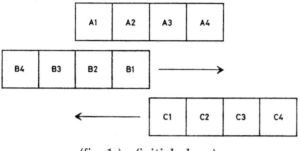

(fig. 1.)   (initial phase)

The squares A, B and C are equal and are lined up four to four. The four A's are stationary, the four B's move to the right, the four C's with equal velocity to the left.

In Aristotle's reading the argument runs as follows:

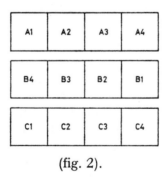

(fig. 2).

When the position of fig. 2 has been reached, B 1 has covered a distance equal to twice A, but at the same time equal to four times C. The measuring of the distance proves that in the same time half a distance and a whole distance have been traversed. Therefore half and whole are equal (*Phys.* 239 b 33 - 36).

99

It is not quite clear from Aristotle's account in what sense he thinks the paradox should be explained. The context in which it is treated by Aristotle suggests that he interpreted the argument as an attempt to prove that motion is unreal. This is in itself incredible if we take into account the mathematical and sober character of Zeno's thought. Brochard perceived a different meaning in the paradox. His interpretation was adopted by Heath (1921, I, 282 - 283). It starts from the assumption that Zeno could satisfactorily distinguish absolute from relative motion, just as in the case of Achilles and the tortoise he must have been aware that the given facts of the problem also included Achilles' actually overtaking the animal.

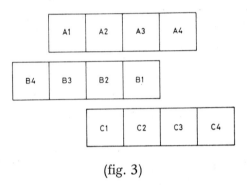

(fig. 3)

We suppose that, starting from the positions of fig. 1, the B's have moved one place to the right and the C's one place to the left. The new positions are those of fig. 3. We must assume that one unit moves one place in the shortest interval of time possible; and also that moving one place means traversing the shortest distance possible. In that case a conclusion follows which is inconsistent with the presuppositions. If we compare the B's to the A's, B_1 has traversed an indivisible distance in an indivisible element of time. The same thing can be said of C_1 if we compare the C's to the A's. However, if we compare the C's to the B's we see that there has been a moment when B_1 was vertically over C_1. This moment is halfway between the positions of fig. 1 and fig. 3. The hypothesis, however, was that the positions of fig. 1 and fig. 3 were separated only by the shortest distance possible, i.e. by an indivisible distance in time and space. The result is that an infinitely short distance can nevertheless be divided anew into two parts.

It is obvious that this conclusion is only the consequence of the axiom which was implicit in the presuppositions, according to which

100

infinite was taken in the naïve sense of "never-ceasing." The operation of bisecting can, even in a infinitely small section, be continued infinitely. When we come to Anaxagoras we shall see that a more conscious application of this principle has developed. Zeno did probably not arrive at a more explicit criticism of his implicit definition of the concept of infinity.

The more consistent treatment of this concept, inaugurated by Anaxagoras, was not further developed by later philosophers. We can see that Aristotle returned to the negative acceptance of infinity, which had come to dominate as a result of the Pythagorean philosophy and of the Zenonian paradoxes. To Zeno the concept of infinity only led to contradictions which, for the moment, could not be solved. The result was that it could not be regarded as practicable in philosophical argument.

In our discussion of the fourth paradox of motion we have followed the explanation given by Brochard and Heath. In this explanation the problem was centred on the concept of infinity exemplified for the special case of infinite bisection. Any distance, however small, continues to be divisible *ad infinitum*. This principle is also found in the presuppositions of another paradox, which is not one of the four paradoxes of motion and has therefore received less attention. It is commonly called the paradox *'on plurality'*.

The paradox has two presuppositions which are contrary to one another: (1) infinite division in the end arrives at a last term having a dimension of absolute zero; (2) any smallest dimension, and therefore also the dimension of absolute zero, can be bisected anew. As we shall see, it is not difficult to find these presuppositions back in the Greek text of the paradox. This Greek text we can read in Simplicius (DK 29 B 1 - 2 - 3). Aristotle makes a passing reference to the paradox in *Met.* B 1001 b 8 - 10.

The argument is as follows: "If things are a multiplicity, then necessarily they are infinite in number; for in that case between any two individual things there will always be other things and so on. Therefore things in that case are infinite in number" (DK fr. 3).

The paradox is based on the conception of a line which is being bisected. In the description of this bisecting, implicitly the following two axioms are at work: (a) if a line consists of discontinuous units, there is no reason why the discontinuity should cease to be discontinuity when a certain small dimension is reached, that is: no reason

101

can be found why the process of bisection should not continue infinitely; (b) the distance between two discontinuous points is not filled with void, but in this distance there is something, because the line there pursues its course. This means that between any two points there is always at least one other point, and so on, *ad infinitum*.

In contrast to this process of infinite bisection (ἡ ἐπ᾽ ἄπειρον τομή, infinity *ad minus*) stands a process of infinitely increasing lengths (τὸ κατὰ μέγεθος ἄπειρον, infinity *ad maius*). Both processes are treated simultaneously in the argument of *frag.* 1 (DK 29 B 1).

"If being has no dimension, it cannot even be something. For if it is something, then necessarily each unit must have a certain size and thickness, and one part of it (i.e. of this unit) must be at a distance from another part. But the same applies to the preceding unit because this unit, too, will have dimension and will be preceded by another unit. Now saying this once is the same as saying it an infinity of times, For no unit will be the last, nor will it occur that in a unit there are no parts having relation to each other. Therefore, if there is a plurality of things, necessarily things will be at the same time small and large; small to such an extent as to have no dimension, large to such an extent as to be infinite."

In the text of this argument there is a certain difficulty due to the word αὐτοῦ in the line: οὐδὲν γὰρ αὐτοῦ τοιοῦτον ἔσχατον ἔσται. If we translate this as: "For no such part of it will be the last" (Kirk-Raven 288), we might be inclined to think that Zeno is describing in these words the process of infinite bisection. This, however, does not go well together with the expression ἔσχατον, and, moreover, it is inconsistent with the tenor of the argument. Zeno wants to prove by one and the same argument that being will be infinitely small and infinitely large at the same time, if once we take it for granted that it has dimensions, and that any dimension can be bisected or prolonged. In the first case, that of bisection, being will be infinitely small, in the second case, that of increasing lengths, it will be infinitely large. That both processes are meant at a time is made clear by the final conclusion. In the text the idea of bisection is formulated by the words: "It will have parts which have a relation (or a distance) to one another," (ἀπέχειν αὐτοῦ τὸ ἕτερον ἀπὸ τοῦ ἑτέρου), whereas the process of increasing lengths is represented in the words μέγεθός τι ἔχειν καὶ πάχος. It seems therefore that αὐτοῦ should be read not with the words τὸ ἔσχατον, but with the expression ἕτερον πρὸς ἕτερον, so that the whole sentence would run:

102

οὐδὲν γὰρ τοιοῦτον ἔσχατον ἔσται οὔτε ἕτερον πρὸς ἕτερον αὐτοῦ οὐκ ἔσται.

We have translated accordingly. Our reading is further confirmed by the fact that ἔσχατον αὐτοῦ would necessarily mean: 'a last part of it', where '*it*' would stand for 'the whole of space'. This latter notion is not expressed or implied in the text which on the contrary takes as the starting-point of the problem the question 'if things are many', εἰ πολλά ἐστιν. Although the idea of an infinite universe in the sense of rectilinear (Euclidean) infinity may come to our mind when we read the text, we must not introduce it into the text, as do DK, who translate: "Denn kein derartiger *Teil* desselben (*des Ganzen*) wird die äusserste Grenze bilden."

In the argument *ad maius* we find the same axioms implied as in the argument *ad minus:* (1) there is no reason why a certain process, in the one case that of bisection, in the other that of adding lengths, should at a certain point come to a standstill; (2) if any infinitely small distance is divisible, then this distance has a dimension, or, transposed to the argument *ad maius*: any dimension, however small, adds length to a dimension to which it is added. This second axiom has its foundation in the notion of dimension, which in the argument is applied in a perfectly consistent way: into whatever argument the notion of 'dimension' may be introduced, it will always have the effect of introducing distance. If space is bisected, bisection will go on as long as space means distance. The very fact that a unit has dimension proves two things at a time: that its parts are at a distance from one another, and that going from one unit to another implies covering a certain distance. If dimensions are added up, all dimensions together will produce an infinite magnitude.

The upshot of the argument must have been the same to Zeno as in the case of the four paradoxes on motion: infinitesimal processes necessarily lead to contradictions. Therefore the principle of infinity cannot be made operational in philosophical argument. It must be avoided altogether, because it does not allow us to pronounce definite judgments on well-determined entities. If infinity is allowed to play a part in our arguments, any magnitude can be infinite as well as zero.

This connotation, implied by the term 'infinite', is, in another form, also found in Plato's theory of πέρας and ἄπειρον in the *Philebus*. In that theory the ἄπειρον is bound to disappear as soon as any well-determined entity comes into existence. The ἄπειρον ceases to exist when πέρας is introduced.

In the order of the fragments given here the argument has preserved the structure it has in the account by Simplicius. Though Simplicius interrupts himself now and then with critical remarks, the order in which he gives the arguments is a logical one. The text of Simplicius' account (*in Phys.* 139, 5 - 141, 8) can be divided as follows:

139, 5-19 = DK 29 B 2

139, 26-140,6 = quotation from Porphyry (not in DK)

140, 29-34 = DK 29 B 3

140, 34-141,8 = DK 29 B 1

In the first of these four fragments the general theme of the argument is given: if things are to be regarded as beings, they must have dimensions; if dimensions are real, there will be infinite extension as well as infinite division. Then comes the fragment which is not in DK. It is given in the form of a statement by Porphyry about the philosophy of Parmenides. The contents, however, make it fairly clear that the quotation is from the work of Zeno, as Simplicius himself remarks afterwards (140, 21-25). This second fragment deals with the question of the so-called 'dichotomy': the result of an infinite division will be either a smallest part, still having dimension, or a smallest part having no dimension at all. In the first case, the original magnitude consists of actual parts, which, however, are infinite in number; in the second case, the original magnitude consists of parts, which are themselves nothing. Both conclusions, that of a thing consisting of an infinity of parts and that of a thing, consisting of mere non-entities, are called absurd in the fragment. The axioms implied have been indicated above. The central notion is, like in the first fragment, that of dimension, and the central question is: is an infinitely small dimension still a dimension, or is it no dimension any more?

This argument is used in the third fragment (B 3 = Simpl. *Phys.* 140, 29-34) in which the totality of all beings is taken as a set. If the set is not larger or smaller than its own size, it is a determined set; if, however, between any two entities, however small, a third entity can be inserted, the result will be that it is an infinite set. (We may notice incidentally that the argument, though concerned with the concept of dimension, here once more demonstrates the contrast between well-determinedness and infinity). The fourth fragment (B 1 = Simpl. *Phys.* 140, 34-141, 8) gives the results of the three former arguments united into one: things will be either infinitely large or infinitely small, depending on whether we take the smallest dimension as still being a dimension or not being a dimension any more.

The conclusion to be drawn is that the internal consistency of the argument requires its being read in the order in which Simplicius gives it. The four fragments discussed above form together the paradox 'on plurality'. Diels-Kranz do not seem justified in reversing the order of the fragments. Their fragment B 2 must be taken as an introduction to the problem. After B 2 should come the quotation from Porphyry, then B 3 and finally B 1, which more or less unites the results of the arguments in one conclusion.

The conclusion is: plurality is problematical, because we cannot say what the smallest unit is. This question perhaps sums up the essence of what Zeno's problems were about. At any rate it was understood in this sense by the ancients. Simplicius (*Phys.* 97, 12-13 = DK 29 A 16) has a quotation from Eudemus, according to which Zeno had declared that he would be able to explain what things were (λέγειν τί ποτέ ἐστιν τὰ ὄντα), if first it could be explained to him what the One was (τὸ ἓν τί ποτέ ἐστιν). The formula of this saying makes one think that it may have originated in the later tradition of the Academy. It runs parallel to the apophthegm ascribed to Archimedes:

δός μοι ποῦ στῶ καὶ κινῶ τὴν γῆν, "give me a fixed point where I can take my stand and I shall move the earth."

This apophthegm served to express what was the crucial point in Archimedes' theory of levers. In the same way the saying, attributed to Zeno by Eudemus, points to what was one of the crucial points in Zeno's problems, even if its formula may be the product of a school-tradition. There are more crucial points in Zeno's arguments. They are all intrinsically bound up with the argument 'on plurality'. The ancient sources often say that the problem of infinite divisibility, ἡ ἐπ' ἄπειρον τομή, was the starting-point for all the problems raised by Zeno. This is true in so far that the whole cluster of these problems pivots on the question, what the ultimate unity or the One is, if things are a plurality, or, put in another form, if reality is discontinuous. This problem of ἓν καὶ πολλά, the One and the many, could only be solved together with the related problems of finiteness and infinity (or indeterminateness), πέρας and ἄπειρον, continuity and discontinuity.

To put Zeno's arguments in their proper historical context, we must also pay attention to the fact that all Zeno's arguments imply a spatial conception of being. In Zeno as well as in Parmenides the concept of being has not yet been completely detached from all associations with spatial concepts, that is, from all material elements.

If we use the word 'material' here, we do not take this word in the sense in which a tangible impenetrable mass is said to be material. This conception of matter corresponds to tactile notions, whereas the term 'material', if we may use it in describing Eleatic theories, must be taken in a spatial sense. The Eleatic concept of being, as we saw in our first two chapters, emerged as the result of a long development, which had started with the conception of a divine and all-embracing infinity, the ἄπειρον, well-rounded and well-determined, and kept in balance from within. The visual or spatial elements in this concept persisted in Parmenides' conception of Being. We may therefore describe the Eleatic Being as a concept from which not all material elements had as yet been eliminated, provided we keep in mind that, in this expression, the term 'material' denotes a spatial concept. It has no connection whatever with a tactile notion of matter. When we shall come to the atomists, we may have to ask the question if theirs is a conception of matter which rests on tactile notions.

Zeno's problem 'on plurality' is clearly to a considerable extent determined by the fact that in the suppositions of the problem the concept of the infinitely divided line plays a part. We find this problem 'on plurality' again in Plato's dialogue '*Parmenides*', where it is given (144 E) as the problem of the ἓν καὶ πολλά. It is discussed in the eight hypotheses of the second part of the dialogue. By their contents, these hypotheses offer a remarkable parallelism to Zeno's paradoxes. It would even be very difficult to see what these dialectical discussions are meant to be, if we do not keep in mind that they are worked out on the lines of Zeno's method. From the very beginning Plato makes it clear by the terminology of the problems, that his discussion takes its starting-point in the Eleatic theories. The formulas εἰ ἕν ἐστιν, ἓν εἰ ἔστιν, ἓν καὶ πολλά, can only be understood if we take them as the formulas of Eleatic philosophy. The expressions ἐστιν and ἔστιν have been derived from Parmenides, but the words ἕν and πολλά rather betray the influence of Zeno. It is not long before the concept of ἄπειρον is also introduced into the discussion (137 D). Afterwards if receives a fuller treatment in combination with the concept of πέρας (158 D). Here and there, there is even an undeniable parallelism between Zeno's paradox 'on plurality' and the discussion in the second part of Plato's dialogue *Parmenides*, especially in the first and second hypotheses. As is so often the case, the points of resemblance draw our attention to the differences. We shall discuss below in what respect Plato's discussion of the problem was an advance on the discussions of Zeno, whose method Plato had so avowedly adopted.

The parallelism is not merely implicit in the discussion, but was consciously designed by Plato, as we can see from the introduction to the hypotheses (135 DE). In the first part of the dialogue the discussion has led up to difficulties to which no solution can apparently be found by the methods of reasoning which Socrates has employed so far. At this point Parmenides remarks that Socrates, however inspired as a thinker, may be in need of a better developed method of thinking, if he wants to avoid the perplexities in which his own theories have involved him. Now it is a striking fact that Parmenides, when asked by Socrates how to develop a more efficient dialectical method, decidedly points to Zeno's: Τίς οὖν ὁ τρόπος, φάναι, ὦ Παρμενίδη, τῆς γυμνασίας; Οὗτος, εἶπεν, ὅνπερ ἤκουσας Ζήνωνος (135 D). "How then, Parmenides, Socrates had remarked, are we to train ourselves? By the method, Parmenides had answered, you heard Zeno making use of." Plato's own words leave us no doubt as to his intention of consciously working on the lines of Zeno's dialectic. The subject chosen is the Parmenidean problem 'if the One is' (137 B). This is, as Parmenides himself remarks, the central theme of his own philosophy: ἢ βούλεσθε ἀπ' ἐμαυτοῦ ἄρξωμαι καὶ τῆς ἐμαυτοῦ ὑποθέσεως; "Or, if you agree, shall I begin with myself, and my own hypothesis?" Presently, however, at the very beginning of the first discussion, this problem of the One is contrasted with the problem of the many: εἰ ἕν ἐστιν, ἄλλο τι οὐκ ἂν εἴη πολλὰ τὸ ἕν; "If there is a One, the One cannot be many, can it?". This means that not only Parmenides' theory, but also Zeno's problem will be discussed. At the end of the next paragraph (137 D) the concept of ἄπειρον is also brought into play. This problem, too, is derived from Zeno. We can only fully understand it if we keep in mind that Zeno's discussion 'on plurality' forms its background. In this discussion, as in practically all Zeno's paradoxes as far as we know them, the infinite divisibility of space was taken as a given concept which was to be tested by argument. As we saw above, this putting to the test was performed by Zeno not by asking questions about the topic, but by using the concept in argument in order to see how far it yielded valid results. This method was pragmatic and adapted itself perfectly to Zeno's mathematical way of thinking. By the same method of using a concept in argument in order to see what are the results Plato also proceeds to test the validity

107

of his concepts. The method is called 'working by means of a hypo-thesis' in 135 E - 136 A, where Parmenides says that the speakers in the discussion must "not only start from the assumption that some particular thing exists in order to see what follows from the argument, but also from the assumption that the same thing does not exist":

μὴ μόνον εἰ ἔστιν ἕκαστον ὑποτιθέμενον σκοπεῖν τὰ συμβαίνοντα ἐκ τῆς ὑποθέσεως, ἀλλὰ καὶ εἰ μὴ ἔστι τὸ αὐτὸ τοῦτο ὑποτίθεσθαι.

The words ὑπόθεσις and ὑποτίθεσθαι are the very characteristics of the Zenonian method. The text of the *Parmenides* makes it clear that the problems discussed in this dialogue, and also the method by which the discussion proceeds, were derived by Plato from Zeno's writings. We must assume that in the 'hypotheses' of the *Parmenides* Plato wanted to test a Zenonian problem by Zenonian methods.

This is not saying that Plato cannot have done more than that. First of all, Plato has worked much more thoroughly. Not only the principles, but also the negation of the principles are amply discussed. It has even been said that Plato set about it far too thoroughly, and that his way of developing every principle to its final consequences only produced a sort of philosophical rhetoric, too much of a verbal character to convey any important philosophical theory. This way of passing judgment on the arguments of the *Parmenides* is, however, contrasted by the fact that the *Neoplatonists* have been eager to make use of the results of Plato's hypotheses. They found in the *Parmenides* the terminology and the arguments by which they could produce a clear formula of their theories about the highest hypostases of being, and their first principle, the One. We may leave out of account here the question how far Plato himself has been conscious of the devel-opments to which his dialectical method was to lead the Neoplatonists. On the other hand it is not necessary to say that Plato's intentions were confined to elaborating some problems within the framework of the Zenonian dialectic.

If we compare Zeno's problems with the text of the hypotheses in Plato's *Parmenides*, we can at any rate see that Plato did more than merely give an exhaustive treatment of a problem already dealt with by Zeno. The text of the *Parmenides* gives us a clue to this in the same introduction to the hypotheses from which some lines have been quoted above (135 D - E). After stating that the method to be followed is Zeno's, Parmenides goes on to say: "Anyhow I admired you when I heard you saying to Zeno, that you did not approve of making investigations in the field of the visible things only, but in the first

108

place in the field of those things, which by their very substance we can only conceive by means of argument, and which we may call ideas." This introductory remark by Parmenides can only suggest that Plato, in writing the dialogue, aimed at something more than Zeno had done, especially in the sense that he wanted to overcome the fixation of the problem to the perceptual field, which we can observe in every line of Zeno's paradoxes. Plato wanted to transcend the visible space-bound things and their qualities, even their most abstract qualities as they were known up to Plato's days, i.e. their mathematical qualities. The most characteristic feature of this undertaking, seen from a historical standpoint, was that Plato made his attempt at transcending the material fixation of our thinking precisely by means of the arguments and methods which had been developed on the basis of material conceptions and by mathematical thinking.

Our exposition justifies to a certain extent the Neoplatonic interpretation, according to which the hypotheses of Plato's *Parmenides* contain a doctrine of hypostases, but at the same time it reduces this interpretation to the historical limits within which it is valid. We need not necessarily assume that Plato, at the stage in the development of thinking that was reached by him, realized to the full every implication for which his philosophy opened the way. It is, however, certain that it was Plato who found the first principles and who developed a fully metaphysical and abstract method of thinking, the concepts of which were valid for both material and immaterial being. As we saw above, the very concept of Being had preserved, in Parmenides' philosophy, its spatial connotations. A spatial connotation is also at work in Zeno's problems on continuity and discontinuity, on the question whether there are one or many beings, on infinitely being bisected and infinitely increasing. Zeno's work did not consist of making additions to the Eleatic metaphysics, but of developing new operational methods for dialectic. Zeno, thus, gave a gigantic impetus to the development of philosophy. The problems developed by Eleatic thinking, whether or not in dialogue with the Pythagorean school, received, through the work of Zeno, a formula which was founded on mathematical reasoning and could be adapted to abstract dialectic. In the mathematical character of Zeno's abstractions lies the last remnant of the fixation to spatial conceptions. In Plato we observe the first break-through to actually transcendent ideas, within a method of thinking which keeps to a strictly rational logic. Plato consciously adopted Zeno's logical concepts and dialectical method, as we can observe in the text of his *Parmenides*. By making use of this method Plato undertook to evolve valid concepts for what was to be the first really transcendent metaphysics.

BIBLIOGRAPHY

Bolzano 1851
Brochard 1888, 1893
Cohn 1896
Covotti 1897
Rodier 1902
Gaye 1910
Cajori 1915
Calogero 1932
Lee 1936
Croissant 1937
van der Waerden 1941
de Rijk 1947
Mondolfo 1952
Grünbaum 1952, 1955

Beth 1953, 1959
Virieux-Reymond 1956
Booth 1957
Owen 1958, 1960
Fränkel 1960
Whitrow 1961
Schramm 1962
Untersteiner 1963
Grünbaum 1963
Benardete 1964
Lee 1965
Vlastos 1966, I and II
Prauss 1966
Szabó 1951, 1954 I and II, 1955, 1967

CHAPTER V

EMPEDOCLES

In the ancient doxographic literature Empedocles is mentioned both as a disciple of Parmenides and as a member of the Pythagorean sect. It is possible to find support for both assertions. The Pythagorean element is to be found in Empedocles' respect for all that lives, his belief in metempsychosis, and his conviction of a retribution in the hereafter. We have evidence of these convictions in the verses that have come down to us under the name of Καθαρμοί or 'Purifications'. If we leave aside the verses which obviously belonged to that work, the fragments we have of Empedocles are, in a number of points, strongly reminiscent of Parmenides, whose typical terminology we even recognize now and then. It has been said, and perhaps with good reason, that there was an Italian school of thinking which, beginning with the Pythagoreans and Parmenides, continued to exist up to the days of Lucretius and of the revival of Pythagoreanism. No doubt there are formulas in Lucretius' verses which may be regarded as Empedoclean in character.

One of the basic convictions of Empedocles was that a determined quantity of primordial matter developed into the universe as we know it by the working of Φιλία and Νεῖκος. Expounding this theory Empedocles emphasizes that the whole of things is not increased by anything, nor can anything actually cease to exist (DK 31 B 11 and 12, DK 31 B 17 verse 32). Even the formula in which Empedocles here expresses himself is taken from Parmenides (cf. 28 B 8, verse 7). The arguments which follow also show Parmenidean influence. "From where should increase have come, or how would it be possible for anything to pass completely out of existence?" This is impossible, says the philosopher of Akragas, for "nowhere in this universe a void can be found", ἐπεὶ τῶνδ' οὐδὲν ἔρημον (31 B 17, verse 33). In this line ἔρημον means the same thing that later on was denoted by the term κενεόν. As has been said above, the term does not occur in Parmenides' verses. The idea, however, is clearly present in the lines where Parmenides emphasizes that the universe is homogeneously filled with Being, which forms a continuous whole, because 'being borders upon being' (28 B 8, verses 22-25). This is a second point in which Empedocles adopts the Parmenidean doctrine. The same view is found in the fragments 13 and 14 where instead of ἔρημον the term κενεόν itself is used.

A third point can be mentioned in which Empedocles adopts Parmenides' views. Parmenides had described the universe as spherical and kept in balance from within (28 B 8, verses 43 - 44). The fragments show that Empedocles followed him in this conception (31 B 27 - 28 - 29). The notion is even older than Parmenides' theory because we find it already in Anaximander and Xenophanes.

In other points of his theories Empedocles is clearly going his own way. His most important contribution to the development of theories of matter is the doctrine that change in the visible world must be explained as a change in the ingredients of a mixture, ingredients which themselves remain what they are. Any change in the quality of a thing can be interpreted as a change in the mixture of its composing parts, be it a different arrangement of these parts or a different proportion. The 'ingredients' in the mixture afterwards were to receive the name of στοιχεῖα or elements. In Empedocles we find them designated as ῥιζώματα, the 'roots' of things. It has been said that the immutable character of these elements reintroduces the immutable Being of Parmenides. This sounds as a preconceived opinion devised in order to bring the theory of elements in line with Eleatic metaphysics. The two theories seem to have rather different roots in the history of thinking. At any rate, starting from the premiss of immutable elements, Empedocles gives a coherent theory of change and becoming. In frag. 17, verses 11-13 he says:

τῆι μὲν γίγνονταί τε καὶ οὔ σφισιν ἔμπεδος αἰών·
ἧι δὲ διαλλάσσοντα διαμπερὲς οὐδαμὰ λήγει,
ταύτηι δ' αἰὲν ἔασιν ἀκίνητοι κατὰ κύκλον.

"In a sense there is becoming as their existence is not stable; but in as far as they never cease their interminable permutations, in so far they have an eternal unmoved existence in the cycle of beings."

'Permutations' is the translation of διαλλάσσοντα, which means literally: 'changing positions'. The term fits in exactly with the doctrine that any process of change is only a change in the ingredients of the mixture. The verses quoted form a sentence in which ἄπαντα is the subject. In the verses preceding our quotation we read:

"The universe (ἅπαντα) is alternately brought to unity by Φιλότης, Love, and dispersed into a multitude by Νεῖκος, Hate." This means that Empedocles, as Plato remarked in the *Sophistes* (242 E), follows Heraclitus' scheme, but with an important difference. In Heraclitus the universe is reigned by the forces of attraction and repulsion simultaneously, whereas in Empedocles they work alternately: having been united by Love, the universe is subsequently disintegrated, that is, scattered into a multitude of beings by Hate. It is to be supposed that in the first of these processes even the primary substances or elements lose their individual character, fusing into one. This, however, is not essential to Empedocles' theory about the 'roots' of things, for his intention is to give an explanation of change and becoming. The question of the ultimate unity of things, as far as our fragments go, is not given further attention, though it must be supposed to be lingering in the background. The opposition of ἕν and πλέονα (31 B 17, 16 - 17) suggests that the problem of ἓν καὶ πολλά may have been in Empedocles' mind, just as the lines quoted above remind us of the Parmenidean one Being. The four elements are indicated in 31 B 17, verse 18 by the names of fire, water, earth and air: πῦρ, ὕδωρ, γαῖα, ἀήρ. This enumeration of four elements is found in numerous other fragments, where, however, they are given other names: γαῖα, earth, is called χθών; instead of ὕδωρ, water, we find πόντος, the sea; the air is alternately called ἀήρ and αἰθήρ, and fire is sometimes referred to as ἥλιος, the sun. Although these names might be thought to be merely poetical metaphors, there is a particular fragment which clearly indicates their mythical origin (31 B 6). In this fragment the four 'roots' are enumerated as Ζεύς, Ἥρη, Ἀιδωνεύς and Νῆστις . Two of these names can at once be identified: Ζεύς represents the celestial fire, and Νῆστις is explained by Empedocles himself as the rain which soaks the earth by its tears. As to Ἥρη and Ἀιδωνεύς the doxographic tradition is not unanimous. Ἥρη is usually taken as the ancient earth-goddess, but the interpretation of Hades as air is less self-evident.

There is, however, a common term connecting the two notions of 'nether world' and 'air'. In the later tradition we find some accounts according to which 'air' and 'night' were the same thing. Stobaeus (DK 31 A 33) says that Empedocles uses the name Ἀιδωνεύς for air because the air has no light of its own. Hippolytus has a remark which plays on the name Ἀιδωνεύς as 'the invisible' (DK *ib*), but which in substance gives the same idea: Ἀιδωνεύς stands for the air "because we see everything through the air without ever seeing the air itself".

Obviously a connection between the concepts of 'night' and 'air' was found in the notion of 'invisible'.

It is true that here and there other explanations are given, mostly in the sense that Ἀιδωνεύς represents the earth (e.g. DK 31 A 33, line 18), probably because Hades was regarded as an old chthonic deity. It seems, however, more plausible to take Ἀιδωνεύς as representing the air, because of a description in Hesiod's *Theogony* in which the same division into four realms is given (*Theog.* 736-738, cf. Kirk-Raven 22 and Dornseiff 1937). The verses clearly represent a more ancient stage of mythical thinking:

ἔνθα δὲ γῆς δνοφερῆς καὶ Ταρτάρου ἠερόεντος,
πόντου τ' ἀτρυγέτοιο καὶ οὐρανοῦ ἀστερόεντος
ἑξείης πάντων πηγαὶ καὶ πείρατ' ἔασιν.

"There are found the sources and the anchorholds of gloomy earth and of Hades filled with air, of endless sea and starry heaven, each and all."

This suggests that there was a tradition according to which the universe, when developing from primeval chaos, was divided into four well-distinguished realms. Primeval chaos is mentioned two verses further on by the name of χάσμα μέγα, the great yawning abyss. The development is the same that we find in Empedocles' description of a universe originally one and afterwards split up into four divisions, called the 'roots of things'. The elements in Hesiod still preserve their condition of cosmic realms. Hesiod calls them γῆ, earth, πόντος, sea, οὐρανός, heaven, and Τάρταρος ἠερόεις, which is usually translated as 'misty nether-world'. The adjective ἠερόεις suggests, however, by its parallelism to the description of Empedocles, a strong connotation of 'invisible'. If we take the translation to be 'invisible Hades', the name of Hades or Τάρταρος represents the only element which cannot be seen, that is, 'invisible air'.

The notion of air as being invisible and also making invisible is also found in the numerous passages of Homer, where a god or goddess causes a person to pass out of sight by hiding him behind a curtain of air, e.g.

ἀμφὶ δ' Ἀθήνη / πολλὴν ἠέρα χεῦε (*Od.* VII, 15).

"Athene enveloped him in a thick layer of air."

Once we have seen that Hesiod's description in *Theog.* 736-738 represents a mythical tradition of four original realms of being into which primeval chaos was split up, another passage in the same work can be accounted for on the same principle. In *Theog.* 116-133 another description is found of primeval chaos. The lines give the

114

impression of a really chaotic enumeration of cosmic powers, moving about picturesquely. If, however, we put the synonymous names together, the picture easily falls into four categories:

(1) Γαῖα, earth
(2) Τάρταρα, Ἔρεβος, Νύξ, night ('the invisible element')
(3) Αἰθήρ, Ἡμέρη, day (the heavenly fire or light)
(4) Πέλαγος, Πόντος, Ὠκεανός, sea

The many synonyms are probably an indication that Hesiod incorporated various strains of tradition, and the same conclusion may be drawn from the fact that the genealogy is very obscure. If, however, we leave out of account the mountains and the mountain-nymphs of verses 129-130, the categories are quite clear. The cosmos appears as divided into four realms, which are ruled by divine powers. The description is in harmony with the oldest mythical conceptions of the structure of the universe: in the centre is the earth, surrounded by the Ocean; over the earth there are the heavens, beneath it there is darkness and night.

The only godhead who does not represent one of the four elements is Eros (Ἔρος, vs. 120). His presence can only be explained as a parallel to the Orphic cosmogonies (see our chapter III). In the Orphic theories Eros stood in the midst of the as yet unanimated masses of chaotic matter as life-giving power, creating order in chaos. In Parmenides (28 B 13) he acts in the same capacity (in 28 B 12 Aphrodite).

If our interpretation of the verses quoted from Hesiod is right, we may conclude that, in a period of mythological thinking, 'night' and 'air' must have belonged to the same category. Because the other three categories clearly represent water, earth and fire, nothing but air is left as the element for the godhead of the netherworld and night.

There is a fragment of Empedocles in which the four elements in the same way represent four cosmic realms. It belongs to the so-called *Purifications*, and describes the fate of the soul when expiating its sins in the hereafter. The elements, in this description, hold sway over the four cosmic realms, and the soul must wander, far from the abodes of the blessed. During the time of its wandering the soul does not only inhabit all sorts of living bodies, but is also driven into the sea by the wrath of the heavenly region; the sea spits it out onto the earth, the earth sends it to the sun, and the sun throws it out again into the whirlpool of the air. It must go on wandering for thirty thousand years, a punishment which has been ordained as a terrible ordeal of Fate, passing judgement on the man that was 'self-confident on account of insane strife'. The line was quoted by Plotinus in the treatise on the soul's fate when the soul goes astray in the inferior realm of matter (*Enn.* IV 8,1).

Summing up, we can say that Empedocles' philosophy in its main features rests on two foundations: Eleatic metaphysics and a theory of the elements which originated from a mythical tradition. Following Parmenides, Empedocles takes the view that things cannot come into being out of nothing or perish into complete nothingness, neither does he admit that there can be a void. The universe, to Empedocles, is spherical and in balance from within. Side by side with these Eleatic doctrines goes the mythical tradition. Not only has the doctrine of the four elements sprung from this tradition, but also the goddess Φιλία. In Empedocles' verses she is also found under the name of Ἀφροδίτη (DK 31 B 17, 24; B 22, 5; B 71); Κύπρις (B 98), and Φιλότης (B 19, B 20, B 26). It is in line with this conclusion to suppose that Νεῖκος, too, has a mythical origin, but this must remain a hypothesis. If the mythical origin of Νεῖκος could be established, at the same time the ὁδὸς ἄνω κάτω of Heraclitus might prove to have been derived from a mythical source. For the moment we must content ourselves with having found the pedigree of Φιλία, who is probably the same godhead that by the name of Ἔρως was found in the Orphic cosmogonies. Plato's description in the *Symposium* of Eros as essential poverty aspiring after fulfilment of desires suggests that even Aristotle's στέρησις or privation, which is distinguished in the being of things side by side with εἶδος and ὕλη, may ultimately have something to do with the Empedoclean and Orphic Eros.

Empedocles did not follow Parmenides in the defence of the unity of Being. Probably he regarded this as a doctrine which was somewhat too ardently vindicated by Parmenides. In the allusions of Empedocles to the defenders of the theory of a unique Being, a mild irony seems to come through: 'Everybody boasts of having found the whole of things' (31 B 2, verse 6).

In the same fragment he says that the universe is beyond the grasp of human senses or human thinking. That is why he prefers to express himself only on things which do not pass human comprehension (31 B 2, 8 - 9). The expression has the ring of a certain criticism, when he says:

116

σὺ δ' οὖν, ἐπεὶ ὧδ' ἐλιάσθης,
πεύσεαι οὐ πλέον ἠὲ βροτείη μῆτις ὄρωρεν,

"but thou, having come so far, shalt learn so much as is within the grasp of human comprehension."

These verses sound as an allusion to 28 B 7, verse 2, where Parmenides says:

ἀλλὰ σὺ τῆσδ' ἀφ' ὁδοῦ διζήσιος εἶργε νόημα,

"but thou, keep they thoughts far from this way of thinking."

The impression is more or less confirmed when we read in 31 B 3 the prayer by which Empedocles beseeches his Muse to send him 'a chariot obedient to the rein', which must come 'from the realm of Piety'. This may also have been aimed at Parmenides, who so self-confidently and prophetically had himself driven around in the chariot of the goddess, while his Muses guided him out of the realm of darkness to that of light. The axle of the car went red-hot when these 'mares of great fame' took the prophet to all towns. It is as if Empedocles wants to state that this is not the course which an authentic philosopher must take, for a man who studies the philosophy of nature must make his judgement subordinate to whatever perception will teach him. The true philosopher, says Empedocles, must not dogmatically boast of having achieved absolute wisdom (B 3, verse 7). His must, on the contrary, be the attentive reflection on whatever presents itself to him from the outer world. Empedocles uses a fine expression to convey this:

ἀλλ' ἄγ' ἄθρει πάσῃ παλάμῃ (B 3, verse 9)

"you must make observations with all five senses."

Not only abstract thinking, but also the observation of the senses must have been of great value to this physicist, who warns us not to be deluded by words, but to appreciate all knowledge, in whatever way it comes to us. The true physicist is manifest in these words, most of all in the expression πάσῃ παλάμῃ, 'with all your hands', for: 'with all five senses'.

BIBLIOGRAPHY

A. Empedocles.

Kranz 1912, I
Bignone 1916
Kranz 1949
Reinhardt 1950
Ferguson 1964
Solmsen 1965
Hölscher 1965

B. The concept of "element".

Diels 1899

Jaeger 1920
Hooykaas 1933, 1947
van Melsen 1948
Vollgraff 1949
Lumpe 1962

C. The concept of "matter".

Gomperz 1932
Solmsen 1950, II
Skemp 1960
Solmsen 1961

CHAPTER VI

ANAXAGORAS

Among the fragments of Empedocles only a very few lines can be found which betray that he had some knowledge of mathematical problems. This may surprise us, because Empedocles was Zeno's contemporary and because he lived in *Magna Graecia*, where he had ample opportunity to know what was going on in the field of mathematics, if at least he had access to Pythagorean circles. He was well informed on the ethical doctrines of the Pythagoreans, as we see at once by casting a glance at his Καθαρμοί or *Purifications*. In antiquity there was a story according to which Empedocles had been an adept of the Pythagoreans and was expelled from the school on a charge of stolen spiritual property. (DK 31 A 1 = Diog. L. VIII 54). The same story was told about Hippasus (DK 18 A 4) which means that some reserve should be made as to its historical truth. If it was manifest from his writings that Empedocles knew the Pythagorean doctrines, a story of this kind could easily become attached to his name. If we leave aside the question whether the story is historically reliable, we may at any rate consider it an illustration of the fact that Empedocles adopted a number of Pythagorean doctrines, as is clear from the extant fragments.

A similar interest as Empedocles's in the phenomena of nature can be observed in a thinker of a quite different character, born nearly at the other end of the Greek world, called Anaxagoras. Although a great distance separated the two philosophers, Anaxagoras, in the Ionian town of Clazomenae, must have been well informed on the philosophical theories of the Eleatic school. What we do not find in Empedocles is manifest in Anaxagoras: a desire to give his theories a mathematical substructure. The fragments put it beyond doubt that Anaxagoras, in formulating the first principles of his philosophy, followed in the wake of Zeno. The central problem in these first principles is that of the ἄπειρον. Anaxagoras offers a new and more thorough treatment of this concept. This could have opened the way for a new treatment of the problem, were it not for the fact that in his own philosophy it plays only a subordinate part, because his thinking was not primarily mathematical but biological in character.

The very first lines of Anaxagoras' work on the philosophy of nature betray at once in what historical connection this work had its place. The text as we find it in Simplicius reads as follows (DK 59 B 1):

ὁμοῦ πάντα χρήματα ἦν, ἄπειρα καὶ πλῆθος καὶ σμικρότητα· καὶ γὰρ τὸ σμικρὸν ἄπειρον ἦν.

"All the many things were mixed up, infinite both in multitude and in smallness; for the smallness too was infinite."

The most important element in these two lines is the repetition of the concepts on which Zeno's problems had centered: the concepts of infinitely large and infinitely small as they played their parts in the problem of the infinite divisibility of being. Anaxagoras, taking over these concepts, does not use them in a mathematical problem of continuity but in a biological theory. Before discussing Anaxagoras' treatment of these matters, we shall consider what other themes come up in the lines quoted above.

The opening words may have been meant as a challenge. They form a reaction to the celebrated verse of Parmenides (DK 28 B 8 vs. 5):

οὐδέ ποτ' ἦν οὐδ' ἔσται, ἐπεὶ νῦν ἔστιν ὁμοῦ πᾶν.

"There is no 'was' nor 'will be', for it is a 'now' being a perfect Whole."

The contrast is in the plural πάντα χρήματα instead of πᾶν, and in the past tense ἦν instead of ἔστιν. Consequently, the word ὁμοῦ acquires a different meaning. In Parmenides it indicated the homogeneity of the one Being, in Anaxagoras the being together of primeval matter in an undifferentiated mass. Anaxagoras wants to dissociate himself from the idea of one immutable Being, which only admits of a present tense ἔστιν and can only be described in the singular as a πᾶν or homogeneous Whole. As if defying a then current view, Anaxagoras replaces the expressions of Parmenides πᾶν and ἔστιν by the plural πάντα χρήματα and the past tense ἦν. The plural πάντα χρήματα, 'all things', can be seen as expressing Anaxagoras' intention to do justice to the multiplicity of the phenomena by taking plurality as a given fact. The use of the past tense suggests, as we shall see, that a theory of evolution is going to replace a static metaphysics. The Ionian cosmology had by that time started a dialogue with western

120

Greek philosophy. Time and evolution were going to play a part in cosmological theories, and, accordingly, the coming-into-being of things would have to be recognized and explained. The universe developed, according to Anaxagoras' views, from an initial state in which 'all things' were together in an undifferentiated primordial mixture: ὁμοῦ πάντα χρήματα ἦν.

The conception is reminiscent of the primeval Chaos from which, in the Orphic and Pythagorean doctrines, the universe had developed. It may seem a somewhat surprising statement if we start the discussion of Anaxagoras' philosophy by saying that his point of view was that of the evolutionist. The ancient authors are in the habit of describing the system of this philosopher as the first attempt at a completely rational cosmology, because they take it that Anaxagoras explained the cosmic evolution as the work of a supreme intelligence or Νοῦς. This interpretation probably came to be generally accepted in antiquity as a result of what both Plato and Aristotle had said about Anaxagoras. As we shall see, it is possible even through the medium of Plato's and Aristotle's accounts to get some idea of what Anaxagoras really wanted to say. Modern historiographers generally adopted the ancient interpretation. Its persistence was probably determined to a large extent by the influence of modern rationalism.

According to this view Anaxagoras had been a kind of Descartes of antiquity who caused a break-through of reason in a one-sided, mythically inspired tradition. His theory of the Νοῦς, accordingly, had been the starting-point of a teleological world-view, in which a highest Providence had designed the order of things. Werner Jaeger e.g. writes (*Theol.* 163): "The idea of this preconceived world-plan is quite worthy of the rational physics of the fifth century." Zeller appreciated Anaxagoras' Νοῦς as the form-giving power, creating an orderly universe and working on a preconceived plan. Zeller thought that the only objection that could be made to this theory was that Anaxagoras had gone halfway, because he had failed to endow his Νοῦς with individuality. If Anaxagoras had availed himself of the opportunity, he would have made his highest principle a personal transcendent God. Zeller was even convinced he could explain the reason of this lost opportunity: the Νοῦς had to be present and at work in every part of the universe, and for that reason could not develop into an independent personality (Zeller-Nestle, ⁶1920, I 1229 - 30). Baeumker (1890, 78) adopted Zeller's interpretation.

121

The very term Νοῦς, intelligence, may easily be a motive for thinking that Anaxagoras did design a system according to which a Providence had created and ruled the universe on the lines of a premeditated plan. If we investigate the scattered evidence, we discover even through the scanty fragments, that the idea of a Νοῦς was inherited by Anaxagoras from a long tradition rather than designed by him on a brand-new rational pattern. It appears that Νοῦς, as the moving force in the evolution of the universe, can be compared with the ancient deity Eros, who according to a mythical view organized the whirling chaos into a cosmos.

In a fragment of Parmenides (DK 28 B 13) we find Eros mentioned as the first-born among the gods, and, parallel to this, we find in *frag.* 12 a female godhead, probably Aphrodite, sitting in the centre of the universe and ruling its evolution. This female godhead cannot have been much different from the principle of Love or Φιλότης which Empedocles assumed to be one of the two supreme ruling principles. In Hesiod as well (*Theog.* 120) we find Eros in the first generation of gods that came into existence from primordial Chaos. The fragment of Parmenides mentioned above is found in a work of Plutarch. It is evident from the remarks added to it by Plutarch that in Parmenides' verses Eros had a cosmic function. This is confirmed by the parallel description in *frag.* 12 where it is said that "in the midst of the cosmic forces a demon resides who rules everything; for she holds undivided sway over horrid birth and sexual copulation." This is a description of a divine cosmic power, ruling the generation of living beings.

In Empedocles we find a good many verses in which, though by different names, this cosmic power is described. In fragment 134 he says that we must not imagine the divine power as having a human shape, a body with a head and hands and feet and hairy parts, but, he says, "it is a holy and ineffable mind, darting through the whole universe by the swift motions of thought." This ineffable mind resembles in many aspects Anaxagoras' Νοῦς. In another fragment of Empedocles we recognize features of the ancient godhead of Anaximander (31 B 135): "that which is the ruling law to the All reaches out through the wide realm of air and that of boundless light." This, moreover, is reminiscent of the Orphic texts in which all-powerful Ἀδράστεια is described as "bodiless and embracing the whole universe."

The term Νοῦς used in a description of this all-powerful godhead is found for the first time in a line of Xenophanes (DK 21 B 25):

ἀλλ' ἀπάνευθε πόνοιο νόου φρενὶ πάντα κραδαίνει.

"Effortless he sets all things going by the will of his Mind."
(cf. Gigon 1936, 40).

To this may be compared Anaximenes fr. 2:

ὅλον τὸν κόσμον πνεῦμα καὶ ἀὴρ περιέχει.

"Breath and air embrace the whole universe."

By the word 'breath' the vital breath of a living universe is denoted. This is also a thinking vital breath.

We may, therefore, feel justified in thinking that Anaxagoras' Νοῦς was a descendant of the cosmic deities, to whom in ancient mythological cosmology the government of the cosmos and the control of the processes of becoming were entrusted. This is the more plausible because nowhere in the preserved fragments the Νοῦς has the function of a Providence, working on a deliberate plan in the management of the cosmic processes. We should rather see it as an ubiquitous force working in the manner of a vital principle, provided we keep in mind that Anaxagoras emphasized its not being mixed up in the substance of individual things (DK 59 B 12: μέμεικται οὐδενὶ χρήματι).

Evolution, according to Anaxagoras, started with an eddy or circular motion in the chaotic mass of undistinguished matter. It was Νοῦς who, even at this first stage, directed the circular motion or περιχώρησις. This περιχώρησις or eddy (DK 59 B 12) even reminds us of the cyclone or vortex, whirling around the primordial Egg from which in the Orphic mythology evolution started. We must assume that the germs of life already existed in the chaotic mass itself, and were not introduced by Nous, for Anaxagoras takes care to distinguish even the soul of the animated beings from the Νοῦς (59 B 12: ὅσα γε ψυχὴν ἔχει . . . πάντων Νοῦς κρατεῖ).

The Νοῦς, then, is a superior being, directing the whole process of evolution. The description, however, of this cosmic evolution makes it clear that the concept of a Nous dominating the universe originated from other sources than the reasoning thoughts of the philosopher. The concept was probably not an invention of Anaxagoras, but was evolved by him from what he found in the tradition. This does not make his achievement less important. The way he describes the dominion of the Νοῦς is a splendid example of the process of rationalizing by which the Ionian philosophers evolved abstract concepts from the mythical tradition. Anaxagoras did not succeed in making the Νοῦς completely transcendent, as many historians would have it. It was reserved to a later development in philosophy to form the idea of a cause of being and becoming which was to be completely detached from any material processes. Probably we are right in saying that Anaxagoras prepared the way for this really transcendent philosophy, and that his Νοῦς stood halfway between an immanent force and a transcendent cause.

It is possible to consider Anaxagoras' Νοῦς the forerunner of Plato's Demiurge, but then we must keep two things in mind. Firstly, as we saw above, the tradition of a life-giving force in a developing universe, alternately called Ἔρως or Φιλία, makes it probable that Νοῦς must be placed nearer to an impersonal force, working ubiquitously, than to a consciously operating creator. Secondly, also the description by Anaxagoras himself suggests this quality of the Νοῦς, for, though Νοῦς is strictly distinguished from any individual being, he is present from the very start at every stage of the evolution as its driving force. It is Νοῦς who directs the development of life by integrating and ordering the vital germs that lie scattered in the original chaos. He does not do so, however, in the way of a craftsman using his skill to a preconceived end. The way in which the universe, according to Anaxagoras' theory, develops, may be compared with the growth of a living whole. It is not the way in which a work of art develops in the hands of a craftsman. It is in Plato's philosophy that we must look for a maker deliberately working in accordance with a preconceived plan. In harmony with that conception is also the notion of a raw material or ὕλη, as Aristotle terms it, which is moulded by the craftsman. The word ὕλη seems to have derived its technical signification in philosophy from that of 'timber', preserving thereby an association with the idea of a carpenter working on a plan (cf. Solmsen 1961).

In Anaxagoras' philosophy it is only the name of Νοῦς which may suggest the idea of a deliberate purpose in the action of an individual person, for the evolution of the universe is rather characterized as a biological process (cf. Kucharski 1964). As we shall see, Plato and Aristotle interpreted Anaxagoras' Νοῦς on the lines of a teleological rationalism. It is all the more interesting to find even in Plato a passage betraying the conception which Anaxagoras actually had on this point. The passage is from the *Cratylus*, 413 C:

εἶναι δὲ τὸ δίκαιον ὃ λέγει Ἀναξαγόρας, νοῦν εἶναι τοῦτο· αὐτοκράτορα γὰρ αὐτὸν ὄντα καὶ οὐδενὶ μεμειγμένον πάντα φησὶν αὐτὸν κοσμεῖν τὰ πράγματα διὰ πάντων ἰόντα.

"... but that justice is as Anaxagoras describes it, when he says that it is Νοῦς: for he says that Νοῦς, being sovereign and not mixed-up in anything, orders all things, pervading the universe."

The most noteworthy terms in these lines are 'τὸ δίκαιον' 'justice', and διὰ πάντων ἰόντα, 'pervading the universe'. They remind us of the old cosmic deity, encompassing the universe and doing justice to all living beings, the ancient ruler of the universe who was the ancestor of Anaximander's apeiron. Anaxagoras' Νοῦς was the lawful descendant of this honourable Ionian ancestry (cf. Guthrie 1965, 320).

Both Plato and Aristotle represent Anaxagoras' theory as if it had been an attempt at the construction of a teleological system. No wonder they felt disappointed at the outcome of the theory. They both imagine the theory of Νοῦς as a brand-new invention of Anaxagoras, and accordingly regret that this philosopher did not make a better use of the principle that Reason was the dominating power in the process of creation. The criticism of both Plato and Aristotle proceeds on the assumption that Anaxagoras, having posited Reason as first principle, then leaves it and allows Nature to go to work in its own more or less arbitrary way. If they had been open to the view that Νοῦς had its forerunner in mythical Eros as driving force and life-giving power, they would not have felt the need to accuse Anaxagoras of inconsistency. It was probably the choice of the very term Νοῦς which to Plato and Aristotle gave the impression as if they had to do with a system of rational and, above all, teleological argument.

Aristotle says that Anaxagoras uses Mind as a device to produce a universe (*Met.* A 4, 985 a 18 - 21), but that "he takes it into account only when he cannot say by which other cause a thing necessarily is, for at all other occasions he adduces anything rather than Mind as a cause for the becoming of things." Taken by itself, it was a brilliant innovation to introduce Reason as a cause of things, as Aristotle says a few lines before (984 b 15): "By saying that there was a Reason in things, not only in living beings, but also in nature, a Nous which is the cause of order and of all arrangement, a certain philosopher (τις, i.e. Anaxagoras) emerged as a sober man in contrast with his predecessors who just spoke at random." Aristotle's irritation already betrays that he is giving one of his typical personal interpretations, and this is made clear by another passage in the same book of the *Metaphysics* (A 8, 989 a 30 - b 21). Here Aristotle states that Anaxagoras, when saying that in their primordial condition all things were mixed, was just talking nonsense, but that we can make sense of it by investigating what he at bottom wanted to say (ἃ βούλεται λέγειν). The method of interpreting texts, put into practice here by Aristotle, is

125

the orthodox method of the non-historians, and the results are surprising. By making use of this method, Aristotle says, we can discern two principles in Anaxagoras' metaphysics: that of the One and that of Otherness. As we must consider the Nous as being simple and unmixed, the Nous represents the principle of the One, whereas the undifferentiated mass of primordial matter represents the principle of Otherness. The interpretation is a disagreeable mixture of Platonic terms and Aristotelean theories, but it must have satisfied Aristotle, for he says by way of conclusion (989 b 19 - 21): "What he (Anaxagoras) means to say is something in the manner of later philosophers and of what we now have come to see as being the right explanation." It is clear that what Aristotle does is framing his predecessor's system of thought on the pattern of his own.

It is not only Aristotle who misread Anaxagoras, for this time the Platonic Socrates, too, offers a striking example of wishful reading. In Plato's *Phaedo* Socrates tells us about his first acquaintance with Anaxagoras' writings. He had heard fragments of these writings read to him and had been very pleased to hear about the theory of the Nous. "I made the assumption", says Socrates, "that if there was a Mind ordering the Universe, it would produce a well-ordered whole and would arrange all individual things in the best possible order within this universe" (*Phaed*. 97 C). It is plain that from the outset Socrates was reading what he wanted and expected to read. He assumed that the theory would come in line with his own philosophy by showing that the Good (τὸ κοινὸν πᾶσιν ἀγαθόν 98 B) was the fixed mark with a view to which all things had been ordered in the cosmos. Further reading, however, had frustrated the expectation of finding a coherent cosmology in which a supreme Intellect, led by the idea of the Good, ordered everything. This is not to be wondered at, because the Nous in Anaxagoras' system is not designed to any teleological purpose.

The cosmogonic doctrine, expounded by Anaxagoras, shows that his philosophical system is that of a theory of evolution in which things develop on a biological pattern. We must keep this biological background in mind if we want to appreciate the meaning of Anaxagoras' theory of infinite divisibility.

Anaxagoras must have known the formulas given to this problem by Zeno. He must also have been aware of the axiomatic character of Zeno's arguments, because he himself designs a theory in which a set of axioms determines the theory very thoroughly and consistently.

126

To Anaxagoras, however, the problem of infinite divisibility was not a mathematical problem, but rather a biological one. In some respects, it was a problem that in our times would be characterized as chemical. His infinite division is not simply applied to spatial distance in the mathematical sense, but to all substances that are found in nature and even to living matter. The transformation of minerals into living matter and of one living tissue into another is the starting-point of the problem. To some extent it is reminiscent of the mixture-theories of the medical schools. How is it possible, for instance, that an apparently simple substance, which is taken in as food, is transformed into all kinds of organic tissues, losing completely its former qualities?

Anaxagoras is too much aware of the complicated character of biological processes to assume that ultimately a substance can be divided into very simple smallest parts. In this respect his theory is in complete contrast with the later atomistic doctrine. He presupposes by way of an implicit axiom that the 'roots' of all substances, as Empedocles would have termed them, cannot be of an elementary simplicity. He combined this implicit axiom with a very outspoken second axiom: if division continues, the composing parts of the substance are not eliminated from it. In a third axiom he formulated a principle from which Zeno had shrunk back: there is no actual end to division. The combination of these axioms results in a theory according to which the complex character of any substance continues to have the same degree of complexity, no matter how far it is divided into parts. Even the smallest parts contain every ingredient of the mixture, and because there is no end to the divisibility of things, there are no actual smallest parts. Every particle, however small, can be divided again infinitely without any change in the character of the mixture. As we shall see, the very strictness of the argument was not quite consistent with the observations which had to be explained by it, but this may have escaped notice because the mathematical argument was subordinate to the whole of the theory, which was constructed on biological patterns (cf. Kucharski 1964, Vlastos 1960, Guthrie 1965, 298 - 9). Anaxagoras' argument on infinity nevertheless deserves our attention.

When we compare Anaxagoras' argument on this point with Zeno's, the question of chronology presents itself. Anaxagoras and Zeno were contemporaries and probably Zeno was the younger of the two by some ten years. We have no indications whatever as to the year of publication of their works. If we are to believe that there is any historical fact behind the literary fiction in Plato's *Parmenides* about Socrates meeting the two Eleatic philosophers Parmenides and Zeno, then there is also room for the hypothesis that Anaxagoras, too, may have met the two Eleatics in Athens. In the beginning of the dialogue a certain Cephalus starts the conversation by telling that he has come to Athens from Clazomenae with some of his fellow-citizens to find out what memories of Zeno still survived in Athens. Clazomenae is the town in which Anaxagoras was born. This might be regarded as an allusion to Anaxagoras, if we were to take everything in the fiction as a symbol. As it is even doubtful whether Parmenides and Zeno actually visited Athens, we should not be too rash to suppose that Anaxagoras had also met them. If we want to do justice to Plato we had better leave aside the question whether the meeting he describes in his dialogue actually took place. If Parmenides, Zeno, Anaxagoras and Socrates did not meet personally, at any rate their philosophies had their meeting-place at Athens.

On chronological evidence only it is impossible to determine whether Anaxagoras' theories were of a later date than Zeno's or the reverse. Luria (1933, 110-111) supposed that Zeno's criticism was aimed at Anaxagoras, but a more current opinion assumes that Anaxagoras reacted to Zeno's problems. A short account of the current tradition can be read in Kirk-Raven, 370-2. The interpretation of Zeno's theories as given by Kirk-Raven differs from ours in some respects, but we share their opinion that the real importance of Anaxagoras' theories stands out better if Zeno's problems preceded them. The principles formulated by Anaxagoras can be explained in a more natural way if we suppose them to have come after Zeno's.

In our fourth chapter we saw that Zeno's axiomatic criticism of the concept of infinity, taken in its naïve sense, did not lead him to a revision of the concept itself. The results arrived at by Zeno did not take the form of a new theory, but were embodied into a new method of philosophical investigation, by which an axiom was taken as a hypothesis and its validity tested by the consequences to be derived from it. This new method soon gave rise to the adoption of new techniques of discussion, in which various and even conflicting hypotheses were tried in order to compare the results. For this reason Zeno may rightly be called the father of dialectic.

The central problem in Zeno's discussions had been that of the infinite divisibility of mathematical space. The discussion on this point had come to a stop at the point when the concepts of 'infinity' and 'determinateness' came into conflict. A line having a determined length could mathematically be bisected an infinity of times, because of the continuity of space. The smallest part could be supposed either still to have a dimension or to have no dimension any more. In the first supposition it could not be explained why the infinite number of smallest parts did not give an infinite length to the original line, which by definition, however, had a determined length. In the second case the consequence was that, if you take an infinity of times a smallest part that has no dimension at all, the operation will never result in a line having a dimension. On the contrary, the line that was supposed to have a determined length would prove to have no length at all.

The criticism formulated by Zeno did not induce him to conceive a new definition of the concept of infinity. It was Anaxagoras who occupied himself with the problem of formulating a more correct and consistent concept of infinity. Anaxagoras tried to find the solution in a theory which was an essential step towards the modern theory of infinite sets as formulated by Bolzano and Cantor (cf. Michel 1950, 663-669).

In the fifth of the preserved fragments Anaxagoras says (DK 59 B 5):

πάντα οὐδὲν ἐλάσσω ἐστὶν οὐδὲ πλείω, οὐ γὰρ ἀνυστὸν πάντων πλείω εἶναι, ἀλλὰ πάντα ἴσα ἀεί.

"The sum total of all things is not a bit smaller nor greater, for it is not practicable that there should be more than all, but the sum total is always equal to itself."

In this translation we have taken the word πάντα in the sense of 'the sum total of the elements of an infinite set'. The only objection that could be made is that the expression τὰ πάντα may have been designed by Anaxagoras as a variation of the expression τὸ πᾶν used by Parmenides. This may be the case, in the same way as in the first fragment (above, p. 120), but a comparison with the next fragment makes it clear that the technical and mathematical meaning is not absent.

In the sixth fragment (DK 59 B 6) Anaxagoras says among other things:

". . . ἴσαι μοῖραί εἰσι τοῦ τε μεγάλου καὶ τοῦ σμικροῦ πλῆθος . . ."

"There are just as many parts in the great as in the small taken as a multitude."

Although in the context of the fragment the idea of the universe taken as a whole persists, the words themselves can hardly be taken in any other sense but the mathematical. The word πλῆθος forms the clearest evidence for this meaning, as it stands for the sum total of the elements of a whole which is taken as a complete infinite set.

When comparing the fragments 5 and 6 we can see that the expressions πάντα and πλῆθος fall within the framework of the same mathematical problem. Πάντα indicates the complete set taken as a whole, πλῆθος the contents of the set, i.e. the number of its elements. The elements themselves are indicated as μοῖραι. The use of these terms in the technical sense of mathematics fits in well with their general use in Greek.

We now may frame the complete argument as follows.

Zeno had already been aware that a set, and an infinite set as well, had to be taken as a complete whole in its own right. He says in *frag*. 3: "If there is a [discontinuous] multiplicity, it must necessarily be as great as it is, not larger nor smaller." In other words: a set, taken as a whole, cannot be greater or smaller than it is by itself. This had formed the starting-point of an argument in which the discontinuous division of space led to inconsistency. In that argument the complete set could be supposed to contain any number of elements, great or small, and a determined or an undetermined number just as well. The solution of the difficulty is that the concept of number changes its meaning according to whether it is used for countable numbers or for the number of elements of an infinite set. In the first case there are discrete units which, taken together, form a determined number, whereas in the second case the number of the elements is by definition not countable. When Zeno in *frag*. 3 speaks about elements which can be inserted between other elements he is talking about discontinuous elements because he treats them as discrete units. This means that implicitly he supposes that the number of elements can be counted. The same conclusion must be drawn from his treatment of the 'Achilles'. In that problem all the diminishing distances covered by Achilles had to be counted, and because the sequence of diminishing distances is infinite, counting must go on infinitely, which means that Achilles cannot overtake the tortoise. A quantity is not countable unless it has discrete units. The discontinuous character of Zeno's concept of infinity was the cause of the paradoxes being unsolvable.

Zeno was obviously aware of the inconsistency of the consequences and even of the necessity of taking any infinite set as a complete whole. Yet he did not arrive at the conclusion that the weak point was that he treated the elements of an infinite set as if they were discontinuous, i.e. countable. Here Anaxagoras takes up the problem. We may even suppose that the text of the fifth fragment of Anaxagoras is directly related to the third fragment of Zeno. In this text Zeno uses the expression τὰ ὄντα, whereas in Anaxagoras' text πάντα is the subject of the sentence. This is essentially the same thing, with this difference that to Anaxagoras πάντα had the connotation of 'the whole of all things'. In both texts, however, the formula is of a kind which makes it impossible to exclude the mathematical sense of the argument.

Making the mathematical sense explicit we get: all elements of any infinite set taken together, i.e. the sum total (τὰ πάντα) of a set must be taken as a determined whole remaining equal to itself and not being greater or smaller than its own quantity. This point of view was a distinct advance towards a solution of the mathematical problem of infinity, when we compare it with the paradoxes of Anaxagoras' immediate predecessor Zeno. On the philosophical side it contains fundamentally the solution of the problem that dominated fifth-century thinking on infinity: how to combine infinity and determinateness. On the mathematical side we may regard the fifth fragment of Anaxagoras as the earliest text in which we find a correct formula of a mathematical definition of infinity, as it has its place in the theory of infinite sets.

So far we have only quoted the premiss of the argument of *frag.* 6, which says that a large and a small set have the same number of elements, that is an infinite number. From this premiss Anaxagoras draws the conclusion that 'everything must be in everything' (καὶ οὕτως ἂν εἴη ἐν παντὶ πάντα). It was the conclusion and not the mathematical argument in which Anaxagoras was interested most. We can observe that in nature different substances and different tissues originate from one another in the most unexpected manner. We shall be able to explain this so much the better if we may start from the assumption that the substances, out of which nature manufactures everything, already contain parts of everything. As we shall see, Anaxagoras subordinated his mathematical theory of infinite divisibility to this biological vision. Before giving a more detailed explanation of this we must add a few remarks on the theory of infinite divisibility.

The term ἄπειρον is not found in the two fragments quoted above. It is, however, beyond doubt that the problem is that of infinite bisection, as is made clear by the terms which appear two lines further on in the same fragment:

τοὐλάχιστον μὴ ἔστιν εἶναι.

"It is not possible for a smallest part to exist."
This means that Anaxagoras wants to take the concept of infinite
bisection in the mathematically strict sense of a never-ending process.
However small a smallest part may be, by itself it can be taken as a new
starting-point for infinite division. The consequence of this is that
the large and the small have the same number of elements, viz. an
infinite number. Only on the strength of this principle it is possible
to conceive of a thing having a determined quantity and nevertheless
an infinite number of parts. The theorem implies the use of the concept of number in two different meanings. In the case of a finite
quantity number is always the counting number, in the case of an
infinite quantity the concept should rather be denoted by a term such
as 'multitude'. Anaxagoras uses the term πλῆθος to convey this
meaning. We may notice that, as far as our sources go, Anaxagoras
did not give a more elaborate development of this different use of the
concept of number.

Our explanation is confirmed by the text of the third fragment
(DK 59 B 3):

οὔτε γὰρ τοῦ σμικροῦ ἐστι τό γε ἐλάχιστον, ἀλλ' ἔλασσον ἀεί (τὸ γὰρ
ἐὸν οὐκ ἔστι τὸ μὴ οὐκ εἶναι) – ἀλλὰ καὶ τοῦ μεγάλου ἀεί ἐστι μεῖζον. καὶ
ἴσον ἐστὶ τῶι σμικρῶι πλῆθος, πρὸς ἑαυτὸ δὲ ἕκαστόν ἐστι καὶ μέγα καὶ
σμικρόν.

"Nor is there a smallest part even of a small quantity, but there
is always a smaller one, for it is impossible that being should change
into not-being, – just as there is always something larger than a large
quantity. This large quantity is equal to the small quantity in multitude (πλῆθος, 'power' in the Cantorian sense), and by itself each thing
is at the same time large and small."

This fragment once more puts it beyond doubt that Anaxagoras
was following the track set out by Zeno. At the same time we can
conclude from it that Anaxagoras wanted to introduce a more consistent use of the concept of infinity, as we have explained above.
In the text the infinity *ad minus* is given the greater emphasis. To
Zeno this had been the main problem. We should also observe that
Anaxagoras does not only give a mathematical argument, but also
an argument which is directly reminiscent of Parmenidean doctrine:
it is impossible to cross the border-line between being and not-being.
However far we may go with our process of division we will necessarily
remain within the realm of Being. Even the smallest parts continue

to belong to actual being and as a consequence continue to be divisible in a mathematical sense. The idea that in a physical sense there may be an actual end to bisection was reserved to a later stage of thinking, when the atomists had advanced their theory of smallest parts. It is however not certain that the atomic theory was inspired by a desire to escape from the difficulties of Zeno's problem of infinite divisibility, which had perplexed the philosophers. It is just as well possible that Democritus' theory was a descendant of the Ionian theories, according to which evolution had started from a primordial mixture of elementary substances. It was probably Aristotle who brought about the connection of the atomic theory with Zenonian problems and Eleatic theory. In our next chapter we shall have to put the question whether Aristotle was right in doing so. It is important to keep in mind that the texts of Anaxagoras which we have discussed prove that the Eleatic problems, in the wording given to them by Zeno, had been incorporated into the Ionian tradition even before Democritus.

Not only the third but also the first fragment confirms our interpretation. In very explicit terms it reads (DK 59 B 1):

ὁμοῦ πάντα χρήματα ἦν, ἄπειρα καὶ πλῆθος καὶ σμικρότητα· καὶ γὰρ τὸ σμικρὸν ἄπειρον ἦν.

"All the many things were mixed up, infinite both in multitude and in smallness; for the smallness too, was infinite."

Two kinds of infinity are being posited here, and once more infinity by division gets the stronger emphasis. Anaxagoras wants to take the concept of infinity in a manner which is consistent with its definition: there is no end to the division. It is this point, together with the more deliberate distinction between a countable number and an infinite multitude, which constitutes the real advance made by Anaxagoras when we compare him with Zeno. Anaxagoras introduces an adjustment of the naïve conception of infinity. In this naïve conception an infinite quantity is a quantity that can infinitely be increased, e.g. the infinity of number means that counting can infinitely be continued. The definition itself implies a contradiction, for in this conception an infinite set will be a set that never achieves its own completeness. The originality of Anaxagoras consists in supposing that the set will reach its completeness. He calls the whole a πλῆθος or multitude, and makes the assumption that the infinite multitude of small parts will constitute a finite whole.

This adjustment introduced by Anaxagoras did not survive its author. Probably the whole problem of infinite division was droppped by Democritus when he framed his atomic theory, at least if we are to suppose that the connection between the Zenonian problem and the atomic theory was an arbitrary interpretation of Aristotle. It was probably for other reasons than those given by Aristotle that Democritus assumed the actual existence of solid smallest particles. The concept of an infinite collection having reached its own completeness was not taken seriously by Aristotle, who probably did not see its originality. He reverts to the naïve conception of infinite quantity as a quantity that can be added to indefinitely without ever actually becoming infinite. It never comes to be actually that which it was supposed to be, viz. *infinite*.

In *De caelo* (271 b 28 - 272 b 7) Aristotle makes use of this never-ending process of counting to prove that cosmic space cannot be infinite. His argument starts from the fact that the revolution of the heavens is completed in a fixed time (ἐν πεπερασμένῳ 272 b 14), and that it is impossible to traverse an infinite distance in a finite time (ἐν πεπερασμένῳ χρόνῳ ἄπειρον 272 b 30). From this he concludes that the universe must have finite and well-determined dimensions; it cannot be infinite. This argument is conclusive as long as ἄπειρον is taken as a process of counting that can be continued indefinitely. This entails another consequence: the term ἄπειρον takes on a merely negative meaning, for whatever is ἄπειρον is unfinished. It is true that the process is on its way to the finish, but the finish is never reached (*Phys.* 206 a 9 - 25). Therefore an infinite number (ἀριθμὸς ἄπειρος) does not exist (*Phys.* 204 b 8 - 10), and the infinite never forms a complete set, for the concept implies that, once a certain set has come into existence new units can always be added to it (ἀεί τι λαμβάνειν ἔξω, *Phys.* 207 a 1 - 8, the word ἔξω indicates that 'from the outside' new elements are taken into that which is being defined. In a definition this is a logical inconsistency). Therefore an actually infinite whole cannot possibly exist (*Phys.* 206 a 18 - 21).

Infinity is to Aristotle something potential, but what is more, it will also remain potential *ad infinitum* (which is a contradiction within the Aristotelean system, for potential is only that which can be brought to actual existence). Therefore, the way in which the bronze is potentially the statue, is not identical with that in which the infinite is potential, for actual infinity can never be realized. In the passage *Phys.* 207 a 1 - 32 we can read to what extent the unfinished character of anything that is infinite entailed a negative appreciation: because it has no τέλος, it could not be τέλειον (*Phys.* 207 b 14). Nor could the

134

ἄπειρον exist by itself unless in our thought, as Aristotle states it in *Met.* 1048 b 14 - 17.

The definition of infinity as used by Aristotle must be considered a step backward if we compare it to Anaxagoras' theory. Aristotle's definition fits in well with the whole system developed in the *Physics*. By analogy we can say the same thing of Anaxagoras: it is the system that determines how the concepts are going to be adapted. To Anaxagoras too, the definition was a necessary presupposition in developing a system of thought. Probably even the requirements of the system as such may have sharpened Anaxagoras' awareness of the importance of the mathematical definitions, which were to give a foundation to his biological and evolutionary theories. These evolutionary views were by far the most important to Anaxagoras, and for his contemporaries they must have been the core of his theories. Possibly this also accounts for the fact that the original contribution made by Anaxagoras to the problem of infinity was forgotten by those who came after him. We may suppose that Anaxagoras' solution of the problems of Zeno did not receive the attention which it deserved, because within the framework of his biological theories the solution seemed so obvious. Anaxagoras' doctrine, moreover, was by its very complexity in an unfavourable position when, within one generation, it had to rival with the atomic theory, which was eminently simple in its principles. Historically, the great influence of Democritus' doctrines on Aristotle's thought may also have contributed to the oblivion into which the more technical points of Anaxagoras' theories were soon to fall.

Surveying Anaxagoras' system and its historical ancestry, it is difficult to believe that it can still be explained as an attempt at a rational theory of nature's processes, conceived as being guided by a supreme intelligence. Both Plato and Aristotle try to find a teleological strain in Anaxagoras' theory of Νοῦς, and both of them complain that the Νοῦς did not meet the requirements of an adequately working universal Mind. We saw that Anaxagoras' Mind was in fact a descendant of the cosmic deities that were active in the cosmic evolution. No more than a rational teleological system was aimed at by Anaxagoras, did he attempt to work out a system of mathematical definitions. His thought is dominated by biological analogies. The universe has developed from an initial state of chaos, in which a vital nucleus condensed in the midst of a rotatory movement of increasing velocity. The analogy of this conception to that of the Orphic cosmogony, in which the universe was a living being developing from an egg, may be

135

somewhat vague, but it is sufficiently recognizable. The primordial mixture in which the vital germs of all things lay hidden (59 B 4: σπέρματα πάντων χρημάτων), and which was surrounded by fire and air (or: by air and void, ἀήρ τε καὶ αἰθὴρ κατεῖχεν 59 B 1), has the same qualities that we have found described in the Orphic traditions of primeval chaos.

Like the ancient cosmogonies, Anaxagoras describes the evolution of the cosmos as if it were the growth of a living being. The biological side of his thinking is also borne out by the fact that, in discussing the problem of the infinitely small particles, he takes his examples mainly from the organic sphere. He asks, e.g., how it is possible that from the same food are produced such different substances as flesh, bones, sinews, hair, nails, and even feathers and horns, if we are to suppose that growth is an addition of like to like (59 A 45 lines 14 - 19, and 59 B 10). Anaxagoras explains this by assuming that in every substance all kinds of substances are mixed. Even the smallest parts into which a substance may be divided retain the composition of the original substance. The biological observation that from our food a broad scale of other substances is produced is thus founded on a theory of infinite divisibility. This theory, originating from a mathematical problem, has taken up a biological function here. It is clear that the mathematical argument, however acute, served to Anaxagoras as a substructure, not as a theory in its own right.

The principle that every smallest particle contains particles of every substance, together with the principle of infinite divisibility were to Anaxagoras a sufficient foundation for a theory which was to explain change and becoming. Anaxagoras did not go so far as to ask how the infinite complexity of all substances was to be reconciled with the differences in their qualities. If all substances are present in everything, it is necessary to ask how the differences can be accounted for. In primordial chaos there was no distinction of qualities. Anaxagoras says (frag. 1): "because all things were together, nothing could be clearly distinguished as a consequence of its smallness." The smallest parts were too small to permit any individual qualities to be perceived. A distinction was not introduced until the vortex set in (περιχώρησις, frag. 12), separating dense from rarefied, hot from cold, bright from gloomy, and dry from moist. Anaxagoras adds, however, that nothing, with the only exception of Νοῦς, is completely separated from other things. Consequently he must assume that the qualities of a thing are determined by the preponderance in the mixture of certain substances (frag. 12, last lines). For the rest, there is nothing that only consists of particles of one quality. This means that in Anaxagoras' system there is no room for the concept of physical element. The condition of things being composed of particles of all substances is in principle the same condition in which they were in primordial chaos: ὅπωσπερ ἀρχὴν εἶναι καὶ νῦν πάντα ὁμοῦ, "just as in the beginning so all things are mixed together now" (frag. 6).

If we combine this theory of universal mixture with that of infinite divisibility, the question arises of how a quality can be constituted by the preponderance of certain particles, because by definition particles of all kinds are present in infinite multitudes. A difference in proportion is only possible if one infinity can differ from the other in quantity. To modern mathematics this does not present any difficulty, because two complete sets can be both infinite while at the same time one contains a greater number of elements than the other (or, in other words, has a greater 'power'). This concept of 'power' as indicating the multitude of elements of infinite sets, may have found its expression in the Anaxagorean term πλῆθος, as we saw above. Anaxagoras, however, offers us, as far as our sources go, no further developments on this point, probably because his presuppositions satisfied him as a foundation for his theories.

BIBLIOGRAPHY

Capelle 1919
Theiler 1924
Peck 1926, 1931
Bailey 1928, 537-556
Schottlaender 1929
Cornford 1930
Gomperz 1933
Gigon 1936
Jöhrens 1939
Bröcker 1943
von Fritz 1945-6
Vlastos 1950
Davison 1953

Raven 1954
Mugler 1956
Mathewson 1958
Bargrave-Weaver 1959
Strang 1963
Lanza 1963
Kucharski 1964
von Fritz 1964
Gershenson-Greenberg 1964
Ferguson 1964
Detienne 1964
Stokes 1965
Romano 1965

DEMOCRITUS OR:
'THING AND NO-THING'

Current tradition says that Democritus laid the first foundations of a really physical doctrine of atoms. This makes him the ancestor of the corpuscular theories of matter, from which modern scientific physics sprang.

We may feel the impulse to verify the tradition of this important theory by studying what authentic texts of Democritus may have been preserved. If we do so, we shall find that in the collection of Diels-Kranz there are 298 authentic fragments, only three lines of which have a statement about atoms, while only five fragments have statements about physical or mathematical subjects. By far the greater part of all that we can still read in Democritus' own version, is about ethical subjects.

These texts give evidence of a mature and sedate wisdom. They give us reason to believe that the renown Democritus earned himself as the 'laughing philosopher' was fully justified. The γνῶμαι or practical maxims show a good-humoured man having a high regard for the value of human life. Diogenes Laertius (IX 43) reproduces a legend according to which Democritus attained the age of 109 and rather faded away than died. The high number of his years was possibly the result of an error in the chronology of the later tradition, but if the statement is historically reliable it seems to be an illustration of the good humour on which Democritus himself made such sound remarks. He called it with one of his special terms εὐεστώ (Diog. L. IX 45, DK 68 B 2c, 4, 140) and once εὐθυμίη (68 B 191). He probably wanted to express the view that a wise man must keep his inclinations under control if he wants to live in good cheer and contentment. He may have spoken from experience when he expressed the opinion that a long life without any feasts is like a long road without any inns:

βίος ἀνεόρταστος μακρὴ ὁδὸς ἀπανδόκευτος (B 230).

The fragments B 9 en B 125 are the only two in which atoms are mentioned:

138

DK 68 B 9 (from Sext. Emp. VII 135): νόμωι γλυκύ, νόμωι πικρόν, νόμωι θερμόν, νόμωι ψυχρόν, νόμωι χροιή, ἐτεῆι δὲ ἄτομα καὶ κενόν.

DK 68 B 125 (from Galen): νόμωι χροιή, νόμωι γλυκύ, νόμωι πικρόν, ἐτεῆι δ' ἄτομα καὶ κενόν.

"As a result of convention we speak of colour, of sweet, of bitter; in reality there are only atoms and void."

The two fragments are so much alike that we may suppose them to be transcriptions from the same source.

On mathematical topics we find two fragments, viz. B 155 and 155 a. The first is from Plutarch. It is rather important, because it proves that Democritus occupied himself with finding a mathematical formula for the solid content of a cone. The text shows that Democritus already saw how important the concept of infinitesimal small sections is to mathematical method. It is possible that one of the titles of the lost works of Democritus, in the list given by Diogenes Laertius, points to the same idea of operating with infinitesimal differences: 'On the contact of a circle and a sphere' (DK 68 A 33, Diog. L. IX 46).

The second fragment, B 155 a, is a statement by Democritus in which he considers the circle as a kind of angle. This probably originated from the set of problems in which theorems about the areas of circles were demonstrated by means of continued fragmentation of the sides of regular polygons. Considering the circle as a kind of angle possibly betrays a working-method in which the fragmentation of a straight line was continued to such a degree that the line approximated a circle.

On physical topics we have three fragments: B 156, 164 and 167. The first of these contains the famous statement:

μὴ μᾶλλον τὸ δὲν ἢ τὸ μηδὲν εἶναι.

"*Thing* does not exist to a higher degree than *no-thing*." (Cf. Matson 1963). The preservation of this sentence we owe to Plutarch, who also added the explication of what Democritus meant by it: "By *thing* he means the bodies, by no-thing the void, because he makes the assumption that also the void has a nature of its own and exists by its own right." This is in harmony with the statements of Aristotle (*Met*. A 4, 985 b 4 - 9 = *Gr. Ph.* 135 = DK 67 A 6) and of Simplicius (DK 68 A 37 = *Gr. Ph.* 141. This latter passage contains a summary made by Simplicius of a lost work of Aristotle *On Democritus*).

The second of the physical fragments, B 164, is an explication of the mechanism of the vortex or δῖνος, a principle which is related to Anaxagoras' περιχώρησις. Democritus says that in this vortex like was added to like, just as on the beach pebbles of the same kind are

139

sorted out by the waves, or as grains of lentils, of barley and of wheat find themselves together as a result of the motion of the sieve.

The third of the physical fragments, B 167, is very short. It reads:
δῖνον ἀπὸ τοῦ παντὸς ἀποκριθῆναι παντοίων ἰδεῶν.
"From the whole a vortex of all kinds of atoms broke away."

The fragment deserves our attention because of the word ἰδέαι, which was probably one of the terms Democritus used to describe the atoms (Burnet EGP 336): they were characterized by their shape.

The authentic texts of Democritus on subjects related to the atomic doctrines comprise no more than the fragments quoted above. We shall therefore try to make an addition to these scanty materials by putting together the various typical expressions we find mentioned in the accounts of Democritus' theory by other authors. Even in antiquity it was noticed that Democritus was very original in his use of language. One often finds the remark that Democritus used this or that peculiar expression for concepts that were central in his theory. Democritus may have taken these expressions from the local dialect of his native town Abdera. Some expressions are certainly of his own coinage, such as e.g. the word-play on δὲν καὶ μηδέν, already quoted above: if the universe is composed of atoms and void, it can be said to consist of 'thing and no-thing'.

The most important terms in Democritus' system of cosmology are:

ἄτομα καὶ κενόν	B 9, B 125	atoms and void
ἀνάγκη	{ A 37 (Simplicius) { Diog. L. IX 45	necessity
δίνη, δῖνος	{ B 164, B 167 { A 69	vortex
		Terms describing the motion of the atoms:
περιπλέκεται, προσκρούει ἀποπάλλεται, διακρίνει	A 49	entangled – collide – are hurled away – separates itself
συγκρίνει περιπαλλάσσεσθαι	A 58	aggregates itself, to be shaken away.
		Terms expressing the characteristics of the atoms:
ῥυσμός, τροπή, διαθιγή translated by Aristotle as: σχῆμα, θέσις, τάξις	{ Met. 985 b 15-19 { A 38	shape, order, position
τὸν σοῦν = τὴν κίνησιν	A 62	motion

140

By the term ἀνάγκη Democritus probably wanted to express our idea of physical causality. It may be classed in the same category as Anaxagoras' Νοῦς. Both are rationalized versions of an old cosmic deity ruling the development of the universe. It is the old deity whose philosophical descendants we find in the hieratic formulas of Parmenides (28 B 8, vs. 30: 'Ανάγκη; 28 B 10, vs. 6: 'Ανάγκη) as well as in the Orphic 'Αδράστεια. The way in which the tradition was rationalized is characteristic of both philosophers. Anaxagoras saw the divine presence as an ubiquitous consciousness, working in a manner which may be compared to the working of the Λόγος in Heraclitus. Democritus restricted the function of the almighty cosmic law to a physical causality, immanent in the atoms. It is interesting to see that Plato in the *Timaeus* tries to correct the one-sided vision of a strictly physical causality or ἀνάγκη by adding to it a craftsman or Demiurge, representing the ubiquitous consciousness of Anaxagoras' Nous.

Anaxagoras and Democritus have in common the concept of a vortex. In the evolution of the cosmos this vortex is the oldest form in which physical causality appears. Accordingly, the concepts of ἀνάγκη and δίνη are more or less identified by Diogenes Laertius (IX 45) and by Sextus Empiricus (DK 68 A 83).

At first sight it may seem to be a matter of course to identify the set of opposites δὲν-μηδέν (B 156) with that of ἄτομα-κενόν (B 9, B 125), and that of ὄν-μὴ ὄν, being-not being. This is what ancient tradition unanimously suggests. We may all the more be inclined to believe this tradition when we read (A 37) Simplicius' account of the typical expressions by which Democritus used to convey his ideas. We get the impression that Simplicius still had the original works of Democritus on his desk. It is, however, not excluded that Simplicius simply repeated what he had read in Aristotle. The fact that the bulk of ancient doxographic tradition was dominated by Aristotelean views should put us on our guard, because the historical accounts in Aristotle himself again and again give rise to critical questions. It is true that Aristotle had practically all the original texts at his disposal and there is reason to believe that he had read them extensively. It is equally true however that Aristotle read them with the intention of finding a confirmation for his own points of view. To this end he even explains the theories of his predecessors in such a manner that they could easily be incorporated into his own system. If a theory offers no possibility of being assimilated, it falls outside his scope and is held up to scorn. Hence the sneering terms in which Aristotle dismisses certain theories, as e.g. those of Xenophanes and Melissus, who are discarded as being on too primitive a level (*Met.* A 5, 986 b 27) or his headstrong interpretations of Anaxagoras, which were discussed above (p. 125-6). The process of assimilating is generally destructive to the historical exactness of the account. As regards historical information we can rely on Aristotle probably to the same degree as we can rely on Heidegger when he gives statements on Aristotle. The theories are completely transformed by the manner in which they are presented to the reader. If we should have to reconstruct a lost Aristotle from the statements given by Heidegger, a strange *monstrum* would be born. Aristotle even when reporting on the doctrines of his own master Plato commits gross blunders, as was pointed out by Cherniss and recently by Ilting (1965).

Bearing in mind this general condition of ancient doxography we are justified in putting some critical questions as regards Aristotle's account of Democritus' theories. Two points especially ask for an investigation: (1) were the terms ὄν-μὴ ὄν used by Democritus himself as synonymous of δέν-οὐδέν? (The latter expression being authentically Democritean); (2) Aristotle is very circumstantial when treating of the atomic theories; he assigns them a more or less directly Eleatic pedigree. Are his accounts, especially the account in *De gen. corr.* 316 a 13 ff., reliable as regards this historical background of the atomic theory?

We may try to approach these problems by drawing up a survey of Democritean terms. Two different identifications can be observed: that of ἄτομα and κενόν with respectively δέν and μηδέν, and that of ἄτομα and κενόν with ὄν and μὴ ὄν. The first of these identifications can easily be verified as historical. The expression δέν-μηδέν (or οὐδέν) was authentically Democritean and synonymous of ἄτομα-κενόν.

In the account by Aristotle and Simplicius (DK 67 A 6 and 68 A 37) and in Plutarch's commentary on the authentic fragment 68 B 156 we find the oppositions stated as follows:

τόπος	
κενόν	ναστόν
οὐδέν	δέν
ἄπειρον	ὄν

In the account by Galen we find the expression δὲν καὶ μηδέν ἐστι τὰ πάντα, "The universe consists of thing and no-thing," explained by the added remark, that δέν must be understood as ἄτομοι, and μηδέν as τὸ κενόν. The opposition therefore is:

| μηδέν | δέν |
| τὸ κενόν | αἱ ἄτομοι |

Because the source is indirect and rather late, we cannot be sure whether there is any meaning in the use of μηδέν instead of οὐδέν, as Bailey would have it (1928, 118).

An account by Aristotle in *Physics* A 5, 188 a 22 - 26 (= DK 68 A 45) has the opposition

| κενόν | στερεόν |
| οὐκ ὄν | ὄν |

The word στερεόν here must be a synonym of ναστόν, for which another synonym is found in *De caelo* Δ 2, 310 a 1 (= DK 68 A 60):

πλῆρες

This short survey can only suggest an observation, which, however, any reader will find confirmed when perusing the complete collection of texts given by Diels-Kranz in 67 A and 68 A. It is the observation that the terms ὄν and οὐκ ὄν (occasionally μὴ ὄν) are only found in texts of Aristotle, with the only exception of ὄν occurring once in a text of Simplicius. This may have some importance, because Simplicius appears to quote directly from Democritus, but even so it is not impossible that Simplicius should have been influenced by what he read in Aristotle. The question whether our observation should lead to any conclusion cannot be answered until we have discussed our second point, the problem as to whether Aristotle was right in giving a directly Eleatic pedigree to the atomic theory.

Aristotle offers a rather thorough treatment of the atomic theory in two passages of *De gen et corr.*: A 2, 316 a 13 - 317 a 31 (incompletely rendered in DK 68 A 48 b), and A 8, 325 a 23 - 325 b 11 (= DK 67 A 7). The first of these passages is about Democritus, the second about Leucippus. He discusses both Democritus and Leucippus, as representing the same doctrine, in *Met.* A 4, 985 b 4 - 22 (= DK 67 A 6).

The passage in *De gen. et corr.* A 2 is the most extensive and the most important. The atomic theory is argued here from the premiss of the mathematical problem of infinity.

In order to obtain a better survey of the whole of Aristotle's argument in A 2, we shall first give a summary of the essentials. Aristotle's argument has three parts in each of which argument and criticism are mixed up. The arguments are given by Aristotle in a way which suggests that they were the original arguments of the atomists.

We think, however, that they should rather be considered as an Aristotelean construction than as the actual substructure of the atomic theory as Democritus framed it. Aristotle's criticism is given on the same lines of thought on which the argument itself is expounded. This makes it difficult to distinguish the contents of the theory from Aristotle's critical remarks on it, and this suggests even more strongly that both the argument and the criticism are given from Aristotelean points of view. This furthermore is borne out by the expressions δοκεῖ, δοκῶν, δόξειεν ἄν, which are found in the text. Aristotle uses these expressions frequently when he is discussing theories which are not in harmony with his own views. Besides the various tenses of the verb δοκέω, Aristotle also uses expressions such as φανείη ἄν, τρόπον τινά, ἔοικε, σχεδόν. The occurrence of these expressions indicates that Aristotle is analyzing opinions of other philosophers in order better to develop his own theories. In such a case it has from the outset not been Aristotle's intention to give us historically reliable information. Mostly the argument takes on an air of self-sufficiency, but if we can stand that and do not ask historical questions, we may be content to see Aristotle analyzing and arguing. If, moreover, we want to form an idea of what the other philosophers may have meant to say, a technique of close reading is required to discern where Aristotelean patterns of thought are at work. In our text the words δοκεῖ and δοκῶν are strong indications.

The three parts of Aristotle's discussion are as follows.

(1) 316 a 13 - 316 b 18: "If we make the assumption that any body is completely divisible, we cannot assume that after complete division a quantity having dimension will be left, for in that case this quantity would still be divisible owing to its having dimension. Therefore we must conclude that division will end at points having no dimension. If, however, a body is to consist of points having no dimension, the body cannot exist at all."

The last sentence of this abridged argument runs as follows in Aristotle's text (316 a 25 - 30): "If, on the other hand, there is no body or quantity any more, and there is actual divisibility, it will either consist of points and in that case the parts out of which it is composed will have no dimension, or, it cannot be anything at all, and this means (ὥστε, 316 a 28) that (1) it could also have come into existence out of nothing, (2) it would be composed of nothings, (3) the whole of it would be no more than a mere appearance, and (4) also, if it consists of points, it would have no dimension." Reading closely, we see that the actual conclusion has already been given in the words preceding ὥστε. Aristotle wants to prove that if there is an actually infinite divisibility, things will eventually consist of nothings. This, in Aristotle's opinion, showed the inconsistency of the atomic theory. The argument can only make sense if Aristotle understood the term ἄ-τομον in its mathematical sense of "indivisible magnitudes which are the result of a process of infinite division". If we read carefully, we see that this meaning of the word 'atom' is tacitly pre-supposed whenever Aristotle is discussing the theories of Leucippus and Democritus. It is precisely this meaning of the word 'atom' which we think is open to question.

The four conclusions following the conjunction ὥστε betray an Aristotelean way of thinking, especially the first of them. The con-clusion that, if atoms are mere nothings, things could have come into existence from nothing, is logically incoherent and can only be ex-plained by Aristotle's desire to see the atomic theory in the light of Eleatic problems. The third of the four conclusions after ὥστε may have some relation to the doctrine of Democritus on sense perception.

Aristotle goes on: "If we suppose that points having no dimension are the subject of qualities or conditions (εἶδος ἢ πάθος), how can a dimension be given to that which is without dimension? (316 b 2 - 6). Moreover, a contact (ἀφή), (and as such a point (στιγμή), too, must be defined), must always be between two things, and therefore there must be something more than mere points (316 b 6 - 9). If, now, we accept that it is impossible for a thing to consist of points, we must neces-sarily assume the existence of indivisible magnitudes still having dimension, which however, is also inconsistent (316 b 9 - 18)." At this point Aristotle stops short, referring to other works in which he has discussed the matter in more detail. The reference is, probably to *Phys.* 231 a 21 and *De caelo* 303 a 3.

We must remark that Aristotle's treatment of the atomic doctrines continues to be a mixture of atomic theory and Aristotelean criticism. Aristotle, as is his way, fails to distinguish between the given facts of the problem and his view of it. This inevitably caused him to think that his view of the problem was identical with the problem as it had been formulated by its author. In our text it is sometimes hardly possible to distinguish between historical information and criticism. The only point which is fairly clear is that Aristotle supposes the atoms to be, as the word says, 'mathematically indivisible units'. This is manifest even from the expressions he uses as synonymous of ἄτομον, such as: μεγέθη ἄτομα, indivisible magnitudes (*De gen. corr.* 316 b 32), and ἀδιαίρετα (*De gen. corr.* 316 b 16, *De caelo* 303 a 6).

A logical inconsistency is found in the last part of Aristotle's argument (316 b 9 - 18): if it is impossible for any dimension to consist of mere points, we must assume that there are smallest units having dimension. The inconsistency lies in the fact that the dilemma is inadequate. In the first proposition the dimensionless points are the subject of the sentence and they are said to be non-existent. In the second proposition the smallest units having still dimension are the subject. The existence of the entities about which the second proposition is formulated, is proved, in Aristotle's opinion, by the non-existence of the entities of the first proposition.

The fundamental misapprehension lies in the conclusion: "We must conclude that division will end at points having no dimension" (316 a 27). This was the very problem that was at issue in Zeno's paradoxes. The point in dispute in these paradoxes was whether an infinite process of division did or did not attain its end, and accordingly whether or not there was a smallest dimension. As we saw in our chapter IV (p. 105) this was understood by the Ancients to be the real meaning of Zeno's paradoxes. Probably this interpretation was canonized by Aristotle's authority and, once canonized, was not brought under discussion any more.

Nevertheless it was a wrong interpretation, which is clearly shown when we see Zeno's paradoxes in their historical situation: the research into foundations (or, as Hasse-Scholz put it: the crisis in the foundations) with which 5th century-mathematics was occupied, and the first development of philosophical dialectic. Zeno did not aim at a solution of the question what was the smallest unit, but what he did aim at was establishing a method for testing such concepts as 'infinite', 'continuous' and 'discontinuous'. Aristotle failed to appreciate this quality of Zeno's thought. He regarded the paradoxes not as a method but as arguments or, in other words, the demonstrations of Zeno, which were intended as aporetical, were taken by Aristotle to be apodeictic. It may be somewhat remarkable that it was a logician like Aristotle who created this misapprehension, but on the other hand it is true that the structure of Aristotle's system of thought often dominates the details of his theory. Perhaps the question may be raised if Aristotle in his logic was not too much occupied with reaching definite conclusions instead of developing a critical method, or, put in ancient terms, an aporetical dialectic.

146

Our analysis of the first part of Aristotle's account has made it clear that Aristotle in his discussion of atomism confounds historical information with his own views, and secondly that there was a fundamental misapprehension in the way Aristotle understood Zeno's paradoxes.

(2). 316 b 19 - 34: "A body can be thought of as potentially divided at any point of its dimension, but not at all points at once. If a body cannot actually be divided at all points at once, it can neither be divided potentially at all points at once. If it is not possible to divide a body at all points at once, the division will go only up to a certain point. This means that there will be a remainder of very small and even invisible last parts, which are the atoms."

It is clear from the use of the concepts 'actually' and 'potentially' that Aristotle is giving a demonstration of the existence of atoms which is valid only within the framework of his own categories of thinking. This is also evidenced by the expression δοκῶν in 316 b 34.

(3). 316 b 34 - 317 a 31: "A body is not simultaneously divisible at all points, because a point cannot be said to be contiguous to a point. This would be inconsistent with the definition of a point as a beginning or end of a given length. It is not possible that only beginnings or endings should follow one another. This means that there must be a remainder of very small indivisible distances."

Leaving aside the question whether the reasoning is logically correct, we can, at any rate, observe that the concepts used in the argument, e.g. the definition of a mathematical point, are Aristotelean in character. It is possible to suppose they were also Democritean, but as far as our sources go we find no evidence for this assumption. The Aristotelean character of the concepts is shown by *Phys.* Z 1, where the same argument is repeated. But *Phys.* Z 1 is not written as a criticism of the atomic theory.

Aristotle concludes by stating what is in his opinion the decisive objection to atomism. Real becoming or γένεσις cannot be explained as aggregation and separation only (σύγκρισις and διάκρισις), as it is in the atomic theory. In that case, Aristotle says, we would have to speak of ἀλλοίωσις or change, and not of real becoming or γένεσις. It is impossible that becoming should consist in σύγκρισις or aggregation (317 a 31).

The latter idea must be considered as authentically Democritean. Aristotle rejects it because it cannot be brought into harmony with his own ideas.

We may now return to the first paragraph of our text (316 a 13 - 316 b 18). The first argument given by Aristotle in order to show the inconsistency of the atomic theory can be summarized in two lines taken from the text itself:

ἀλλὰ μὴν εἰ μηδὲν ἔσται σῶμα μηδὲ μέγεθος ... ἢ ἐκ στιγμῶν ἔσται ... ἢ οὐδὲν παντάπασιν (316 a 25 - 27).

"Now if division ends at a thing which is neither a body nor a dimension, it will consist of points or it will be nothing at all."

ὥστε κἂν πᾶσαι συντεθῶσιν, οὐδὲν ποιήσουσι μέγεθος (316 a 34).

"This means that, even if all the points are taken together, they will produce no dimension."

Aristotle's argument is: if the smallest parts at which division ends, still have dimension, the division was not complete, for then it can be continued; at the moment when division is complete, the particles lose all dimension, and are reduced to mere points. This would mean that a body or a dimension is built up out of nothings. Therefore the supposition that there are smallest particles having no dimension is inconsistent, for in that case any body (or dimension) will be without any dimension.

The argument can only make sense if it pivots on the idea that an atom is, as the word says, an indivisible last unit in the mathematical sense. It is this idea which, if we read closely, is implicit in the paragraphs of the text which we have indicated by (1) and (2). At the end of paragraph (2) the implicit idea changes, because Aristotle here changes his outlook and starts talking on the problem of coming-to-be and passing-away, taken by the atomists as processes of aggregation and dispersion. Accordingly the underlying notion makes way for the physical notion of solid invisible particles having dimension, and this only for a moment, for in the course of the third paragraph the argument once more changes into a mathematical one.

There is a remarkable parallelism in Aristotle's argument to Zeno's argument on plurality. One line of Aristotle is almost literally found in Zeno's text:

(De gen. et corr. 316 a 26) ἀλλὰ μὴν εἰ μηδὲν ἔσται σῶμα μηδὲ μέγεθος, which reproduces DK 29 B 1:

εἰ μὴ ἔχοι μέγεθος τὸ ὄν.

Aristotle's conclusion: ἢ ἐκ στιγμῶν ἔσται ... ἢ οὐδὲν παντάπασιν (316 a 27) reproduces the words οὐδ' ἂν εἴη of DK 29 B 1.

There is at the same time a difference, which in our opinion is characteristic of the difference in dialectical thinking between Zeno

148

and Aristotle. To Zeno two conclusions were possible which were drawn only hypothetically in order to test the axiomatic principles. Of these two conclusions Aristotle needs only one, viz. the conclusion that things will be reduced to nothingness if we make the assumption that they can be divided infinitely. Aristotle needs this conclusion because he wants to prove by it that atomism is an impossible thing. By restricting the demonstration to one conclusion only, the aporetical argument of Zeno changes into an apodeictical one, or, in other terms, a critical problem changes into an argument. Zeno's paradoxes were intended as an invitation to find a better formula for the concept of infinity. Aristotle only makes use of the argument in order to reach the conclusion that the concept of infinitely small atoms is contradictory. This concept, in Aristotle's view, literally comes to nothing.

Having seen the identity and at the same time the difference between Zeno's arguments and Aristotle's, we may conclude that Aristotle made use of one half of Zeno's dilemma in order to prove the inconsistency of the atomic theory. Next to the question of whether Aristotle had a right understanding of Zeno's arguments, we must put another critical question. Aristotle's arguments against the atomic theory can only make sense if the atomic theory was really founded upon the form given by Zeno to the Eleatic problem of the one Being. The current view is that the atomic theory had been prepared by the Eleatic problem of infinity. Though this is the current view, we must ask if it does not represent an inheritance from ancient doxography, inspired by the views of Aristotle and transmitted to us by way of an hereditary corruption. There are two reasons to ask the question: the first is that Aristotle, as we saw, misunderstood Zeno. The second is that, as we shall see, the atomic theory may indeed partly be seen as a development which was inspired by the influence of Eleaticism, but then it was not the problem of infinite division which supplied the link between the two, but that of the μὴ ὄν as a concept indicating spatial void.

In our opinion the contribution of Eleatic thought to the development of the atomic theory must be acknowledged, but only in the restricted sense that in the period preceding Democritus the Ionian school had assimilated a certain amount of Eleatic thought. As we saw in our sixth chapter, the wording in which Anaxagoras expressed his ideas on the divisibility of material substances shows that he knew the form which Zeno gave to the problem, while some other expressions reveal that he wanted to criticize the opinions of Parmenides. This makes it clear that Democritus could already find certain Eleatic views transformed into components of Ionian doctrine. This was not a predominantly metaphysical doctrine, like Parmenides's, but a physical one. An example of this was the way in which Anaxagoras made the mathematical theory into a substructure for his biological doctrine. It is not probable, though Aristotle thought so, that the atomic theory was framed by its authors on the model of the paradox on plurality, which had been left unsolved by Zeno. The fact that Aristotle tries to establish the connection between Eleaticism and atomism exactly in an ontological theory must give rise to the question of whether Aristotle was not adapting the historical development to the framework of his own theories. It is true that the absence of authentic fragments of Democritus containing ontological theories is not a strong argument. On the other hand, however, it is possible to describe the Eleatic origin of Democritus' ideas on being and not-being in such a way that the interrelation of the two can be illustrated by the authentic fragments.

Besides the long text from *De gen. et corr.* quoted above, there is a text on atomism in the *De caelo*, 303 a 3 - 303 b 3. In this passage Aristotle repeats his mathematical argument in two variations, the first of which is more or less identical with the argument given in *De gen. et corr.* 316 a 13 - 316 b 18, which was discussed above. Aristotle here says of it (*De caelo* 303 a 20 - 24): "Moreover, if they want to assume the existence of indivisible bodies (ἄτομα σώματα), they inevitably come into conflict with mathematics, and, in that case, must also reject many now famous conceptions which are founded on the evidence of the senses, which we have discussed in an earlier work on time and motion." This refers to the *Physics*, which is often mentioned as 'a work on time and motion'. Aristotle's criticism, here as elsewhere, is centred on a mathematical inconsistency which in his opinion is found in the atomic theory. The mathematical views with which the atomic theory is brought into contrast, must have been Aristotle's own views.

The discussions on the mathematical concept of infinity, to which Aristotle refers, are found in *Phys.* III 4 - 8, 202 b 30 - 208 a 24, and in *De caelo* I 5 - 7, 271 b 1 - 276 a 17. They offer a fairly constant doctrine with slight variations and a small number of inconsistencies. Actual infinity is non-existent to Aristotle because the definition of infinity (*Phys.* III 6, 207 a 7 - 8) says that "infinite is that which, regarded as a quantity, can always be increased by something outside it." The definition is a curious one, because in it certain things are included that are outside that which is being defined. The sequence of integers is infinite because one can always go on counting in the direction of the infinite. A number which is infinite by itself, can never be actually reached. This is why infinity only exists potentially (See p. 134 in our chapter VI). The sequence of integers is an example of infinity by addition (τὸ κατὰ πρόσθεσιν ἄπειρον). The opposite of this is infinity by division (τὸ κατὰ διαίρεσιν ἄπειρον), an example of which is found in the process of continued bisection of a line. This second kind of infinity never becomes an actual infinity either, because mathematically the process of bisection can always be continued. In harmony with this point of view is Aristotle's conviction that it is impossible for actually smallest units to exist, unless they are dimensionless, i.e. unless they are mere points (οὐκ ἔστιν ἀδιαίρετα μήκη, De caelo III 1, 299 a 12, cf. Phys. VI 1, 231 a 24). As we saw above, this argument also serves Aristotle to prove that the atomic theory is impossible.

Transferring the concept of infinity from the field of spatial extension to that of temporal extension, Aristotle says that infinity by addition cannot be traversed in a finite time, but infinity by division can (Phys. VI 2, 233 a 24 - 28). The latter opinion is inconsistent, because the number of parts of an infinitely bisected line can never be actually traversed by counting. The difference of the two statements is an indication that Aristotle has changed his point of view when passing from infinity by addition to infinity by division, because in the first case he sees the infinite sequence as a series of countable discontinuous units, whereas in the second case he sees the divided length as a continuous unit which can be traversed in a finite time. Probably we must say that he was deceived by the evidence of the senses. Aristotle makes a similar abrupt transition a few lines before (233 a 18), when he seems to deduce the infinity of space from the infinity of time. Ross, in his commentary points out that "The statement that if time is infinite ... μῆκος must also be so, is a dangerous one for Aristotle to make; for he denies the infinity of extension (III 5) and asserts that of time (VIII 1,2)."

There are more inconsistencies than this one in Aristotle's treatment of the concept of infinity (see above). Probably Aristotle did not notice them. For the moment, it is not so much important to reveal the inconsistencies, as to point out that Aristotle is implicitly making the assumption that he can use his mathematical ideas in arguments on physical space. This in the more remarkable because we can read in *De caelo* 299 a 14 - 18 that Aristotle was aware of a difference between mathematical and physical quantity (cf. *Met.* K 3, 1061 a 28 and *An. post.* 87 a 35).

In whatever way we shall have to interpret these ambiguities, for the moment we may confine ourselves to stating that in *De Caelo* 303 a 20-24 Aristotle's objections to the atomic theory pivot on the incompatibility of the physical theories with mathematical principles. It is not so much important to see the details of this incompatibility as to note that, by making the objection, Aristotle implicitly acknowledges that the atomic theory is to be taken in a sense differing from the mathematical.

The second variation of the mathematical argument is given next (*De caelo* 303 a 24 - 29). It confirms the conclusion we have drawn from the first variation. Aristotle says that if the elements are taken to be indivisible units (ἄ-τομων ὄντων), the theory cannot account for the difference in size between various kinds of atoms such as those of air, earth and water. The argument implies that there were differences in size between atoms, and this again means that the atoms were not indivisible units, as Aristotle supposes them to be, probably owing to the term ἄ-τομον. If Aristotle did not make this assumption on his own account, but found it in Democritus, we should have to suppose that Democritus, following the example set by Anaxagoras, prefaced his doctrine by drafting a mathematical theory of smallest parts, and afterwards left it at that and used the atomic principle as he needed it. This is a mere hypothesis, which is not borne out by the texts of Aristotle. Another remark which we may make in passing is that Aristotle's description of the differences between the atoms does not only imply that the atoms were different in size but also in shape, for he says that the sphere and the pyramid were fundamental atomic forms. This may induce us to think that in this respect a certain parallelism was to be found between Democritus' atomism and Plato's theory of the fundamental structure of matter in the *Timaeus**.

The third part of Aristotle's argument (*De Caelo* 303 a 29 - b 2) says that the atomic theory is inconsistent in assuming an infinite number of elements. This is superfluous, Aristotle says, for it implies an unnecessary multiplicity of shapes, as there is a limited number of mathematical ground-patterns into which the various shapes can be

* See the next chapter.

152

divided. The argument once more implies that the atoms were not the mathematically indivisible units which Aristotle elswhere supposes them to be.

In the text we also find a valuable indication as to the description which Democritus probably gave of the atoms. Aristotle uses the term σχήματα for the shape of the atoms. We find the same term in *De gen. corr.* 315 b 11: τὰ σχήματα ἄπειρα ἐποίησαν, "They (the atomists) made the shapes of the atoms infinite in number." A few lines before we find the word σχήματα simply denoting the atoms themselves (315 b 7). It is not quite certain whether the word was used in this sense by Democritus himself. It may be that Democritus used the word ἰδέαι as a synonym of ἄτομα. Burnet (*EGP* 201 n. 5, 228 n. 1, 336 n. 5) adduces a number of quotations which make this probable. If ἰδέα was really used by Democritus, Aristotle may have dropped the term in order to avoid its being mistaken for Plato's ideas. The passages adduces by Burnet are convincing enough to show that μορφαί and σχήματα could denote the atoms. The words illustrate the fact that Democritus gave his atoms different shapes. As they also had different sizes, it is impossible to give credit to the view that they were products of the mathematical problem of infinite division.

We cannot make sure whether μορφαί and σχήματα as synonyms of 'ἄτομοι' were introduced by Aristotle in his discussion of the atomic theory, or were found by him in the authentic writings of Democritus. Aristotle uses a third synonym, viz. 'ἀδιαίρετα', 'indivisible units'. In contrast to the other two words, this term is most probably Aristotelean in origin, because it represents an interpretation which was characteristic of Aristotle. The term suggests a relation to mathematical problems on infinity. It is true that Democritus' atoms were indivisible, but not in the mathematical sense of infinitesimal small parts: they were indivisible because they were solid and impenetrable smallest particles of tactile matter.

The view that the atomic theory was prepared by the development of the problem of infinity in its Zenonian form may be considered as an Aristotelean corruption for the reasons given above. This still leaves us with the problem of the real origin of the atomic theory. We may try to find an answer by once more drafting a list of the terms which may be considered characteristic of Democritus (cf. p. 140). Most of these terms at once betray their Ionian origin.

DK 68 B 164, 167
Ar. *Phys.* 196 a 26   δῖνος
Diog. Laert. IX 45   and
DK 68 A 67, 83   δίνη

Anaxagoras:
59 B 9 and 12: περιχώρησις
59 A 57: δῖνος

DK 68 A 49: σύγκρισις "aggregation"
         διάκρισις "dispersion"

Anaxagoras:
59 B 4:
59 A 41 and 43:

DK 68 A 71: τὸν γὰρ χρόνον ἀγένητον εἶναι, 'Time is unbegotten,' (from Aristotle); ἀΐδιον τὸν χρόνον, 'Time is eternal', (from Simplicius).

Anaximander (see Ch. I).

DK 68 A 82: τῶν κόσμων ἀπείρων ὄντων καὶ ἀλλήλους διαδεχομένων, 'There are innumerable worlds, succeeding each other.'

Anaximander:
Χρόνος – ἄπειρον and innumerable worlds: see Ch. I.

Ar. *de gen. anim.* 742 b 17-23
(not in DK): ὥστε τὸ ἐρωτᾶν τὸ διὰ τί ... τὸ ζητεῖν εἶναί φησιν τοῦ ἀπείρου ἀρχήν.
'Therefore he (Democritus) says that asking why in these matters is the same as asking for the beginning of eternity.'

This text, compared to *Phys.* 252 a 34, makes it probable that the term ἄπειρον was used by Democritus.

Because of the scantiness of these fragments it is impossible to draw a decisive conclusion. If they suggest anything at all, it is that atomism had its place in the tradition of Ionian natural philosophy. Once more we get the impression that the connection with Eleatic theory in the sense that ὂν καὶ μὴ ὂν can, in the ontological sense, be identified with δὲν καὶ οὐδέν, and also the connection with mathematical demonstrations, was an Aristotelean construction. We found this already implied in Aristotle's accounts. In analyzing them it appeared that we had to do with Aristotelean theory rather than with historiography. Though authentic fragments are utterly scanty, the terms used by Democritus give us a hint that his doctrine was Ionian.

Our interpretation can further be corroborated by an analysis of two somewhat longer accounts of the atomic theory, which may have been written before Aristotle's later system of thought took shape, or, in the second case, without the influence of the Aristotelean tradition. They are found in DK 68 A 37 and 49.

The first text can be read also in Ross, *Fragmenta selecta* p. 144. It is from a lost and probably early work of Aristotle Περὶ Δημοκρίτου, *On Democritus.* The text consists of short summaries given by Simplicius directly from the original work of the young Aristotle, as we may infer from the words with which Simplicius introduces the text: ὀλίγα ἐκ τῶν Ἀριστοτέλους Περὶ Δημοκρίτου παραγραφέντα, "We shall give some transcriptions from Aristotle's work on Democritus." In the Oxford-translation (vol. XII 148-149) the first paragraph is translated as follows:

"Democritus thinks the nature of the eternal entities consists of small substances (μικρὰς οὐσίας), infinite in number (πλῆθος ἀπείρους); as a place for them he supposes something else infinite in size (ἄπειρον τῷ μεγέθει), and to this he applies the name 'void', 'nothing', and 'the infinite' (κενῷ, οὐδενί, ἀπείρῳ), while to each of the substances (οὐσιῶν) he applies the names 'thing', 'solid' and 'real' (δέν, ναστῷ, ὄντι). He thinks the substances are so small as to escape our senses, but have all sorts of shapes and figures (μορφὰς καὶ σχήματα), and differences of size. From these substances, as from elements, are generated and compounded visible and perceptible masses (ὄγκους)."

The text confirms the conclusion we have drawn above (p. 153) from our analysis of *De caelo* 303 a 29 - b 2: Democritus' atoms were physical quantities: they are not to be placed in the category of mathematical problems. In harmony with this is the fact that the word ἄτομον occurs only once, at the end of the fragment (not quoted here). The atoms are denoted as οὐσίαι, 'substances' and ὄγκοι 'solid particles', and they have all kinds of shapes and figures (μορφὰς καὶ σχήματα, terms in other accounts rather frequently used for the atoms themselves; *De gen. corr.* 315 b 7, see above p. 153). Single atoms are denoted as δέν, ναστόν and ὄν, the void as κενόν, οὐδέν, ἄπειρον. The word ἄπειρον is used in the first line in the sense of 'innumerable' and 'infinite in size'.

The text shows that Democritus' theory was physics, not mathematics. The atoms are solid particles having different shapes and moving in infinite empty space. There is no trace whatever of a mathematical ground-pattern for the theory. This means, incidentally, that Democritus' infinite space was probably also derived from the Ionian tradition of the unbounded heavens.

Our second text can be read in DK 68 A 49. It is from a work by Galen. Its first line is the well-known authentic fragment, quoted at the beginning of this chapter: "As a result of convention we speak of colour, of sweet, of bitter; in reality there are only atoms and void." The account is in the first place an explication of this theory of knowledge. Next Galen says that the universe consists of 'thing and nothing', which means 'atoms and void'. In the void the atoms are moving. Their motion is described in the current terms: 'whirling', 'aggregation', 'dispersion', 'colliding and bouncing off'. Then Galen returns to his subject and goes on explaining sensorial impressions by the motion of the atoms. This account as well gives us a theory which is completely physical, and does not in any way remind us of a mathematical problem.

The results of our analysis may be used as a stepping-stone to a probably more correct historical explanation of the term 'atom'. As we saw, the current view, originating from Aristotle, is that the word ἄ-τομον served to denote the indivisible smallest part resulting from the process of infinite division. On the ground of this interpretation of the term Aristotle uses ἀδιαίρετον, 'indivisible unit', as its synonym. These indivisible units, then, were the smallest elements out of which a universe is built up. In harmony with this view, and also on the authority of Aristotle, 'void' and 'atoms' were taken as representing the Eleatic 'not-being' and 'being'. This opened the way to a metaphysical inter-pretation of Democritus' doctrines. On this view, the atomic theories were a reaction to the Eleatic ontology. On the strength of this view one might even suppose that they prepared the metaphysical doctrine of the μὴ ὄν in Plato's *Sophistes*. Melissus' doctrine is generally regarded as the last step leading up to the theory of Democritus (Kirk-Raven 304-306 and 406-407).

We shall have to discuss this problem of the metaphysical pedigree later on. For the moment we must point out that it is very well possible to explain the choice of the word ἄτομον as a result of the Ionian tradition only. Anaxagoras had made the assumption that, just as all things had been mixed up in primordial chaos, so in the now existing universe all things still contained particles of every substance. According to Anaxagoras this universal mixture continued to exist in the infinitesimal small parts. Even then division could be supposed to continue without changing the character of the substance as a mixture, simply because no reason could be found why division should come to a stop at a certain point, or why the mixture of the ingredients should change as a result of the division. The argument shows that Anaxagoras' way of thinking may have been more strongly influenced by strict mathematical consistency than Democritus's. On the other hand Democritus' theory outweighs that of Anaxagoras by the greater simplicity of its construction. From a systematical point of view the construction of the atomic theory is characterized by the

156

tendency to reduce the number of principles to a minimum. Void and atoms, shape, order and position, and the motion of the atoms are the ultimate building-stones out of which a universe comes into existence. In any theory of cosmology it is of great use to have a limited number of first principles, and these must be of a relatively simple character, not giving cause for confusion or unnecessary complication. The infinitesimal small particles of Anaxagoras could not be very useful in a physical theory, because they were still of a complicated character and did not possess the necessary simplicity for things to be explained. This may have been the reason why Anaxagoras' theory was dropped by his immediate successors. Democritus replaced the infinitely complicated and infinitely divisible small parts of Anaxagoras by solid units, only externally differing from each other in shape and size. If we take this as the historical connection between Anaxagoras and Democritus, the term ἄτομον can be explained as the expression of a criticism aimed at Anaxagoras. It may have been chosen to express the idea that division cannot go on indefinitely. Physically there is an actual end to division at the point where atoms are found to be the smallest building-stones of matter. At the same time this supposition answers the need for structural simplicity by reducing the principles of the system to a well-determined small number.

In Democritus we find quite a few qualities which reveal the scientist. His doctrine is constructed on a pattern of three or four first principles which by their very simplicity eliminate any axiomatic problem. It has a mechanistic feature: motion of solid particles is the cause of all change and becoming. It contains a theory of perception: the qualities of a thing are only appearances, because in itself the thing is only an aggregation of atoms. Democritus designed it consciously on a physical basis by positing that atoms do have size but nevertheless have no parts, thus avoiding the complication of mathematical problems. Dimension implies divisibility in the mathematical sense, but if a measurable dimension is assigned to the atoms while divisibility is rejected, we have a physical theory.

We may find a confirmation of the view that the atomic theory must be seen against the background of Ionian cosmology by analyzing the accounts given by Diogenes Laertius of Democritus' and Leucippus' theories (Diog. Laert. IX 30-32 = DK 67 A 1 on Leucippus and Diog. Laert. IX 44-45 = DK 68 A 1 on Democritus).

Diog. Laert. IX 30-32	Diog. Laert. IX 44-45	*to be compared*:
LEUCIPPUS	DEMOCRITUS	
ἄπειρα τὰ πάντα καὶ εἰς ἄλληλα μεταβάλλειν 'All things together form an infinity and they are transformed into one another.'		Anaximander: 'all things passing judgement on one another.'
τὸ πᾶν ἄπειρόν φησιν		Anaximander
ἀπείρους κόσμους 'innumerable worlds'	ἀπείρους κόσμους ἀπείρους ἀτόμους	Anaxagoras (59 B 4): 'many worlds.'
τούτου δὲ τὸ μὲν πλῆρες εἶναι, τὸ δὲ κενόν, ἃ καὶ στοιχεῖά φησιν· κόσμους τε ἐκ τούτου ἀπείρους εἶναι καὶ διαλύεσθαι εἰς ταῦτα 'of this apeiron a part is full, a part is void, and so he also calls the elements. Out of the apeiron innumerable worlds arise and they are dissolved again into the elements.'	πῦρ, ὕδωρ, ἀέρα, γῆν 'fire, water, earth, air.'	full and void: apparently the Pythagoreans, more probably the Eleatics. the four elements: Empedocles; (the word στοιχεῖα probably of a later origin)
κατὰ ἀποτομὴν ἐκ τῆς ἀπείρου the elementary substances 'are segregated from the apeiron.'		Anaximander.
μέγα κενόν	κενόν	Pythagoreans and Eleatics, or Anaximander's apeiron?
δίνη 'whirl'	τὰς ἀτόμους φέρεσθαι δινουμένας 'the atoms move about in a whirl'	Anaxagoras
διακρίνεσθαι τὰ ὅμοια πρὸς τὰ ὅμοια 'Like is segregated with like.'	συγκρίματα 'compounds'	Anaxagoras
σύστημα σφαιροειδές 'a spherical whole'		Anaximander

ὑμένα 'membrane'   the primordial Egg of
                                                    the Orphics

πάντα κατ' ἀνάγκην
γίνεσθαι 'All things oc-
cur by necessity'
τῆς δίνης αἰτίας οὔσης
τῆς γενέσεως πάντων
'The vortex is cause of
the becoming of all
things.'
ἣν ἀνάγκην λέγει 'He   in contrast to Anaxa-
calls the vortex neces-   goras who represents
sity (= physical cau-   physical causality
sality).'   (περιχώρησις) and evo-
                              lution as dominated by
                              a divine power, Νοῦς.

In the survey here given we have left aside the expressions related
to theory of knowledge.

In the two accounts by Diogenes Laertius of respectively Leucippus' and Democritus' theories only once (IX 44) an expression is found
which may suggest that there was a direct connection between the
doctrine of Democritus and that of Parmenides:

μηδὲν ἐκ τοῦ μὴ ὄντος γίνεσθαι μηδὲ εἰς τὸ μὴ ὂν φθείρεσθαι.

"Nothing comes into being out of not-being, nor can it pass away
into not-being."

The words give the impression that Diogenes Laertius did not
quote them directly from a text of Democritus. Even if the words
should be authentic, we need not assume that Democritus was directly
inspired by an Eleatic source. We find the doctrine in the extant texts
of the philosopher who in the historical sense was nearest to him,
Anaxagoras. In DK 59 B 17 Anaxagoras says that nothing comes into
existence or passes out of it; on the contrary it is always composed
of existing things (ἀπὸ ἐόντων χρημάτων) or is disintegrated into the
composing parts. This and other texts prove conclusively that the
essentials of Eleatic philosophy had been absorbed by the Ionians well
before Democritus' days. The most direct way in which Democritus came
to hear of it may have been through the works of Anaxagoras. Incidentally we may remark that most probably it was in Athens that Anaxagoras had become familiar with Eleatic theory and Zenonian problems.

For the same reasons for which we may doubt whether the atomic
doctrine was prepared by Eleatic thought, we may feel justified in

159

assigning it an Ionian pedigree. If the indirect sources are to be relied upon, it was Anaximander who for the first time introduced the principle of condensation and rarefaction in cosmological theory. After him this principle was combined with that of aggregation and separation, according to which the qualities of a thing were to be explained by the special mixture of its composing parts. This theory may have been influenced by medical thinking. We find it even represented in the western Italian school where Empedocles introduced it along with his theory of the four elements. Anaxagoras designed a theory of evolution in which at every stage the condition of things had to be explained as a mixture of very small composing parts. It does not seem improbable at all that the cosmology of Anaxagoras should have been the last step to Democritus' doctrine of indivisible atoms.

In our analysis of Aristotle's arguments we saw that it was Aristotle's own system of thought which induced him to represent the concept of atom as prepared by the Zenonian problems. We must add that this interpretation may have been suggested to Aristotle by the Eleatic elements which beyond any doubt were present in the Ionian tradition.

The very term "atom" may have induced Aristotle to describe the concept of "atom" on the pattern of the Zenonian problems. Anaxagoras had criticised these Zenonian problems and had tried to find a new solution. His theory, however, was predominantly physical and permeated by a biological way of seeing the problems. In the same way the atomic theory may have been in part prepared by the Eleatic influence upon Ionian thinking, but the theory in its essentials was not founded on mathematical patterns of thought but on a physical problem.

Apart from the question whether the atomic theory originated from Zenonian paradoxes, Aristotle's account of atomism gave rise to a second problem. We saw (p. 142-3) that the formula δὲν καὶ οὐδέν was taken by Aristotle to be synonymous with ὂν καὶ μὴ ὄν. We may feel inclined to think this is also due to Aristotle's habits of interpreting. A glance at the history of the concept of μὴ ὄν will teach us that our second problem has a background quite different from the first.

The opposition of ὄν and μὴ ὄν was a burning question as early as the days when Parmenides came to oppose the Pythagoreans. In the verses 4-9 of *frag.* 6 Parmenides pours forth his wrath upon the "doublethinking blockheads to whom Being and not-being have the same value". This means, among other things, that there must have been

160

opponents using the concepts of being and not-being in this confused way. It is possible that Parmenides is referring to the Pythagoreans here. In Pythagorean theory the cosmos came into existence when a primordial germ began to take breath from the surrounding void. Parmenides may have had the Pythagorean void in mind when talking about not-being. Another possibility is that he is giving vent to his irritation at a certain kind of possibly Sicilian rhetoric, which was aimed at confusing the audience. In that case Parmenides would be referring to precursors of Gorgias, which would explain his remarks on the audience: "Stupid hordes, drifting about blind and deaf, in whose breasts helplessness controls the navigation of their staggering minds: people dazed and devoid of any discernment, who take being and not-being as having the same value." Afterwards the Sophists did confuse reality and delusion in order to make unacceptable propositions acceptable to their audience. In the well-known adage of Protagoras we find the two concepts of ὄντα and οὐκ ὄντα juxtaposed in this sense (DK 80 B 1):

πάντων χρημάτων μέτρον ἐστὶν ἄνθρωπος, τῶν μὲν ὄντων ὡς ἔστιν, τῶν δὲ οὐκ ὄντων ὡς οὐκ ἔστιν.

"Man is the measure of all things, of things being in the sense that they are, of things not-being in the sense that they are not".

In this sentence ὄντα and οὐκ ὄντα are opposed in gnoseological sense, denoting what is true and what is not. The expression ἔστιν is the famous ἔστιν of Parmenides, but it is used by Protagoras in a quite different sense from that intended by Parmenides. The theories of the Sophists generally betray a certain knowledge of explicit logical methods, which they may have learnt from the Eleatics.

Parallel to the meaning 'true and false' for ὂν καὶ μὴ ὄν the meaning 'real Being and void' is developed. In Parmenides' verses we do not find the word κενόν, but now and then his argument suggests the idea. In fragment 8 verse 10 the words τοῦ μηδενὸς ἀρξάμενον, to be translated as 'starting from not-being', suggest the idea of 'starting from a void.' In verse 12 the words ἐκ μὴ ἐόντος γίγνεσθαι imply the connotation of 'coming into existence out of a void'. In verse 24 Parmenides says: 'The all is full of being'. We may conclude: there is no void. The first philosopher to state the conclusion in this formula was Melissus. In a long fragment (DK 30 B 7) Melissus argues that the universe is eternal, infinite, one and homogeneous (§ 1), and goes on to prove one by one all the characteristics of true Being and of the universe as Parmenides had defined them. In the seventh paragraph

161

he says: οὐδὲ κενεόν ἐστιν οὐδέν· τὸ γὰρ κενεὸν οὐδέν ἐστιν· οὐκ ἂν οὖν εἴη τό γε μηδέν. "Nor can there be a void; for the void is a nothing; now if a thing is a nothing, it cannot even exist." The terms used by Melissus are worth noticing because they are the same terms which we find in the texts on the atomic theory.

Melissus rejects the existence of a void in order to prove that motion is impossible. He argues that, if the all is a *plenum*, there is no empty space to move into. This is in harmony with Aristotle's state-ment about Melissus in *Phys*. Δ 6, 213 b 12 - 15: "Melissus proves by this argument that the all is unmoved; for if there is motion, there is necessarily a void, he says, and void is a not-being." Empedocles denied the existence of a void (DK 31 B 13 - 14). Though B 14 seems to suggest it, we cannot ascertain if Empedocles rejected the void with the intention of rejecting motion as well. Whether Anaxagoras gave his opinion on the problem is open to question, because only in the A-fragments he is said to have rejected the existence of a void.

Coming to the atomists we must consult the statements Aristotle gives us. There are a number of passages in which the terms ὄν and μὴ ὄν (occasionaly οὐκ ὄν) are found in the context of a statement on atomism. Leaving aside the shorter or incidental remarks, the most important are the following:

De gen. et corr. 315 a 2 - 6 and 23 - 29.

Phys. A 3, 187 a 1 - 6 (if, as Ross takes it, ἔνιοι here denotes the atomists).

Met. A 4, 985 b 4 - 15.

The text from *De gen. et corr.* reproduces the argument we also found in the fragments of Melissus: depending on whether we accept the existence of a void or not, the possibility of motion must be admitted or denied. Aristotle adds a second argument: a void is necessary, if things are to be a multiplicity. This second argument is not much stressed by Aristotle. It may have a Pythagorean origin, if it was intended in the sense that the void has the function of separating individual things. Without this separation things would be a homo-geneous mass, and this was what the Pythagoreans accused Parme-nides of admitting.

The text from the *Physics* only repeats this second argument. Explaining it, Aristotle only uses the term μὴ ὄν, in contrast to the text from *De gen. et corr.* where he uses indiscriminately μὴ ὄν and κενόν.

The passage from the *Metaphysics* gives neither argument. Aristo-tle is comparing the atomic doctrine with his own theory of ὕλη and εἶδος, trying, as is his habit, to reconstruct the atomic doctrine on the framework of his own thought. Aristotle thinks the concepts of both πλῆρες and κενόν, i.e. both the full and the void, have in Democritus' system the function of a ὕλη or matter, whereas the qualities of things, generated by the shape, order and position of the atoms, represent the principle of form. As synonyms of πλῆρες the text has σῶμα, στερεόν and ὄν, as a synonym of κενόν it has μὴ ὄν. The full or solid, together with the void or empty, are taken by Aristotle to represent his own ὕλη, a brilliant example of *interpretatio aristotelica*.

The summary of texts given here allows us to epitomize the history of the concept of the void. As early as in the works of Parmenides the idea of the void was formulated in terms of not-being. The confusion of the concepts of spatial void and not-being has persisted even in the accounts given by Aristotle of the history of this problem. This is only natural, if, as we have seen, the concept of Being itself had to be evolved so slowly from its spatial connotations, a process in which generations of philosophers took part. There is no reason to doubt that it was the atomists who created a terminology in which the atoms and the void were denoted by respectively ὄν and μὴ ὄν, οὐκ ὄν or μηδέν.

A glance at the same texts, however, makes us see at once that these expressions have, within the framework of the problem, always been used in a spatial sense or with a spatial connotation. It is important to state this, because the same terms ὄν and μὴ ὄν are used by Plato when he is developing his theory of the highest categories of being in the *Sophistes*. The parallelism of the terminology might easily induce us to suppose a historical connection between Plato's and Democritus' theories, if we do not keep in mind the widely divergent use to which the same expressions are put in the two systems. The similarity of the expressions is not fortuitous. It is, in both cases, an inheritance from the Eleatic theories. However, Democritus takes the expressions in their spatial sense, whereas Plato turns them into metaphysics.

It might be objected that, though an analysis of Aristotelean texts may prove to a certain extent the views expounded here, a demonstration founded on authentic fragments of Democritus would be more satisfactory. In the absence of authentic fragments we have tried to reconstruct Democritus' views from the scanty remnants of his own words, setting them against their most probable historical background. We may summarize our argument as follows.

163

It is improbable that Democritus should have designed his atomic theory in order to reconcile the Eleatic theory of an immutable being with the real existence of multiplicity and change. The first reason to regard this as improbable is that the way in which the concept of the atom is formulated and used in the philosophical system can be explained in a much more natural way by referring it to Anaxagoras. The second reason is that everything we know about Democritus suggests the scientist. In the numerous indirect accounts there is hardly any line intimating that he occupied himself with metaphysical speculation. On the contrary, all we gather from the extant descriptions is that he was devoted to physics and mathematics. Thirdly, even granted that certain elements in his theories betray an Eleatic inheritance, these elements prove to have their organic place in a cosmological doctrine, not in a metaphysical. Fourthly, not a single account, whether direct or indirect, can be adduced to prove conclusively that Democritus intended his theories to be solutions of metaphysical problems. The concepts 'empty space' or 'void' as opposed to 'full' or 'solid' are fundamental in the atomic theory, but they are no metaphysical concepts, despite their being denoted as 'being' and 'not-being'.

If our arguments are sound, they give us reason to doubt whether Kirk and Raven were right in their description the development leading up to the atomic theory (Kirk-Raven 302-306, 404-406). Their explication follows that of Burnet (EGP 173), who in his turn is following Aristotle, whose accounts he considers reliable. Burnet principally has in mind the texts found in *De gen. et corr.* A 8, 324 b 35 - 325 a 32 and *Physics* A 3, 187 a 1 - 6 (see our discussion on p. 143 -148). In the first of these texts Aristotle derives the genesis of atomism from the consideration that both multiplicity and motion will be impossible if the existence of a void is denied (325 a 4 and 27). This argument has its place in cosmology, and as we saw, the first development of it can be traced in the texts of Melissus and Parmenides. There seems to be a probability that Democritus' use of it was indirectly a reaction to Eleatic doctrine. This is even suggested by the polemical tone of the sentence in which Democritus affirms that "thing has not a higher degree of existence than nothing."

The next argument we find in Aristotle's text is that on infinite division (325 a 8 - 9). Burnet takes this as proving that Democritus is aiming at Zeno with his arguments. In the course of this chapter we

164

have given our reasons for thinking it more probable that it was Aristotle who constructed this antagonism.

Finally Aristotle says that a solution both of the problem of motion and of that of multiplicity was found by Leucippus (325 a 23 - 30). His theory, Aristotle says, was in harmony with sense perception, and the solution consisted in his replacing the one and homogeneous Eleatic Being by the multiplicity of invisibly small solid particles (ὄγκοι). The argument has an ontological ring, which diminishes its chance of being historical. On the other hand Aristotle's use of technical terms suggests that he may have reproduced an authentical text of Leucippus, possibly quoting from memory (παμπλῆρες, ἀόρατα, ὄγκοι). It is possible to think that this special argument did not originate from Democritus but from Leucippus. In that case Leucippus would have been the more metaphysically minded of the two atomistic philosophers. A certain reserve must remain, because it is still possible that it was Aristotle who constructed this ontological argument.

The second passage adduced by Burnet is *Physics* A 3, 187 a 1 - 6. Aristotle here indicates in what respects the atomists adjusted the Eleatic doctrine: they introduced a μὴ ὄν in order to explain multiplicity, and ἄτομα μεγέθη in order to avoid the difficulties of Zeno's problems. The first point is given by Aristotle in an ontological sense, but in reality it belongs to the history of the concept of the Void. The second point reproduces the Aristotelean construction of a historical connection between Zeno's paradoxes and the atomic theory.

Following in the wake of Burnet, Kirk-Raven took this historical connection for granted. Like Burnet, they consider the account given by Aristotle as plausible (p. 406: "This assessment is so plausible in itself that . . .") and they add a text of Melissus to confirm their historical explanation. Melissus had said (frag. 8): "If a multiplicity of things were to exist, things would necessarily have the same characteristics as I say the One has." According to Kirk-Raven this theorem has been the bridge from Eleatic theory to atomism. Leucippus had only to replace the conditional 'if' by the causal conjunction 'because'. This interpretation is not self-evident, for in that case it does not follow that the many things existing must inevitably be atoms. Another text of Melissus was the starting-point for Bailey's historical reconstruction (1928, 74). In fragment 7 § 7, Melissus says that there is no void, and that the universe is a *plenum*. Bailey thinks that Leucippus was reacting to this sentence when he stated boldly:

full and empty together are the elements of all things (cf Kirk-Stokes 1960).

As far as our sources go, we do not dispose of sufficient evidence either to prove or to disprove these views. The historical explanations trying to prove that atomism was essentially a metaphysical development appear to have had an overcharge of Aristotelean thought. It seems better, for the moment, not to attribute to atomism an ontological background in history. The most obvious reason for this is that this interpretation is found exclusively in Aristotelean texts, where it is embedded in Aristotelean argument. In Aristotle's own works we find at the same time a number of accounts which illustrate the Ionian character of atomism. What is more, this Ionian character is also borne out by what we still have of authentic Democritean texts. Accordingly, we shall dismiss the ontological background suggested by Aristotle and take it that the expressions ὂν καὶ μὴ ὄν, when used in relation to atomism, have no metaphysical signification, but simply mean: 'atoms and empty space'.

We may summarize the various historical problems as regards atomism as follows.

There are four problems which according to the current historical explanation atomism tried to solve. (1) The problem of multiplicity and (2) that of motion. Neither multiplicity nor motion can exist, if there is no void. The history of the concept of the Void makes it clear that in this point there was a real connection of atomism with a tradition originating from Eleaticism. (3) The problem of infinite division. The connection of atomism with this problem cannot be considered historical. It was constructed by Aristotle on the basis of a misapprehension of Zeno's paradoxes. (4) The metaphysical problems formulated by Parmenides and Melissus. The relation of atomism to these problems cannot be proved conclusively, but its possibility cannot be eliminated either. If the relation exists, it may be due to the work of Leucippus, who, according to the tradition, attributed Eleatic Being not to an immutable whole of things, but to a plurality of immutable smallest parts. The explanation has too much an ontological and therefore Aristotelean ring not to give cause for reserve.

It is not difficult to find out why the atomic theory was interpreted by Aristotle against a background which was not the historical one. Aristotle designed his own theory of matter and form as a solution of the problem of coming-to-be and passing-away. The

166

formula of the problem was this: how is it possible for that which is, to have come into existence out of a condition in which apparently it was not, in other words, how can being come into existence out of not-being. Aristotle gives the answer that not-being precedes being, but not in an absolute sense. Not-being means not-yet-being or being potentially, δυνάμει. Therefore he calls the potential being of matter a not-being-actually, μὴ ὂν ἐνεργείᾳ (*Met.* Λ 2, 1069 b 18 - 20. *Phys.* A 9, 192 a 3 - 5). Aristotle's theory continued a tradition of thinking which originated from Parmenides and had come to him via Plato. The formula of the Parmenidean principle is recognizable: Being cannot come into existence out of not-being.

Aristotle consciously worked on the line of this tradition, as we can see when he is quoting the Parmenidean doctrine. In *Met.* N 2 1089 a 2 - 6 he states that the problem originated from Parmenides, and that Plato attempted a solution which implied the necessity of showing that not-being also existed. Aristotle is referring here to Plato's *Sophistes* (see Ross and Tricot *a.h.l.*). Pursuing his explanation he says that not-being must be taken as not-being-something, e.g. not being human, not being straight etc.

To Aristotle's system of thought this theory is essential, because it is intended as an explanation of the problem of coming-to-be and passing-away. There are few exceptions to the rule that Aristotle, whenever it is possible, tries to find back the essential elements of his own thought in the systems of other philosophers. We may feel confident of not committing *hybris* by supposing that Aristotle interpreted the Democritean use of ὄν and μὴ ὄν in a metaphysical sense as a result of the metaphysical investigations in which he was absorbed.

Empty space and solid particles were to the atomists the things that mattered. The empty space was a later development of the Eleatic concept of the void or μὴ ὄν. It is, however, not excluded that it had a double ancestry, for we may wonder if the Ionian ἄπειρον did not play a role as well.

In the doxographic tradition constant mention is made of the infinity of empty space in the atomic theory. This characteristic of being infinite cannot be explained by relating the concept to the Eleatic theory, for if anything was all-encompassing to the Eleatics it was Being and not the Void. In the structure of the atomic theory the infinite empty space is absolutely indispensable. The whole of Democritus' doctrine offers a picture which is in many essentials in harmony with the traditional Ionian world-view. We may suppose that the idea of infinite empty space in the last resort goes back to Anaximander's conception of the boundless heavenly space, from which all things emerge and into which they perish. The idea had already undergone important transformations when it came to be adapted to the atomic theory. The work of Melissus may have been one of the junctions at which the Eleatic influence came into the Ionian tradition.

It is not clear from the fragments of Melissus whether he still regarded the universe as spherical. His defense of the Parmenidean conceptions suggests this to a certain extent, but at the same time the concept of an ἄπειρον, which in this expression is absent in Parmenides, is frequently discussed by Melissus. The general development in early Greek philosophy was from a spherical to a rectilinear universe. To the early Presocratics the cosmos was spherical, as it still was to Plato. Democritus clearly conceived the cosmic space as infinite in the rectilinear sense. To Aristotle the heavens were spherical, but his use of the concept of ἄπειρον in cosmology betrays an underlying notion of rectilinear infinity. We may ask if it was Melissus, who introduced the change in outlook.

The fragments of Melissus (DK 30 B) give a systematic defense of Parmenidean Being. In the second fragment he argues that Being is infinite in the temporal sense, in the third fragment that it is infinite in the spatial sense. In the fifth fragment we find the expression which has been considered as evidence that to Melissus the universe was not determined from within nor kept within boundaries:

εἰ μὴ ἓν εἴη, περανεῖ πρὸς ἄλλο.

"If it is not One, it will be bordered upon by something else."

The expression "bordered upon by something else" was in this interpretation taken as implying that outside the universe there would be something, for instance empty space, to which the universe then would be contiguous. From this the conclusion was drawn that Melissus had been the first who had consciously argued that outside the cosmos an empty space is extending into infinity. If we consult the text of the fragment it is not evident that this was implied by Melissus. The point in discussion in the fragment is not the question of whether the all is bordering upon something else, but whether it is a unity or has internal lines of division. This is what Simplicius says in his preliminary remark to the fragment, and it is also made clear by the sixth fragment. Here Melissus says: "If the all were a duality, it could not be infinite, but it would have boundaries where the composing parts would border upon one another." This means that we have the traditional picture here: the universe is internally a Whole, and this Whole is infinite from within. The question whether there is something outside the Whole is, within the framework of this conception, meaningless.

Burnet (*EGP* 167) takes the fragment as implying the view that reality was spatially infinite. He writes: "Melissus saw that you cannot imagine a finite sphere without regarding it as surrounded by an infinite empty space." The question itself, Burnet says, would have been meaningless to Parmenides, for "no one knew better than he (Parmenides) that there is no such thing as nothing." Nevertheless Melissus did put the question of what was outside the spherical universe, and thus opened the way to the conception of the infinite empty space as the atomists described it. Burnet's interpretation was influenced by a statement of Aristotle, which is found in *De gen. et corr.* 325 a 15:

τὸ γὰρ πέρας περαίνειν ἂν πρὸς τὸ κενόν.

"(The universe is infinite;) for any limit would make it border upon the Void."

The view that infinity meant the absence of outer boundaries, is not supported by Melissus' text, and was probably given by Aristotle as an addition of his own.

Burnet's interpretation gives rise to another problem in as far as the term πέρας is implied in it. In Parmenides this term had a double meaning: that of spatial boundary, and that of perfection or determinateness. If Burnet's interpretation is right, the word πέρας as it is used by Melissus would have lost definitely its ambiguity and henceforth would only convey the meaning of "spatial limit". It is not altogether impossible that this was the case, but even then the texts do not prove that πέρας indicated the outer boundary where empty space begins.

Without attributing the argument in its explicit form to Melissus it is best to suppose that Melissus, by the very acute form of his arguments, contributed indirectly to the development we can observe in the notion of the ἄπειρον. Melissus uses the methods of Eleatic logic to analyze this ancient concept. The concept itself probably had an Ionian origin. In Melissus' argument three terms at least were Anaximander's: the word ἄπειρον itself, the expression ἀρχὴν οὐκ ἔχει (fr. 2) and the expression ἀΐδιον καὶ ἄπειρον (fr. 4 and 7).

In Democritus any notion of a spherical universe has vanished.

The sphericity of the all, as we found it in Anaximander and in Parmenides, has made way for a universe, moving in an empty space which is completely infinite in a rectilinear sense. In this infinite space an infinite number of atoms move about. In our survey of characteristic terms given on p. 158-9 we could recognize quite a few expressions which were reminiscent of Anaximander. There is every reason to assume that the cosmological theories of Democritus did not only incorporate a certain influence of Eleatic thought but also set forth the essentials of the Ionian tradition.

The problem whether there is empty space outside the boundaries of heaven still survives in a remark made by Simplicius (in *Phys.* 648, 12-14): "The followers of Democritus and Leucippus admitted that there was empty space not only within the cosmos but also outside it." The argument is not completely in harmony with what we know about Democritus' cosmology. Simplicius himself adds a quotation from Porphyry to the effect that according to Democritus there was no empty space outside the universe. This is more consistent with his theory, for to Democritus all the empty space taken together was by definition the universe.

Not only do we find in Simplicius' account the term ἄπειρον, which is common to all the ancient accounts of atomism, but even the term ἀΐδιον emerges. Simplicius says (*in Phys.* 1153, 22) that Democritus regarded time as eternal:

ἀΐδιον εἶναι τὸν χρόνον.

The notion of an eternal Time belongs to the Ionian worldview, in which, in its most ancient stage, an all-encompassing Time-deity dominated the process of coming-into-being and perishing. If the line, found in this late authority, contains an authentic statement, it completes our account of the Ionian character of Democritus' cosmology.

BIBLIOGRAPHY

Natorp 1884
Lasswitz 1890
Natorp 1890, I and II
Hammer-Jensen 1910
Reinhardt 1912
Kranz 1912, I and II
Sachs 1917
Stenzel 1920

Bailey 1928
Philippson 1929
Robin 1933
Luria 1933
Howald 1934
Luria 1936
Vlastos 1945-6
Mau 1949

Wilpert 1950
Van Melsen 1952
Davison 1953
Mau 1954
Kranz 1954
Samburski 1959
Gershenson-Greenberg 1961
Moorhouse 1962

Van Melsen 1962
Mugler 1963
Matson 1963
Von Fritz 1963
Schreckenberg 1964
McGibbon 1964
Luther 1966
Klowski 1966

CHAPTER VIII

PLATO

A. ATOMISM AND PLATO'S TIMAEUS

Since the days of Zeller it has been a hotly debated question whether or not Plato knew Democritus. The reason for putting this question was obvious. In his *Timaeus* Plato had elaborated a theory of the fundamental structures of matter, which could not fail to suggest the idea that it ran parallel to Democritus' atomic theory. As was so often the case, the general idea of the theory suggested a parallelism which was not borne out by the details.

In the *Timaeus* Plato distinguishes four ultimate elements, each of them possessing a typical structure. Plato nowhere talks about smallest solid particles, as Democritus did. He tries to visualize the characteristics of the four elements by drawing up patterns of regular constructions, which remotely resemble the patterns of modern crystallography. Nor does Plato talk about any opposition between smallest particles and empty space, a feature, which was indispensible to the conception of Democritus. All the same, the idea of ground-patterns for the elements inevitably suggested a comparison between Plato and Democritus.

The number of four elements was traditional. Though the historical roots of the conception are much older, Empedocles was the first to work out a coherent doctrine based on it (see our chapter V). Plato adapted the idea in its Empedoclean form, but he added a mathematical theory. In Plato's days probably for the first time in the history of mathematics the theory of the regular solids was completed. Though regular solids had been known for at least some centuries, it was then established that there were five and only five regular solids capable of being inscribed in a sphere. This complete theory was the work of Theaetetus, a young and brilliant mathematician, whom we find as a speaker in Plato's dialogue of the same name (cf. Heath 1921, I 158 - 162, 209 - 212). The famous thirteenth book of Euclid's

Elements is generally considered to be based on the work of Theaetetus.

The pentagram and the division of a line into extreme and mean ratio had early attracted the attention of geometers. The pentagram is found in Mesopotamia as early as circa 3000 B.C. (see de Vogel 1966, 292 - 297). By joining twelve regular pentagons a regular solid, the dodecahedron, could be obtained. This construction must have been known as early as the sixth century B.C., for in an Etruscan tomb a stone copy of such a dodecahedron was found, which could not be of a later date than 500 B.C. (v. d. Waerden 1966, 165, Heath 1931, 107). The regular solids aroused the special interest of the Pythagoreans. According to tradition they knew three of them. The other two were discovered by Theaetetus.

The history of the theory of the regular solids explains why Plato took such a lively interest in it. Plato tried to combine the theory of the four elements with that of the five regular solids. To each of the elements he ascribed the fundamental form of one of the regular solids. Fire consisted of regular pyramids, earth of cubes, air of octahedrons and water of icosahedrons. One of the five regular solids was left: the dodecahedron. Probably this was not fortuitous but in harmony with tradition. Though it cannot be proved, it seems probable, as de Vogel points out (1966, 293) that in Mesopotamia the pentagram had a cosmic significance. Plato considers the dodecahedron as a kind of ground-pattern for the structure of the universe. He says so in two lines of the *Timaeus* (55 C 4 - 6) without adding further explanations.

The context of Plato's *Timaeus* suggests that the background of this doctrine should be looked for in Pythagorean cosmic and mathematical speculation rather than in the Ionian mixture-theories from which Democritus derived his doctrine. Nevertheless, at the end of the nineteenth century, a comparison was made between the two theories of Plato and Democritus. This comparison has produced a general and persistent conviction that the intuitions of the two philosophers presented a close resemblance, and that it would be difficult to deny the historical connection. The question calls for a critical examination, because it appears that in the comparison an important element was forgotten. Plato's intuition can be characterized as mathematical, whereas Democritus' theory was physical. Moreover, the idea that Plato's theory was inspired by that of Democritus, has been demonstrated by arguments which imply certain unproved presuppositions derived from nineteenth-century philosophical historiography.

The problem was raised, in a more general form, as early as in antiquity. It had been noticed that Plato nowhere quotes Democritus or makes allusion to his theories, though he does so with regard to practically every great philosopher who had preceded him. Diogenes Laertius (IX 40 = DK 68 A 1) has a tradition according to which Plato had been jealous of Democritus, whose fame was far greater than his own. He says that Plato had even intended to burn Democritus' work. The story looks more like an aetiological myth, invented in order to explain an otherwise inexplicable fact. The fact was that Plato seemed to ignore Democritus, whose writings at any rate must have preceded Plato's Although the chronological dates are somewhat at variance, it is impossible to suppose that the works of Democritus did not yet exist when Plato wrote his *Timaeus*. If we wanted to classify Democritus' theories chronologically after Plato's we should have to resuscitate the ancient Time-deity Chronos to have him perform this Herculean feat of anachronism. Nor is it easy to imagine that Democritus' works had not found their way to Athens. There is one authentic line of Democritus alluding to his visiting Athens:

ἦλθον γὰρ εἰς ᾿Αθήνας καὶ οὔ τίς με ἔγνωκεν.

"For I came to Athens and nobody knew me." (DK 68 B 116, cf. Skemp 1942, 34). In Plato's works he seems to be absent.

Starting an investigation of this problem we must put a number of questions. The first is whether the use of certain terms or expressions may betray that Plato is referring to Democritus. The second question is whether Plato and Democritus used parallel arguments in the construction of their theories. The third question is a historical one: when we take the theories as a whole, to what historical development do the essentials of their structures correspond? The first of these questions can only be dealt with incidentally, because hardly any fragments of Democritus' physical works are extant. The second and third question may be introduced by a general outline of the problem.

When Plato raised the problem of the ultimate building-stones of matter, three explanations were possible. The first was the atomic hypothesis, worked out by Leucippus and Democritus. We saw that this hypothesis agreed with the general characteristics of the Ionian tradition, which was biological and evolutionary. Mixture-theories and theories on infinitesimal small particles had played their parts in the development which led up to atomism. The second explanation was that which, somewhat later in history, was given by Aristotle in his criticism of the atomic theory. According to this explanation the idea of an atom had been conceived by the atomists as a result of a mathematical process of infinite division, and not in the first place as a concept of very small solid particles, which were ingredients of a mixture. We saw that this explanation was an Aristotelean construction. The third theory is Plato's. Here the characteristics of material things were explained by the theory of the four elements, specified according to a geometrical pattern. Plato nowhere talks about smallest parts or solid particles. What he does attempt is to explain the characteristics of the elements by giving them a geometrical structure. The inspiration of his theory is Pythagorean.

Besides the Pythagorean tradition the Eleatic theory had a decisive influence on Plato. While Eleatic theories are practically ubiquitous in Plato's works, it is a remarkable fact that Zeno's paradoxes are absent, that is to say, not in their value as a dialectical method, but regarded as a mathematical problem on infinite divisibility. If this problem would have led to the atomic theory, we would have to expect that it was Plato who developed it on this line because Plato was so well acquainted with Zeno's thought. In Plato however, there is no development to this effect. This means that the problem of infinite division cannot be taken into the comparison, even if we were to believe Aristotle who held that it played a part in atomism. In that case it would have been the atomists who started from this problem, not Plato.

We may divide the passages in which Plato is referring to the theories of other philosophers into two extensive categories: (1) all those places where Plato mentions the other philosophers by name, (2) all the places where this is not the case. Because in Plato's work not a single line can be found where Democritus is explicitly mentioned, all references to Democritus or to the atomic docrine must be looked for in the second category. This means that a wide field is opened for speculation. If the reference to the atomists is not beyond doubt, the question whether or not a certain passage refers to Democritus must depend on its interpretation. The most important investigations in this field have been those by Natorp (1884 and 1890), Ingeborg Hammer-Jensen (1910), and Eva Sachs (1917).

Archer-Hind and Zeller were probably the first to notice that a certain number of passages in Plato's works might be explained as containing references to Democritus' theories. Nineteenth century philosophy saw this parallelism mainly in the field of ethics and of theory of knowledge. Once the investigations seemed to have yielded results in these fields, the way was open to the supposition that also in cosmology and atomic doctrine Plato had been influenced by Democritus. It was even thought possible that he had elaborated ideas first formulated by the latter. The idea of atoms having a characteristic shape, it was argued, might have induced Plato to conceive his theory of the fundamental geometrical forms of the elements.

The texts belonging to the field of ethics must be used with circumspection. There is a very great number of pages in which Plato has an argument with unnamed opponents. These opponents mainly appear to have been adherents of doctrines according to which human knowledge was restricted to sense-data. In line with this gnoseological point of view are their ethical theories on pleasure and pain. Plato's opponents are described as people who think that the sense-data are decisive to our knowledge of things, and accordingly that any appreciation of the value of things is entirely subjective. Man had to seek for happiness in the changing and deceptive illusions of his senses. This ran counter to Plato's conviction that a philosopher has to seek for things which are permanent and essential, and which do not change their identity, so as to offer a reliable starting-point to man's search for happiness. Metaphysically speaking, the opinions of Plato's adversaries were in permanent conflict with his ideas of true being, inspired by Eleatic thinking.

An adversary whom Plato practically always mentions by his name is Protagoras, the fellow-countryman of Democritus. When Plato does not name his opponents, we have, as a rule, to do with wide-spread opinions, which are attacked by Plato as such. In such cases he does not identify the points of view of the opponents as the opinions of any particular philosopher. Probably, it was not even his intention to make us think of certain persons. We are always free to guess whom Plato may be aiming at, but if in the text only the general tendency of an argument is given, we are likely to draw arbitrary conclusions if we fix our choice upon one or another philosopher. We may take as an instance the idea that sense perception is unreliable. If in a text this idea is discussed in a general form, it is possible to think of Protagoras as well as of Heraclitus or Democritus. To the three of them the idea was fundamental, yet they applied it in their philosophy in a different sense. It is, therefore, a better method to pay attention not only to the contents of a doctrine but also to the expressions by which it is formulated. Only when two doctrines agree in these two respects we have a chance of finding a real historical connection.

176

The question whether Plato knew any Democritean theories was amply discussed by Natorp in two works, published in 1884 and 1890. The first study deals with ethical and gnoseological problems, and with the texts of *Philebus* 44 B, 51 A and *Republic* 583 B. Natorp thinks that Plato in these texts, in which he discussed pleasure and pain and the distinction between true and false pleasure, is following Democritus. The distinction is given by Plato as that of ἡδοναὶ ἀληθεῖς, true pleasures, and, opposed to these, the "seeming pleasures, which are by no means real, only imaginary", δοκούσας, οὔσας δ' οὐδαμῶς, φαντασθείσας (*Phil.* 51 A). These false pleasures are also described as γοήτευμα, οὐχ ἡδονή, "a bewitchment, not real pleasure" (*Phil.* 44 C - D), or as ἐσκιαγραφημένη τις ἡδονή, "a phantasmagoria of pleasure" (*Rep.* 583 B). Natorp compares these expressions with the term: εὐεστώ (DK 68 B 2 c, 4, 140), and with Democritus' distinction between σκοτίη καὶ γνησίη γνώμη, "bastard-knowledge and real knowledge" (DK 68 B 11).

The parallelism which Natorp wants to establish is rather superficial. In Democritus' text the distinction between bastard and real knowledge has no bearing on pleasures, but on our perception of the outer world. What we suppose to perceive is completely different from the reality of the thing perceived. Reality is only atoms moving in a void. In Plato the distinction has a different background, because it is based on Eleatic metaphysics, and, in as far as pleasure is concerned, possibly on Pythagorean ascetic practice. It is not obvious that Plato should have taken his ideas from Democritus. The term which, in Plato's dialogues, comes nearest to εὐεστώ, "well-being", is γαλήνη, "serenity". This latter term however, is so common in Greek that it can hardly be used to show that Plato took the idea from Democritus.

Natorp thinks the parallelism sufficiently proved, and in addition he points to the fact that both Plato and Democritus expressed themselves on the existence of not-being (Plato, *Sophistes*, Democritus B 156). Natorp thinks we have to regard Democritus at least as a forerunner of Plato's theories, but presumably as the philosopher whose influence on Plato was decisive. Moreover he thinks that both Plato and Democritus founded their metaphysics on Eleatic and mathematical principles. As far as Democritus is concerned, Natorp is still under the spell of Aristotle's authority. According to the picture Aristotle gives us, we would have to consider the atomic theory as a development originating from Eleatic theory and Zenonian paradox. As we saw in our seventh chapter, this was an Aristotelean

177

construction. The historical background rather suggests that, if there was any Eleatic influence in atomic doctrine, it was incorporated into the Ionian tradition before the days of Democritus.

A second study was published by Natorp in 1890. Here he bases his argument on two previous suppositions: first, in certain passages of his *Theaetetus* Plato is referring to Aristippus; second, Aristippus' theory about the absolutely subjective character of sense perception was inspired by Democritus. Natorp's study consists of two parts. In the first part he discusses the two presuppositions of his theory, in the second he tries to ascertain where in Plato's dialogue traces of Democritean influence can be found. To the testimony of *Philebus* 44 B and *Republic* 583 B is added that of *Phaedo* 69 B, 81 B, 84 A, where Natorp finds the same ideas expressed in the same terms: "bewitchment", "phantasmagoria", "serenity". In the *Philebus* (44 B) Plato informs us, as Natorp takes it, that these expressions were borrowed from philosophers who were regarded as δεινοὺς τὰ περὶ φύσιν (44 B), "great men in natural philosophy." Natorp argues that this must include Democritus and that, therefore, Democritus must have been known to Plato even when he wrote his *Phaedo*.

As in the case of his publication of 1884 we may object that the parallels are of too general a kind to permit of any strict conclusion with regard to Democritean influence. The problem of real and false opinion, and that of the reliability of sense perception was widespread and not in any way peculiar to Democritus. Moreover, the sense Plato gives to these problems is widely divergent from the sense they have in Democritus' philosophy.

Passing from ethics to cosmology, Natorp adduces three other texts. He thinks that in the *Parmenides* (164 B) the concept of atom is in the background. In the *Philebus* the concept of ἄπειρον, in Natorp's opinion, is an *analogon* of Democritus' empty space, and, finally, the concept of χώρα in the *Timaeus* has, as Natorp states it, an unmistakable affinity to the μὴ ὄν of Democritus. This latter relationship, moreover, is also found in the *Sophistes*. Natorp thinks the evidence is conclusive. In his opinion Plato is, compared to Democritus, in a position of "Fortarbeit an seinem Werk", that is, Plato was building on foundations laid by Democritus (1890, 531).

The weak point in Natorp's argument is essentially the same throughout his various studies: any parallelism in the contents of a theory is taken by him as a proof of their historical connection. He generally forgets to mention the important differences by which the

178

parallelism is accompanied, and pays insufficient attention to the way the theories are formulated. Moreover, the parallelism is, in the majority of the instances given by Natorp, too superficial. There is hardly any passage that cannot succesfully be related to more than one philosopher, and nowhere the conclusion that Democritus was the inspiring source of the idea is inevitable. Natorp's method shows a confusion of systematical philosophy and historical investigation.

A more critical approach to the subject is found in the work of Ingeborg Hammer-Jensen. Her investigation on *"Democritus and Plato"* was published in 1910 in the *"Archiv für Geschichte der Philosophie"*. She methodically confines her study to the cosmological theories of Plato and Democritus, leaving ethics aside. The argument is based on the following specified details.

(1) The concept of ἀνάγκη is typical of the atomists. Plato, on the other hand, very positively rejects any type of causality which is not the deliberate working of a Mind, or, in the organic sphere, of a Soul. We find this conviction of Plato elaborately argued in the *Phaedo*; but even in the *Laws*, which is a work of his old age, the doctrine has not changed (891 sq.). It is, then, a remarkable fact that in the *Timaeus*, where he gives such ample teleological arguments, Plato juxtaposes ἀνάγκη to his Νοῦς (47 E). This, Hammer-Jensen argues, can only be explained by the influence of Democritus.

(2) In the *Timaeus* Plato accepts the theory that there are four elements. He adds a theory of his own in order to explain that the elements can change into one another. This means that Plato accepts the idea that in the last resort there is one unqualified material substratum. This latter idea, Hammer-Jensen argues, is found before Plato in only one system of thought: the atomic theory. It is true that Plato changes the conception, but he must have borrowed the fundamental idea from the atomists. Hammer-Jensen finds support for her argument in Aristotle's account of atomism, which she interprets as implying that the atomists assumed the existence of one unqualified substratum of material things.

(3) In the middle of the *Timaeus* Plato interrupts the course of his own argument (48 E - 49 A). So far, Plato says, two factors sufficed to give an explanation of things, the idea as the archetype, and things perceived by the senses as its images. "We thought these two were sufficient as an explanation, because we failed to distinguish a third factor. It appears now that the argument (ὁ λόγος) compels us to elucidate a dark and difficult form (εἶδος) by arguments (λόγοις)."

179

This 'dark form', the 'third factor', is the receiving medium, which Plato denotes by the expressions ὑποδοχή, 'receptacle', τιθήνη, 'nursing mother', ἐκμαγεῖον, 'recipient' (49 A, 50 C). There are two current theories to explain these terms. One theory says that Plato wanted his 'receptacle' to be understood as 'space' (τὸ τῆς χώρας ἀεί, ἕδρα, 52 AB). The other prefers to interpret the terms in the sense of a mouldable substratum (ἐκμαγεῖον 50 C). We shall have to discuss the question further on. For the moment it must suffice to state that in Plato's own explications two similes occur, which are apt to suggest that it was the mouldable material which was meant by Plato. These are the simile of gold that is moulded by the goldsmith to represent all kinds of figures (50 A), and the simile of the work of the perfumers, who try to make the ointment which is to receive the perfume as odourless as possible (50 E). Aristotle, who sometimes takes the expressions of his master in too concrete a sense, may have been induced by these comparisons to formulate his own theory with the expression 'ὕλη', timber, as a material from which all kinds of figures are made. Hammer-Jensen follows in Aristotle's track, without mentioning the possibility of the other explanation. Accordingly she supposes, firstly, that what Plato intended was a material substratum, secondly, that Plato found the example for this substratum in Democritus. She takes the fact that Plato interrupts the course of his own argument to insert the theory of a material substratum as evidence that Plato came to know Democritus' theories when writing the *Timaeus*.

Hammer-Jensen's arguments have an unequal value. The first of the three arguments is the best. To the atomists, ἀνάγκη represented the immanent determining rules of nature, as we can infer from the fragments with reasonable certainty. In a text of Leucippus (67 B 2) we find ἀνάγκη brought into opposition with λόγος. Though the account is of a late date it probably reproduces a distinction made by Leucippus between teleological causality, exercised by a conscious agent, and the causality of the physical laws. The account of atomic theory of Diogenes Laertius (IX 45) and Simplicius (DK 68 A 37) give us the impression that after Leucippus every teleological conception vanished. In the philosophy of Democritus no deliberating ruler of the universe is found, no Νοῦς, no Λόγος. The construction of his theory leaves no room for any conscious causality. Democritus' way of thinking, characteristic of the scientist, betrays that he did not feel the need of a divine ruling of the universe. Its function has been taken over by τύχη (68 A 70), a concept which probably comes near to our concept of

180

statistical probability. This characteristic feature of Democritus' thought can be observed in all the later schools that were inspired by the atomistic cosmology, for instance in Lucretius.

The fact that the atomic theory was the first doctrine which essentially grasped the concept of a law of nature adds probability to Hammer Jensen's hypothesis. It is possible that, when Plato in his *Timaeus* introduced the conception of an ἀνάγκη as an autonomous ruling force in Nature, he did so after the example of Democritus. This is, however, not the only possible explanation. The term ἀνάγκη is found as early as Parmenides, who designates by it the iron laws of cosmic order: "Ananke keeps it all fastened firmly within the boundaries of limit" (28 B 8, verse 30; B 10 verse 6). If it were true that Parmenides was a physician by profession (Merlan 1966), we may assume with all the more probability, that even he must have had a clear idea of the working of a law of nature . It does not seem necessary to assume that the metaphysical meaning of the concept of ἀνάγκη was not replaced by a physical meaning until it passed from Parmenides' philosophy into that of Democritus.

The concept of natural law is more clearly marked out in the work of Empedocles. Though there are quite a number of mythical elements in his verses, we can observe his attemps at developing a scientist's point of view. In 31 B 8 he says: "There is no Nature, only aggregation and segregation." The vortex is the starting-point of evolution, and Empedocles designates it by the same term which is used by Democritus: δίνη (31 B 35, verse 4, Anaxagoras has περιχώρησις). Plato was influenced by the Italian thinkers in many of his conceptions, and we can see that he was aware of it. In the *Sophistes* (242 D) he calls these western philosophers "Sicilian Muses", obviously referring to Empedocles by the words: "The universe is kept together by Love and Strife." The doctrine of the four elements in the *Timaeus* was taken from Empedocles. Even the concept of 'natural law' has, as we saw, its forerunners in the systems of Parmenides and Empedocles. As long as we can point to these two philosophers as the source from which Plato took his conceptions, the hypothesis that Plato borrowed from Democritus cannot be put on a higher level than that of possibility. The possibility must, on the other hand, not be excluded altogether, in the first place because the conception of ἀνάγκη worked out in the *Timaeus* reminds us so strongly of Democritus.

The second of Hammer-Jensen's arguments is an unfortunate one. The conception of one receiving medium in which the images of the ideas appear, is by its very nature only possible within the framework of an idealistic philosophy. The attempt to reduce this receiving medium to a unity may have been suggested to Plato by the dominating search for unity of Eleatic philosophy. It seems probable that Plato was the first to introduce a distinction between form and receiving medium, and that he was also the first to conceive this medium as a homogeneous unity. It may also be possible that before Plato's days some philosopher had formulated thoughts implying the unity of a material substrate. Aristotle, with all his might, tries to explain earlier theories as having this meaning. Even if the notion existed, however, it is certainly not found in Democritus' theories. Hammer-Jensen thinks, Democritus really had the doctrine of a universal material substrate. She thinks so on the authority of Aristotle's account in *De gen. et corr.* I 2, 316 a 13 - 34. If this text were a reliable account, we would have to assume that to Democritus atoms were the smallest parts at which the infinite division of Euclidean space came to a stop. Hammer-Jensen accepts this Aristotelean interpretation. It provides her with an argument which is to justify her conclusion: if there are smallest parts, these must necessarily all be of an equal dimension. This would mean that Democritus assumes the existence of a homogeneous material substrate.

Even leaving aside the question of how Aristotle's account is to be interpreted, it could have been clear to Hammer-Jensen from other evidence that Democritus by no means had a theory of a unique material substrate. Aristotle's own texts refute this interpretation. In *Met.* A 4, 985 b 14 - 19 (= DK 67 A 6) he says, reproducing Democritus' own words, that the atoms differed in shape, order and position. In *De gen. et corr.* 315 b 11 he says that the atoms had an infinity of different shapes (σχήματα), and that the atomists assumed this to be so in order to explain the processes of change. We may conclude from this that to Democritus all kinds of different qualities continued to be present even in the smallest particles, just as in Anaxagoras' theory the qualities of a mixture remained the same even in infinitely small parts of it. Aristotle mentions one of the shapes of atoms. In *De anima* 404 a 1 - 3, 405 a 11 - 13 and in *De respiratione* 472 a 4 - 5 we can read that in the atomic theory the souls and the fire consisted of atoms which were spherical in form.

It may also be considered impossible from a theoretical point of view that the atomists should have admitted a unique material substrate. Absolutely unqualified matter cannot be admitted in a theory

182

unless previously all the different qualities of things have been classed under one category as images of Ideas, which are assigned a place in an incorporeal realm. Democritus certainly did not think about incorporeal realms. In a systematic sense a homogeneous matter is the remnant of a procedure in which qualities are sundered from the individual things in which they appear. If we take this into account, we can say that it is highly improbable that it should have been Democritus and not Plato who first postulated some kind of homogeneous substratum, which was to be devoid of any quality. At any rate the established facts of the atomic doctrine prove that the idea of a unique substrate-matter did not belong to the atomic doctrine. Plato cannot have found it in Democritus.

The question whether Plato could find the doctrine of the four elements in Democritus is of secondary importance. If it was a theory of Democritus, it is not necessary to assume that Plato owed it to him. The oldest form of the theory is found in Empedocles. Plato was so well acquainted with this Italian philosopher that there is no reason whatever to suppose that he must have borrowed it elsewhere. It is plausible that Plato's Sicilian Muses told him about it. The problem leaves room for one argument only. Plato was the first to reduce the four elements to a common factor, that is to say he tried to do so. Hammer-Jensen supposes that he found this idea in Democritus. This only holds good if we admit that Democritus actually assumed the existence of a unique substrate. As we saw this is not borne out by the texts.

There are a few reliable accounts informing us that the four elements had a place in the atomic theory. Diogenes Laertius (IX 44 = DK 68 A 1) incidentally mentions them, when he says that in the vortex the atoms generate all kinds of aggregations, fire, water, air and earth, "for", he adds, "these also are a concretion of atoms." Aristotle (*De Caelo* III 4, 303 a 12 - 16 = DK 67 A 15) criticizes the atomists because they gave their atoms different shapes but failed to make clear by which form every element was determined. To the atoms of fire they attributed a spherical form, to the atoms of air and water different dimensions only. Simplicius (*in Phys.* 35, 22) has the statement that "the atomists did not oppose the conception that there were four elements as principles of things. However, seeing that fire, air and water and perhaps earth as well, could change into one another, they tried to find simpler and more general causes in order to explain the differences of the elements." Simplicius is confusing the conceptions of Plato with those of the atomists, as is made clear by the following lines, where he states that "Timaeus and, following him, Plato regarded the geometrical forms as the elements of the elements."

Simplicius' account might confirm the opinion of Hammer-Jensen if it could prove that the atomists assumed a unique material substrate. His statement, however, leaves the possibility that there was a multiplicity of atomic forms, as we know from other sources. As regards the four elements, we may conclude from Simplicius' account that these only played a subordinate part in the atomic theory, though they were present in it, probably as a traditional feature.

Hammer-Jensen's third argument is not so much an argument as an attractive possibility, which could be added to the hypothesis if first it could be proved conclusively, that Plato derived some of his theories from Democritus. In that case it might be supposed that Plato had come to know Democritus' theories while writing the *Timaeus*. He then would have stopped to insert a new point of view. The hypothesis must have appeared tempting to Hammer-Jensen. How convinced she was of her own theories may be seen from the last part of her study. Here she even uses the text of Plato's *Timaeus* to reconstruct missing links in the theories of the atomists.

The study of Hammer-Jensen has the merit of drawing our attention to specified details in Plato's thought, which may make it possible to suppose that they are related to Democritus. Her best argument is that based on the double causality of Νοῦς and 'Ανάγκη in Plato's *Timaeus*. The theory of Νοῦς Plato probably derived from Anaxagoras. As to that of 'Ανάγκη, which represents immanent physical law, it is possible to think that he found it in the writings of Democritus, but this cannot be proved strictly.

To the evidence adduced by Hammer-Jensen in 1910 more material was added in 1917 by Eva Sachs in her dissertation on *"The Five Platonic Solids"*. In this book pp. 185-234 are devoted to a detailed study of the theory of the elements in Plato and in Democritus.

Eva Sachs rightly remarks that the theory of the four elements is in the atomic system essentially an unconnected ingredient. The elements are found in Democritus' theory by way of a traditional feature, but they serve no essential purpose. The important difference with Plato, Eva Sachs argues, is that to the atomist the elements are things or substances, whereas Plato wants to see them as qualities. In *Timaeus* 51 A - B he says that we are not justified in designating the receiving medium by the names of earth, air, fire or water, but that the part of it which is ignited appears to us as fire, the moistened

184

part as water, and so on. Fire, earth, water and air he calls solid bodies (σώματα) in 53 C. Because bodies can change into one another we may not designate them as a "this" (τοῦτο), but only as a τοιοῦτον, a thing that has a certain quality (49 D). Eva Sachs thinks this must be explained as a criticism aimed at Democritus.

It is true that a criticism of a theory of elements need not in particular be directed against Democritus, but none the less Eva Sachs' argument must be considered very acute. It is possible to think of Heraclitus if the question is about elements changing into one another, because in the cosmic process as Heraclitus describes it all things gradually change into fire and afterwards, when the fire cools down, are again separated from it as sets of opposites. There is a rather general tradition of condensation and rarefaction in Ionian philosophy and we even find the idea in Empedocles. Plato alludes to this tradition in *Timaeus* 50 A when speaking of "opposites such as hot and cold, black and white and so on." In three ingenious remarks Eva Sachs further argues that Plato is referring to Democritus here. In the passage where Plato is explaining that elements can only be qualities of an underlying substrate, there is a pun on an incompetent thinker who would have been more competent if he had omitted to speak of an infinite number of worlds (55 C - D, cf. 31 A). The words for "incompetent" and for "infinite" are the same in Greek: ἄπειρος. Eva Sachs thinks that Plato is referring to Democritus, who assumed an infinite number of worlds to be generated in infinite space.

Her second remark is a conjecture. In *Timaeus* 49 E a slight alteration in the text suffices to make Democritus' typical term τὸ δέν appear. The third remark regards an expression in *Timaeus* 48 B-C which, according to Eva Sachs, can only refer to Democritus. Plato here says that we are in the habit of considering the elements as first principles (ἀρχάς), but that in reality they cannot even be compared to the syllables in a word. If we want to know what the real "elements" of a word are, we must go back to the letters. This comparison of the elements with letters must have been typical of the atomists, as was pointed out by Diels (1899). The comparison had a certain renown in antiquity. Aristotle mentions it, saying that the atomists used it in order to explain how by a different order many different things can condense out of the same atoms. A comedy and a tragedy, they said, are written with the same letters (*De gen. et corr.* 315 b 14-15). Cicero adds something to the argument by saying (*De nat. deorum* II 37, 93): if everything would come into existence by chance, it would even be possible that by throwing a great number of letters on the ground we might cause the *Annals* of Ennius to appear in the sand. Cicero takes advantage of the simile to prove the existence of a Providence.

The conjecture in 49 E is a correction of a *passus* where the manuscripts have the untranslatable text τὴν τούτου or τὴν τῷδε. If the conjecture could be turned into certainty the whole problem whether Plato knew Democritus would have been solved at a blow. The highly original term τὸ δέν would prove conclusively that Plato had read Democritus' works. In reality, things are the other way round: if first it can be proved that Plato knew Democritus we may feel sure of the reading τοῦ δέν. Nevertheless, we must grant to the hypothesis the same right every conjecture has. If the conjecture provides a plausible solution for a complex textual problem, this in itself is an argument in support of it. However, the text allows of a much simpler solution, if we accept that the untranslatable words τὴν τούτου (or τὴν τῷδε) have been inserted as an alternative reading (and a mistaken one) of the immediately preceding words. When correcting the proof-sheets of her book, Eva Sachs herself again doubted whether the simpler solution should not be preferred, as she admits in an added note (1917, 204). Rivaud, in his edition of the text, has printed the reading τοῦ δέν (Paris 1949).

The comparison of the elements with the syllables and the letters of a word has a fair chance of having originated with Democritus, but there are no authentic fragments to prove this. Linguistic analysis was not a privilege of the school of the atomists, as we may see from Plato's *Cratylus* and from many of the discussions of the sophists.

A parallel remark may be made on the supposed allusion to Democritus in the question of the plurality of worlds. It cannot be proved that this was a specifically atomistic doctrine. Burnet (EGP 59-60, 269-270) has pointed out that a doctrine of "innumerable worlds" was traditional in the Ionian schools. Possibly Burnet's arguments have been more or less invalidated by Kirk-Raven (1962, 121-126), who, with a certain reserve, admit that the attribution of a doctrine of innumerable worlds to Anaximander may have originated from an interpretation of Theophrastus. The validity of Burnet's argument can, however, not be doubted as far as Anaxagoras is concerned. We still have the authentic words of Anaxagoras (DK 59 B 4), which say that, as a result of a process of condensation in the primordial mixture, elsewhere also human beings must have come into existence, who have towns and arable land and a sun and a moon.

186

It is difficult to interpret this but as part of a theory of innumerable worlds. Moreover, the doxographers so often mention this type of theory that it cannot have been a monopoly of the atomists. It is possible, though not certain, that its attribution to Anaximander was due to an interpretation of Theophrastus, and the same can be said with regard to Xenophanes (cf. Diog. Laert. IX 19 = DK 21 A 1). On the other hand it agrees too well with Anaximander's doctrine that the cosmos developed from the Infinite by a process of condensation and rarefaction, and with the Ionian tradition in general, to make its attribution to Anaximander and Xenophanes impossible. To this may be added that there can be no doubt whatsoever as regards Anaxagoras. This invalidates the principal argument of Eva Sachs. The doctrine of innumerable worlds was not specific to atomism.

We may conclude from our survey that practically every passage which has been explained as a tacit reference to Democritus, has a much broader correspondence in the Ionian tradition than only in the theory of the atomists.

There are a number of passages in Plato's dialogues, which, taken at their face-value, seem to imply a reference to Democritus but which, on investigation, prove to represent rather current ideas. With a view to this we shall stick to the opinion of Taylor (1928, 84) that "there is no passage anywhere in Plato which shows beyond doubt that he knew of Democritus."

Besides the very thorough investigations of Natorp, Hammer-Jensen and Eva Sachs, mention must be made of a few studies by Pohlenz (1918) and Taylor (1928, 83-85). Pohlenz thinks that *Laws* 889 A might aim at Democritus. Taylor thinks that it is rather Empedocles who is criticized here, but that ten pages further on (899) the discussion is possibly with Democritus. Both texts have too broad a field of correspondence in the Presocratic tradition to make it plausible that they are specially related to Democritus. The same must be said about the arguments of Kranz (1912, II) on the theory of colours which is found in *Timaeus* 61 C-68 D. The work of Theophrastus informs us about a theory of colours of Democritus (DK 68 A 135), and Kranz thinks the two are parallel.

Stenzel (1920) supposes that Plato must have found examples for his method of διαίρεσις in Democritus. His arguments are not strict enough to make his evidence conclusive. Wilpert (1950) and Kranz (1954) follow in the track of a by now accepted interpretation without adding new material to the discussion.

The question whether Plato knew Democritus' theories is not only of historical importance. On the answer to this question the interpretation of Plato's *Timaeus* is, to a certain extent, dependent. If ever it could be established as a fact that Plato's discussions in this dialogue (and also in *Laws* X) are discussions with the atomists, in many cases the traditional interpretations of Plato's view would have to be changed. They would at any rate ask for a different historical description. The constant and unavoidable stumbling-block in these matters is the scantiness of authentic fragments of Democritus. However, we have at our disposal the complete works of Plato. From the text of the *Timaeus* we can draw many conclusions as to the influences assimilated by Plato. By drawing up a survey of these influences, it may at least be possible to state whether there is a probability that Plato, when using certain expressions, may have had atomism in mind. Tracing out the recognizable allusions, we shall try to determine to what extent it is possible that Democritus, too, should be in the picture.

In the *Timaeus*, especially in that part of the dialogue which deals with the question out of what substance the material universe is built, there are many expressions reminiscent of the Presocratic thinkers. The universe is eternally young, Plato says, using an expression of Anaximander's: ἀγήρων, 'never-aging' (33 A), and it is spherical (σφαιροειδές, 33 B), having in all directions the same distance from the centre to the circumference. This latter feature was characteristic of both Xenophanes and Parmenides. In the *Timaeus* (33 B) we find the typical expressions which the doxographic tradition uses to designate their theories (Xenophanes 21 A 1, Parmenides 28 A 7 and 31). The term κυκλοτερές, used by Empedocles (31 B 27 - 28) occurs in the same passage. The description reminds us of the spherical Being of Parmenides. The characteristic terms of Parmenides are present: the well-rounded universe is perfect (τέλεον), and it is One and a Whole (ἕνα ὅλον 33 A).

The life which fills the universe contributes to its perfection. The cosmos is a ζῷον τέλεον, a perfect living being, of which even the composing parts are perfect (ἐκ τελέων τῶν μερῶν 32 D). This conception originated in the ancient Orphic and Pythagorean philosophies, in which the universe was described as an animated being, developing from a primordial germ by inhaling the breath of life. The living universe even comprised other animated beings as a necessary factor of its perfection: τῷ τὰ πάντα ἐν αὑτῷ ζῷα περιέχειν μέλλοντι ζῴῳ (33 B).

188

The adjustment of this conception which was brought about by Xenophanes (see our p. 59), is repeated by Plato: the universe is not surrounded by any breath which could be inhaled: δεόμενον ἀναπνοῆς, 33 C.

In *Timaeus* 48 E - 49 C we can recognize Anaximenes' theories. Of this text Taylor (1928, 314) says: "The whole passage is full of echoes of early Ionian cosmology." Plato gives a description of the processes of condensation and rarefaction which account for the fact that material substances can change into one another. This was what Anaximenes had done. In the account by Simplicius (DK 13 A 5) we find the same terms in which Plato expresses the doctrine: μανότης, πυκνότης, or also μάνωσις, πύκνωσις, and the participles ἀραιούμενον, πυκνούμενον (cf. 13 A 7). Plato has: πυκνούμενον, συμπιλουμένων, διακρινόμενον. It is true that the theory is not specifically that of Anaximenes. It is rather frequent in the Ionian tradition, and Anaxagoras is also in the background when Plato speaks of the processes of aggregation and dispersion (συγκριθέν, διακρινόμενον). The terms are an exact parallel to the expressions συμμισγόμενα, ἀποκρινόμενα, διακρινόμενα, by which Anaxagoras (59 A 12) describes the same process.

Plato describes the universe as a well-ordered whole, kept in balance from within. He expresses this idea in terms which reproduce the expressions of Parmenides: ἰσοπαλές (63 A), τὴν πάντηι ὁμοιότητα (63 A), ἐκ μέσου ἴσον (34 B). Parmenides (28 B 8, verse 44) had described the universe as μεσσόθεν ἰσοπαλὲς πάντηι, "from the centre evenly balanced in all directions". This conception is also found in the *Phaedo* where Socrates explains that the heavens are in a state of equilibrium or ἰσορροπία (109 A). Besides Parmenides, this notion is also found in Anaximander. Kahn (1960, 78-79) even thinks that the words by which Socrates introduces his cosmology contain a reference to Anaximander: πέπεισμαι ὑπό τινος, "the views of a certain philosopher appear to me convincing" (*Phaed.* 108 E).

There is hardly any dialogue of Plato's in which we do not find back the Eleatic way of thinking. Most of all it manifests itself in Plato's search for absolute principles. The subjects of the dialogues often show his preference for Eleatic themes, but it is even more manifest that Plato's method of thinking is Eleatic to the core. In the so-called metaphysical dialogues, from the *Parmenides* onwards, Plato is largely building on Eleatic foundations and using the methods of Eleatic philosophy. In the *Timaeus*, a work which belongs to the same period of Plato's creative activity, he incorporates into his philosophy many

Pythagorean and mathematical theories. This may obscure our view of the presence of Eleatic principles, which, nevertheless, are unmistakable in the *Timaeus* as well. A systematic treatment of those elements has been given by Theiler (1924). In *Timaeus* 32 B-C Plato explains how the maker of the All manufactured the 'body of the cosmos' by joining the four elements in the proper proportions. Doing so he produced a whole, which was in harmony with itself and was kept together as a unity by Love. The word Φιλία for Love as a unifying principle makes it certain that Plato derived the theory of the four elements from Empedocles. Plato calls the whole of the cosmos a 'living being which is complete and perfect', ὅλον ζῷον τέλεον (32 D, 33 A, 34 B). This Whole is composed of parts which in their turn are perfect and which together form a unity (ἕν, 33A). This is straight from Parmenides, who had said that the whole of Being was complete (οὐλομελές) and perfect (τετελεσμένον ἐστίν) (DK 28 B 8, verses 4 and 42).

In the construction of the cosmos, the available quantity of each of the elements was used up (*Timaeus* 33 A). That is why it is impossible that another universe should have been created outside the universe we know. In this universe, as in a perfect and complete cosmos, all things have been incorporated. As a result of this, there are no forces outside which might attack or weaken it or make it grow old. Plato developed this world-vision on the basis of Parmenides' doctrine. To Parmenides as well, nothing could exist outside this cosmos, which was a spherical and perfect whole.

The same mixture of Empedoclean and Parmenidean elements is found in 58 A-B. Plato wants to explain here how the elements ceased moving at random and found their natural place in this universe. This was a result of the revolution of the All. By this revolution all things were tightened up as in a bundle and pressed together so as not to leave any empty space (σφίγγει πάντα καὶ κενὴν χώραν οὐδεμίαν ἐᾷ λείπεσθαι, 58 A). Plato's universe is a closed, well-rounded whole like that of Parmenides. To express its spherical form Plato uses the terms κυκλοτερής (58 A, 33 B), σφαιροειδές (33B) and εὔκυκλον (40 A), reminding us of Parmenides (fr. 8 verse 43):

εὐκύκλου σφαίρης ἐναλίγκιον ὄγκωι,

"in the shape of a well-rounded solid sphere."

Plato adds that this sphere has from the centre to the circumference the same distance in any direction:

33 B: ἐκ μέσου πάντῃ πρὸς τὰς τελευτὰς ἴσον ἀπέχον,

34 B: πανταχῇ τε ἐκ μέσου ἴσον,

once more borrowing his expressions from Parmenides (fr. 8 verse 44):

μεσσόθεν ἰσοπαλὲς πάντηι.

The time-cycle in this cosmos is taken by Plato to be the image of the immutable eternity of its divine archetype. The terms Plato uses are directly reminiscent of Parmenides:

37 E: λέγομεν γὰρ δὴ ὡς ἦν ἔστι τε καὶ ἔσται, τῇ δὲ τὸ ἔστι μόνον κατὰ τὸν ἀληθῆ λόγον προσήκει. "We say that it *was* or *is* or *will be*, but in relation to eternal being only 'is' is the proper expression, if we are to speak the truth."

This is an echo of Parmenides (fr. 8 verse 5):

οὐδέ ποτ' ἦν οὐδ' ἔσται.

It is probable that Parmenides did not treat the subject of time at great length, because his universe of Being is in essence a static universe. We may suppose that Plato discussed this point in more detail. His theory of time was part of a cosmology which was based on the theory of ideas. This visible world is created on the model of a divine and eternal world of ideas. The universe is characterized by the fact that its motions are ordered by time. The processes of change and coming-to-be suppose a before and after, but all this is only imitating the never changing eternity of the divine model. By making the distinction between the two worlds, that of eternal Ideas and that of sensible things, Plato marks off his own philosophy from Parmenides's. As a result of this we can observe an important difference along with the similarity. To Plato as well as to Parmenides this universe is a perfect Whole. Plato describes it as a perfect living being, even containing other living beings as its composing parts. In contrast to Parmenides, however, it is not a Being in its own right, but an imitation of a divine and eternal Being which in the same way contains within itself all incorporeal living beings (30 C). In Plato's description of the universe there is a term which shows the likeness and the difference between his and Parmenides' system of thought. In *Timaeus* 31 B Plato says that the Maker of this world made it after the likeness of the eternal perfect Being, and made it one world, not many. The heaven in this world is the 'one and only-begotten heaven', εἷς ὅδε μονογενὴς οὐρανός. If we compare this expression with that of Parmenides: ἀγένητον, "un-begotten", we see that Plato partly repeats and partly corrects him. To Parmenides there is no duality of the universe and its more divine model. Plato speaks of a perfect living cosmos, which exists in time and was begotten by a timeless Living Being.

The Pythagorean inspiration runs parallel to the Eleatic. Though

Plato derived the elements, and the principle of Love by which they are harmonized, from Empedocles, he gives the description of this harmony in a mathematical formula (*Timaeus* 32 A - C). Between the most solid element, earth, and the most rarefied, the elements of air and water come in as the two mean terms which are required between two cubic numbers in order to form a continued proportion:

$$\pi\tilde{\upsilon}\rho : \dot{\alpha}\acute{\eta}\rho = \dot{\alpha}\acute{\eta}\rho : \ddot{\upsilon}\delta\omega\rho = \ddot{\upsilon}\delta\omega\rho : \gamma\tilde{\eta}$$
$$a^3 \ : a^2b = a^2b : ab^2 \ = ab^2 \ : b^3$$

The cubic numbers denote the three-dimensional character of spatial things. The formula may at the same time be an echo of the famous problem of the duplication of the cube, which in antiquity was reduced to the problem of finding two mean proportionals in continued proportion between two given straight lines (cf. Heath 1921, I 244-270).

Having harmonized the elements in this way, Plato calls the formula an ἀναλογία (32 C).

As we saw in our chapter III, the Pythagoreans did not only occupy themselves with mathematical theory, but also had a very special cosmology. Their theories about the evolution of the universe were related to the Orphic myths. In these myths it was assumed that the universe was an animated being, which had developed from a primordial germ, or, as the Orphics called it, a primeval Egg. Taken at its face-value, this mythical cosmogony may seem to have little relation to Plato's theories about the construction of the universe by the Demiurge. Perusing the *Timaeus* we can discover that even the mythical tradition is not absent. Plato does not only, on the Pythagorean example, attempt a mathematization of his cosmology, he also incorporates into this cosmology the view that the universe is a living being (33 B - 34 A). In a truly philosophical spirit he undertakes to adjust the image. The cosmos has a spherical shape, because a perfect creation should have the most perfect of all shapes. It is self-sufficient and therefore it needs no organs for assimilating food, which, moreover cannot exist outside the cosmos itself. It has neither eyes nor ears, because nothing can be seen or heard outside itself. It has no respiration because there is no air to be inhaled from outside. This way of correcting the ancient mythical image was in itself part of the Ionian tradition. In our first two chapters we have seen examples of it in the philosophy of Anaximander and Xenophanes. As a method of thinking it is found throughout the history of ancient Platonism. Bréhier, in his introductions to Plotinus' *Enneads*, designed it as the method of "adjusting the images".

192

From the short survey here given we can see that Plato built his cosmology on the firm foundations of Eleatic philosophy, to which were added a method of arithmetizing inspired by Pythagorean traditions, and the theory of the four elements which had been developed by Empedocles. If we are to look for a possible Democritean influence, we shall have to discover this influence in Plato's theory of the fundamental structure of the elements. This theory was worked out by Plato on the pattern of the geometrical theory of the regular solids. It shows that Plato made an attempt at a mathematization of cosmology, clearly inspired by the Pythagorean school. In our opinion no element of this theory is related to any element of the atomic theory.

First of all, there is no trace in Plato's dialogues of any problem of infinite divisibility as a starting-point for an atomic theory. This may seem a superfluous remark because there was no trace of this problem in Democritus' theories either.

Secondly, an essential difference between the two theories consists in the fact that to Democritus the atoms have a great variety of shapes, whereas to Plato there were only four fundamental figures. This is the same number as that of the elements. To Plato these elements were not the ultimate substrate. He tries to develop a theory in which the elemental patterns are reduced to one first principle of spatial configuration. In the atomic doctrine the atoms have an infinity of shapes, and no attempt is made to reduce these shapes to an ultimate unity.

Thirdly, in Plato's *Timaeus* not a single word is found which could convey the idea of "atom" or could remind us of this conception of Democritus. Plato uses the expressions σώματα, "bodily figures" (53 E), and εἶδος, "characteristic shape" (54 D). This latter term is the same which he uses for his Ideas. It is true that there is a probability that Democritus used the term ἰδέαι for his atoms (see above, p. 140, 153). Even so, the term must have had a quite different sense in the two systems, and, what is more, the relationship would not have escaped Aristotle's notice. In the *Timaeus* we find two more terms designating the first principles of material substance: στοιχεῖον and σπέρμα (56 B), the latter being reminiscent of Anaxagoras (fr. 4). According to Eudemus (Simpl. in *Phys.* 7, 13) the term στοιχεῖον was coined for philosophical use by Plato himself.

The most important difference lies in the function which is attributed to the fundamental principle of atoms, respectively elements, within the framework of the theory. In the atomic doctrine the charateristics of the atoms themselves are constant, only their order and position can be changed. This, together with the principle that the number of atoms is infinite and that the empty space, too, is infinite, means that the number of possible combinations is infinite. The atoms have their natural function in a theory in which combination is the decisive factor. Therefore, the theory is essentially a continuation of the traditional mixture-theories of the Ionian philosophers. Differences in the combination of the composing particles produce different characteristics in the thing produced. In contrast to this Plato tries to explain that even the ground-patterns of the four elements are such that they can change *into one-another*. His theory is, in essence, not a physical theory, but a mathematization of the theory of the elements, by which he attempts to find the existence of a last unique substratum for all sensible bodies. In this point, Plato was probably inspired by what was the dominating element in his thought: Parmenidean metaphysics and its search for unity.

In order to show by what process the elements can be changed into one another, Plato assumes the faces of the regular solids to be divided into triangles as follows:

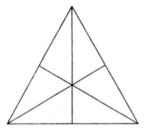 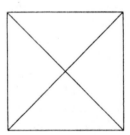

By thus dividing the faces of one of the regular solids into the elementary triangles it is possible to rearrange the triangles so as to form one of the other regular solids. We can see at once that these solids, which Plato calls "figures" and "shapes" are not ultimate smallest particles, like the atoms, but rather fundamental structures, characteristic of each of the elements. Plato says nothing about the dimensions of these structures, nor about the question whether or not the division will go on indefinitely.

The elementary triangles into which the faces of the solids can be divided are only two:

194

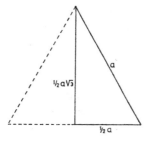
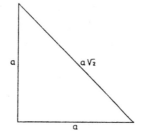

The first of these two, the half of an equilateral triangle, is described by Plato (*Tim.* 54 B) as the triangle of which the square on the one side is three times the square on the lesser side, that is, the right-angled triangle in which the sides are in the proportion of $1 : \sqrt{3}$. In the second triangle the side and the hypotenuse are in the proportion of $1 : \sqrt{2}$. It seems plausible to suppose that Plato's choice of these two elementary triangles was determined by the fact that they contain the irrational lengths of $a\sqrt{2}$ and $a\sqrt{3}$, representing the two most elementary instances of irrational proportions. It is possible that they were, historically, the first proportions the irrationality of which could mathematically be proved (cf. Von Fritz 1945). Even without deciding this question we may suppose that the two triangles were attractive to Plato because of the simplicity of their forms. A division of the equilateral triangle and of the square naturally results in these two types of triangles.

Plato was aware that his division, resulting in these two types of triangles is only half-way a solution of the problem how elements can change into one another. By this method only three of the elements can be changed into one another. These are fire (tetrahedron), air (octahedron), and water (icosahedron), because only in these three cases the regular solids have faces consisting of equilateral triangles. The element of earth (the cube) has squares as its faces, which cannot be divided into triangles in such a manner that these triangles can be rearranged into the faces of the three other elements. Plato explains this in *Timaeus* 54 C, and he repeats in 56 D that earth cannot be transformed into another element (cf. Rivaud, éd. Timée p. 77-79).

The construction of the regular solids explains how the other three are transformed into one another (56 D - E). One unit of water, if broken up by the sharp atoms of fire, can be reconstituted into one unit of fire and two units of air. Water is an icosahedron having in its faces 40 elementary triangles. Fire is a pyramid having in its faces 8 elementary triangles. The 40 triangles of water can be regrouped into one unit of fire $= 8$, and two units of air $= 2 \times 16 = 32$ triangles. In the same way, the segments (τμήματα) into which air (octahedron) can be divided produce two units (σώματα) of fire (tetrahedron). A third example (56 E): two-and-a-half units of air ($= 2\frac{1}{2} \times 16 = 40$ elementary triangles) can produce one unit of water. The last of these three instances once more proves that Plato intended to give a transformation-theory, not a mixture-theory. In the atomic system the idea that an atom could be halved is out of the question.

Plato confined the number of his ground-patterns (εἴδη, σώματα, στοιχεῖα, σπέρματα) to four. It was clearly his intention to find a last unifying substratum for the elements. As far as our sources go, it is not possible to find in Plato's theory any parallel to the way in which the nature of matter is dealt with in the atomic system.

B. IONIAN ELEMENTS IN THE TIMAEUS. PLATO'S χώρα

Our survey of the various traditions incorporated by Plato in his *Timaeus* has still to be completed by what we can trace of Anaxagorean influence. Anaxagoras' presence in the *Timaeus* is unmistakable, and it is the presence of a philosopher whose views have been adopted. This might cause some surprise if we take into account what Plato, in earlier dialogues, said about Anaxagoras' theories. As early as in the *Apologia* he is mentioned (26 D). The public prosecutor, Meletus, here accuses Socrates of not venerating sun and moon as gods, because, he says, Socrates thinks the sun is a kind of stone and the moon something like our earth. Socrates answers that the prosecutor must have mistaken Socrates for Anaxagoras, whose books could be bought in Athens for a few pennies. We must take this as an indication that Anaxagoras' theories were very popular in Athens. Socrates is critical of them and says that, if these theories were really his it would be easy to ridicule him, because the theories were so utterly stupid. We get the impression that what the prosecutor apparently had in mind, was in accordance with the general opinion in Athens.

If Anaxagoras' philosophy was very popular, it is possible that Socrates, simply because he was a philosopher, fell a victim to the same suspicion which had resulted in Anaxagoras' being banished. Philosophers must have been looked upon in Athens as either dangerous or ridiculous persons. We can still see in Aristophanes' *Clouds* that making fun of a philosopher must have been to the taste of the Athenian audience. It has been observed that, as a matter of fact, it was not the philosophy of Anaxagoras but that of Diogenes of Apollonia which was represented in Aristophanes' comedy. Because Diogenes was of the school of Anaxagoras, we may assume that a special denomination of Ionian philosophy was dominant at Athens for some decades. This would explain why Socrates' own convictions were not understood by his judges. If the description given by Plato in his *Phaedo* (97 C - 99 D) applies to the historical Socrates, we must assume that Socrates opposed some of Anaxagoras' doctrines. Plato makes Socrates say that, when first hearing of Anaxagoras' theories, he had been pleased to notice that the dominating principle in his philosophy was a supreme intellect or Nous. He had supposed that this Nous would order all things with a view to what was best, and accordingly had been disillusioned when the Ionian philosopher failed to explain things on this principle. It was just air and fire and water and the vortex that were given as causes of the universe, whereas the question why the universe should be as it is, and why it was necessary that it should be so, was not paid attention to. Socrates thinks Anaxagoras should have made a distinction between the real cause and the concomitant cause, the latter being described as the necessary conditions for a cause to come into action (*Phaed.* 99 B).

In our sixth chapter (p. 126) we saw that it was probably wishful reading that induced the Platonic Socrates to expect a causal theory of this kind in Anaxagoras. One should not forget, after all, that Plato's *Phaedo* was a literary work, and that the author himself knew better about Anaxagoras. There is a passage in the *Cratylus* (413 C, cf. above, p. 124) which categorically confirms that the Nous had a function quite different from that which Socrates required. Anaxagoras conceived the universe as having developed from an initial turbulent state, from which all kinds of substances were separated by a rotatory movement or vortex. By a process of separating and mixing a great many things were produced. The evolution was, from its initial state, directed by the Nous, an immanent divine force, probably a rationalized version of older mythical deities, who governed life (see our Ch. VI). Plato follows Anaxagoras in the outline of his theory, adding, however, other elements, and introducing some alterations. He adopts Anaximander's Nous, but he lays more emphasis on its teleological function by incarnating it, so to say, in the figure of the Demiurge. Moreover, to Plato a Nous must be in a Soul, just as human reason can only live in a human soul, and, accordingly, he admits the existence of a World-Soul. Most important is that the Demiurge builds the Universe according to an eternal archetype, which is the world of Ideas. When building the universe, the Demiurge did not take whirling smallest particles as the ultimate substratum out of which things were created. Plato drafts a theory of fundamental material structures by which he clearly aims at finding a last and unique metaphysical principle for material being.

Besides Anaxagoras' Nous we also find his undifferentiated primordial mass (πάντα ὁμοῦ, B 1, B 6) as the starting-point for evolution in the *Timaeus* (30 A). The Maker and Father of this universe took the whole visible cosmos in his hands, not in a condition of rest but as a turbulent mass. He ordered its disorderly motion by giving it a Soul and putting this Soul under the guidance of a World-Reason. By doing so he made the cosmos into a ζῷον ἔμψυχον ἔννουν τε, an animated Being, endowed with Reason. We can see at once that Pythagorean elements have been joined to the views which Plato derived from Anaxagoras. The universe as an animated being is a Pythagorean inheritance, whereas the conception of a World-Reason inhabiting a World-Soul is Plato's own.

The disorderly moving primordial mass is found once more in *Timaeus* 52 D as part of the description of the "nursing mother of all becoming." Anaxagoras' vortex is here compared to the motion of a sieve for the winnowing of corn, probably because in Plato's theory the agent is a consciously working Demiurge. The description of the process, however, offers a clear parallel to Anaxagoras. The "nurse of becoming" received the forms of fire, water, earth and air, but she moved unsteadily in all directions (52 E), and her characteristics could not be identified. The movement of the sieve caused the four elements to be separated from the mass (διακρινόμενα 52 E, the same term as in Anaxagoras B 12) and find their natural places. After that the construction of the cosmos was started. It was given shape by means of "forms and numbers", εἴδεσί τε καὶ ἀριθμοῖς (53 B). The numbers, as a Pythagorean concept, and the elements, derived from Empedocles, have been added to an evolutionary theory on the pattern of Anaxagoras'. The characteristic forms or ideas (εἴδη) are Plato's own.

In the construction of his theories, Plato constantly unites different conceptions into one vision. He gives them a characteristic form and orders them on the pattern of his own essential doctrines. This

198

way of integrating various points of view into the texture of one argument may be observed in other dialogues as well. In *Laws* XII 967 Plato has an argument with those philosophers whose theories are "full of stones, earth and other inanimate bodies determining and ruling the development of the universe." Some lines might even suggest that the argument is directed against Democritus, but then Plato says that some of those philosophers assumed a Nous to be the cause of all things in the universe. After having posited this cause of all things, they later abandoned it and again attributed all causality to material things. This criticism runs so exactly parallel to that given in the *Phaedo* (97 C) that it is impossible to think of other philosophers than Anaxagoras.

A similar case is *Laws* X 889. Here he starts the discussion by mentioning the four elements, which may make us think of Empedocles. The adversaries are indicated as philosophers who say that the material elements exist "by nature and by chance" (φύσει καὶ τύχῃ), but not in any way as a result of craftsmanship (τέχνη 889 B). On the same page the accusation turns into an attack on philosophers who say that the gods exist "not by nature (φύσει) but as a result of craftsmanship and convention" (τέχνη καὶ νόμοις 889 E). The two accusations could be brought to agree if we suppose that Plato puts forward as his own opinion that the material elements are a result of divine craftsmanship, which is in harmony with the *Timaeus*, and, secondly, that the gods exist by nature (φύσει), which is a somewhat unfortunate expression for conveying Plato's notion of gods. In 889 C the objection is that in these philosophies life is not under the guidance of a Nous. The discussion in 889 D suggests that Plato is attacking theories of the Sophists. Throughout the passage the expressions are such that any materialistic doctrine may have been meant, for they cover the whole range of typical expressions, such as φύσει, τύχη, τέχνη, νόμῳ, κρᾶσις τῶν ἐναντίων, ἐξ ἀνάγκης, which remind us respectively of the Sophists, of the Ionian school, and, possibly, even of Democritus (ἀνάγκη). England (*ad Laws* 889 b 4) says about this text: "The mention of the four elements suggests that it was not the Atomistic system, of either Leucippus or Democritus, against which the Athenian's arguments are specially directed. It is against any system which denies ψυχή or νοῦς to have had any share in creation, that he is fighting, and though the arguments put into the mouths of his opponents remind us now of one school, now of another, he probably had no particular school in mind." Tate (1936) has analogous comments.

199

It seems best to assume that what Plato is attacking are the materialistic elements in various cosmologies at once. He does not reject these cosmologies as a whole, as is clear from the fact that he derives important elements in his own theories from the same philosophers whose materialistic views he rejects. Plato took the doctrine of the four elements from Empedocles, but he added a theory of his own to give it another meaning. He borrowed the evolutionary point of view from Ionian philosophy, but the whole process of evolution had to be ordered according to "numbers and ideas", that is, a theory of evolution was combined with Pythagorean mathematics and Platonic metaphysics. It is not strange that Plato should attack the materialistic views of Anaxagoras, while at the same time adopting his principle of a Nous and adapting it to his own doctrines.

There are two conceptions in Plato's philosophy which we may rightly attribute to the influence of Anaxagoras: the doctrine of the two kinds of αἰτία, and that of Νοῦς. Neither doctrine is found in Plato's dialogues in the form it had in the work of Anaxagoras. Plato's method of adapting them is perhaps best described when we say that Anaxagoras' theories were the direct occasion for Plato to formulate his views on these two points.

Plato makes a fundamental distinction between cause and concomitant cause (αἰτία-συναιτία). The two causes are found as early as in the *Phaedo* (99 B), where they are described respectively as the "cause for the being of a thing", and "that without which the cause never could be a cause" that is: the necessary condition for its working. In the *Timaeus* (46 C - D) he says about the concomitant causes that the God accepted their assistance when he wanted to realize his idea of the best possible. The secondary causes, Plato says, are regarded by the majority of thinkers not as secondary causes but as first causes of all things, realizing a universe via processes of heating and cooling, condensation and rarefaction, and the like. These causes, however, can only be secondary, because neither a Nous nor a reason can be in them. A Nous can only live in a soul. Therefore the cosmos has a soul, as Plato has argued in more detail earlier in the dialogue (30 B, 34 B). In *Timaeus* 68 E - 69 A the distinction between first and secondary causes is once more dealt with. Here he calls the latter the "subservient causes", and "the necessary causes", probably indicating that what he means by this is the natural laws inherent in the material world. The first cause is divine and brings about whatever is good in things.

Plato's theory of the two kinds of causes is closely connected with that of the Nous, as is evident from the arguments in *Philebus* 28 C - E and 30 A - E. In the latter passage Plato points out that in our bodies a cause is at work which provides them with a soul, sets the bodily organism going and cures whatever is hurt. He designates this cause as a "complete and multiform wisdom", πᾶσαν καὶ παντοίαν σοφίαν. In the same way the animated body (σῶμα ἔμψυχον) of the universe is ruled by a powerful cause, which may be called "wisdom and Nous", σοφία καὶ Νοῦς. This Nous or supreme cosmic wisdom lives in a soul, the World-Soul (*Phil.* 30 D), which makes the body of the cosmos into an animated body (σῶμα ἔμψυχον, *Phil.* 30 A). Throughout the passage the Nous is said to be a cause or αἴτιον, by which expression clearly the first kind of cause is meant, because it is emphasized that it orders all things with a view to the good. The argument runs parallel to the arguments in *Timaeus* 30 B, 34 B, 46 C. In *Phil.* 30 D it is expressly stated that the Nous is of the category of what is called a cause, a statement which is repeated in *Phil.* 31 A.

In the argument two lines are found which can hardly be related to any philosopher but Anaxagoras. Plato says in *Phil.* 30 D that his doctrine "is in harmony with what the ancients have explained, namely, that a supreme Intellect rules the universe." From the texts quoted above we can see (1) that Plato's theories of Νοῦς and αἰτία in the *Timaeus* and in the *Philebus* are closely related, and (2) that Plato elaborated these theories by taking those of Anaxagoras as a starting-point. We get the same impression when in the *Phaedo* the theory of the two kinds of causes is developed in a discussion with Anaxagoras. Plato's theory of the two kinds of αἰτία originated from his criticism on Anaxagoras' conception of causality. The cosmological principle of a Nous was found by Plato in Anaxagoras' philosophy, but then incorporated into a quite different vision of the universe.

So far the texts quoted have a wider scope than just that of the material substratum. We have given the essentials of some of Plato's cosmological doctrines in order to show the framework within which his notions must be explained. We saw that, above all, Plato was inspired by "Italian and Sicilian Muses", that is, by Pythagorean and Eleatic philosophy. Besides this Western inspiration we find the influence of Ionian philosophy (cf. Skemp 1942, Ch. II on: Ionian elements in the *Timaeus*). Plato derived the theory of the four elements from Empedocles, and perhaps also that of the vortex or δίνη, which is found in Anaxagoras as well. From the text of Plato's works we can

201

perceive Anaxagoras' influence, when Plato describes the evolution of the universe in terms of aggregation and dispersion, μῖξις and διάκρισις. The discussion with Anaxagoras gave rise to Plato's theory of a dual causality. The conception of a cosmic Nous was taken by Plato from Anaxagoras.

In the texts we have adduced, the references to the Italian philosophers and to Anaxagoras are unambiguous. Of Democritus no trace can be found. It is true that a certain reservation must be made, because we have so few authentic texts of Democritus. In the texts of Plato's dialogues, however, there is, in our opinion, no passage which can prove with reasonable certainty that Plato had Democritus' theories in mind when writing it. Our arguments are essentially of two kinds: (1) when a certain expression seems to be related to the atomic theories, it can generally be found in the theories of more than one philosopher, and (2) the internal structure of Plato's theories suggests quite different analogies from those which atomism can offer.

As regards Plato's theory of the mathematical ground-patterns of the elements, it is hardly possible to find any parallels in it to the doctrines of Democritus. At first sight Plato's theory makes us think that he is giving his particular version of an atomic doctrine. When reading carefully, however, we see that Plato did not speak of smallest particles having inalterable shapes and constant qualities. The fundamental structures which he describes can be broken up into parts, which may again be joined to build up a different whole. This explains how the elements, that of earth excepted, can be constructed out of the composing parts of one another. Even the term "atom" or any equivalent expression is not found in the *Timaeus*. What we do find is the term εἶδος, the same which elsewhere denotes the Ideas. Plato's theory of matter is inspired by the desire to find a common undetermined substratum which will be determined by "ideas" or "forms" (εἴδη), in this case by the mathematical configurations of the regular solids.

We have given a somewhat circumstantial account of Plato's theory of fundamental structures in order to show how Plato's theory of matter is to be set in perspective. From what we have found it may be possible to throw some light on another problem.

When Plato has finished his exposition of the workings of the

Demiurge and of the function of the Nous, he goes on to deal with the processes of becoming in this world, where ἀνάγκη and the secondary causes play their parts. The Demiurge must persuade these resisting forces to give some voluntary contribution to his aims (*Tim.* 48 A). As we saw in the first part of this chapter (p. 179-180), the abrupt transition made Hammer-Jensen think that Plato had found a new theory when he was writing the *Timaeus*. She assumed that it had been a theory of Democritus. Her argument is that, from 48 A onwards, Plato introduces a new principle of being, a "third kind" (τρίτον γένος, 48 E). This third kind is the "receiving medium", characterized by Plato as an ὑποδοχή, "receptacle", τιθήνη, "nursing mother", ἐκμαγεῖον, "matrix", or simply as χώρα, "space". Hammer-Jensen understood this as an adaptation of a theory of Democritus. She supposed that Democritus had assumed a common material substrate for all sensible things.

We saw that attributing a theory of this kind to Democritus was an Aristotelean fiction, and, moreover, that the empty space in Democritus' theory, though it had an indirect relation to Eleatic thought, was essentially a descendant of the Ionian ἄπειρον (p. 166, 169, 170). The question, then, rises, what Plato's χώρα was meant to be. Starting from the conviction that Plato must have known the atomic theory, one might be inclined to suppose that his χώρα was a new version of Democritus' principle of infinite empty space. We shall try to elucidate this problem by tracing the probable origins of Plato's χώρα.

The space out of which the configurations of the elementary solids are built, is, in the framework of Plato's theory, quite a different thing from the empty space in which, according to Democritus, an infinite number of atoms is moving. The way in which Plato constructed his theory suggests that he wanted to explain in what ultimate substratum the material things find their unity. This is confirmed by his remark in *Timaeus* 48 B, that, though his predecessors had posited the four elements as first principles (ἀρχάς), nobody had as yet dealt with the question of how the elements were generated. Plato here uses a remarkable expression: πρὸ τῆς οὐρανοῦ γενέσεως, "before the heaven was generated" (48 B). In the mythical style of ꞁPlato's exposition this can have no other meaning but: the elements find the ultimate foundation of their existence in some kind of being which is not material. The expression "before the visible universe came into existence" can make sense only if we are to understand that there is a more basic origin from which the elements have sprung. Till now, Plato says, we have talked about fire, water, air and earth, assuming that everybody knew what these things were, and so they were even assigned a place as στοιχεῖα τοῦ παντός, "the elements of the universe" (στοιχεῖα: the letters of a word). We shall try, therefore, Plato says (48 D), to make a fresh start in order to put forward a theory of the ultimate substratum of the elements.

The same argument is repeated in 49 CDE. Plato here describes, in terms which betray the Ionian origin of the theory, the processes by which the elements are supposed to change into one another: condensation and rarefaction, heating and cooling, aggregation and separation. The result of all this is that there is a cyclical process by which the elements are transformed into one another. Nevertheless, we are accustomed to designate fire and water as a "this", whereas their incessant changing should have induced us to designate them as a "such", that is, as passing conditions of things. By calling them a "this" we fail to see what the underlying subject of these conditions is.

This argument is essentially Eleatic. Changing things are only passing conditions or appearances, they have no being of their own. It is not possible to say of these things what they are by themselves, αὐτὰ καθ' αὐτὰ (51 C). This last expression is characteristic of Plato's theory of ideas. Plato takes fire as an example and asks the question: "Are we to assume that there is a fire-by-itself?" Then follows an outline of his traditional theory, with the addition, however, of the "third kind" (51 E - 52 A).

When we survey the whole exposition, we see that it starts at 47 E, when Plato interrupted the course of his own argument in order to "make a fresh start." Plato first discusses the theory of the elements, emphasizing that the elements do not suffice as first principles, and that we must look for an ultimate unique substrate of the elements. This makes it necessary (48 E) to introduce a third principle or "kind" which had, so far, not been taken into consideration. With the aid of this third kind Plato is able to explain that the elements are not a "this" but a "such", not substances, but conditions of an underlying substrate. He compares the substrate with a mouldable stuff such as gold, out of which all kinds of forms are made (50 A), and with the neutral ointments of the perfumers (50 E). This passage is concluded by a reference to the theory of ideas (51 E - 52 A), immediately to be followed by the enumeration, repeated here from 49 A, of the "three

204

factors" (52 A - B). The "first kind" is that of the realities which always remain identical with themselves, that is, the Ideas. The second is that of the perceptable things, which have been generated and are always moving, now appearing now disappearing. The third kind is that of "ever-existing space" (τὸ τῆς χώρας ἀεί), imperishable and providing a place for all things that come into existence. This brings the argument back to its starting-point in 47 E.

The argument taken as a whole makes it clear that, if we want to see things in perspective, we should place the doctrine of the "three factors", as it is exposed by Plato, against the background of the theory of Ideas and of Eleatic philosophy. This implies an important conclusion. If to the exposition of the theory of Ideas and of the Eleatic doctrine of true being the enumeration of the "three factors" is added, we may wonder if the "third kind", that of χώρα or space, should not also be explained by an Eleatic background.

The third kind, the "receptacle", is a necessary condition for things to come into existence, while it is not incorporated into the material existence itself of things. It may, therefore, be included in the category of the "secondary causes", because the receptacle is that, without which the images of the Ideas could not come into existence. It may call for some closer argument, if we suppose that Plato's receptacle was a version of the Eleatic concept of the Void. The difficulty lies in the fact that the Eleatics denied all real existence to the Void, which was regarded as "not-being" or μὴ ὄν. The concept of μὴ ὄν, however, received a new development in Plato's philosophy. Moreover, Plato's description of the "third kind" has many features in common with a description of not-being. We can see from the texts of the *Timaeus* that Plato considered his receptacle as a spatial reality (52 B): "The third kind is the concept of eternal space, not admitting any perishing and offering a place for all things that come into existence; ... we say, therefore, with a dreamlike expression, that it is necessary for all things to exist in a place and to occupy a certain space."

As far as we know Plato did not have any examples of earlier thinkers for this systematic analysis of the process of becoming, resulting in the description of three principles. It must be considered his own work, just as the theory of Ideas. Aristotle, in his theory of εἶδος, ὕλη and στέρησις, adapted Plato's conception to the requirements of his own system of thought.

It is a difficult problem to determine how Plato came to admit a spatial substrate as a necessary third principle for things to come into existence. The general tendency of Plato's theory of matter, however, may give us a hint. We saw that this theory had two characteristic qualities. Firstly it was an attempt to find an underlying unity in the multiplicity of material things. In this respect the theory was inspired by the dominating trend of Plato's philosophy: the Eleatic way of thinking. Secondly it was worked out on the pattern of a mathematical theory. Here the inspiration was clearly Pythagorean: material things are characterized by geometrical figures, by "forms and numbers." When the geometrical figures are broken up into their components, we find an ultimate spatial substructure of the elements. The ultimate elements, the "letters" out of which material things are composed, are the triangles, that is, the ultimate substructure of matter is a spatial configuration.

The concept of space has, as we have seen, its own history (cf. above pp. 161-170). It started with the Pythagorean concept of "unbounded breath or void", which was rejected by Parmenides on the ground that it was a not-being, μὴ ὄν. We saw that Melissus expressed himself on the subject in terms which have induced some scholars to think that Leucippus was reacting to Melissus when he stated, for the first time in history, that "full and void" are the elements of material things (above, p. 165-6). It is possible that by this way the impulse of Eleatic thinking reached the atomists. We think it more probable, however, that Democritus was following the Ionian tradition, and that he was reacting in particular to Anaxagoras' doctrine of very small, indefinitely divisible particles. We may, for the moment, leave aside the development leading up to the atomic theory, because, if the history of empty space is continued in Plato's work, Plato at any rate is building on Eleatic foundations and reacting directly to Parmenides.

When we compare the Eleatic theories to Plato's, one of the differences we cannot fail to notice is, that Plato paid much more attention to the multiplicity of things in the visible world. The difference is not so much one of doctrine as one of emphasis. Parmenides had tried by powerful arguments to establish the doctrine that Being is immutable and unique. To Plato the changing things of this world themselves deserve attention as images of the eternal being of the Ideas. At a critical point in his development he even framed a theory which was to account for the processes of change and coming-to-be. The core of this theory is found in the *Sophistes* on the well-known pages where Plato argues for the existence of not-being. In this dialogue not-being or μὴ ὄν coïncides with the category of Otherness or ἕτερον. Not-being in the sense in which Plato explains it here designates the characteristics which in every being are added to those qualities which are thought essential to it. The doctrine, therefore, is a metaphysical one. It is designed as a general theory, which applies to all kinds of being, in the first place to the Ideas.

We must emphasize this general character of the doctrine of the μὴ ὄν in the *Sophistes*, because it must be excluded beforehand that the principle of the μὴ ὄν should have been intended by Plato as the principle of sensible things as opposed to the ὄν of the Ideas. The μὴ ὄν is found in both realms, in that of incorporeal being as well as in the sensible things of this world. On the other hand the μὴ ὄν had a long history as a term that conveyed the idea of not-being in the spatial sense, that is the idea of a Void or empty space. It is not too hazardous to think that in the *Timaeus* two lines come together: that of Plato's own metaphysical principle of the μὴ ὄν as Otherness, and the historical influence of the concept of μὴ ὄν as empty space. Plato's theory of χώρα was conceived within the framework of the theory of Ideas, and it is easy to recognize its Eleatic background. It seems obvious that, if the Eleatics had dealt with the problem of a spatial μὴ ὄν and if Plato had accepted a metaphysical principle of μὴ ὄν, he may have thought of the Eleatic problem when framing his theory of χώρα in the *Timaeus*.

Though our argument cannot be conclusive, it is in harmony with the texts. If it is sound, and if the χώρα in Plato's *Timaeus* is to be regarded as Plato's version of the Eleatic principle of the Void as a not-being, we must at any rate give attention to a point where the theory comes on the verge of inconsistency. The receptacle is described as formless or ἄ-μορφον (50 D), because it is devoid of all form, and has no communication with the ideas (πάντων ἐκτὸς εἰδῶν, 50 E, 51 A). However, the receptacle has a function of its own as a necessary condition for things to come into existence. This at least suggests the idea that the receptacle is a substance itself, not simply an ontologically necessary element in the constitution of things. Moreover, in describing it Plato must inevitably state that it has the character of Sameness, ταὐτόν, just because it remains true to its own function (ἐκ τῆς ἑαυτῆς οὐκ ἐξίσταται δυνάμεως, 50 B). This logically induces one to think that it exercises an action by its own, being a reality in its own right. Therefore, Plato must grant that, "it even partakes of the nature of the ideas, though in a very poor and clumsy way."

The view that Plato's χώρα in the *Timaeus* is an adapted form of the Eleatic concept of the not-being of empty space, must necessarily remain a hypothesis. It may, however, receive some further confirmation from the historical background. The conception of a theory in which three principles are required to explain the being of material things, viz. the Idea, its image and the receptacle, is Plato's own work. This does not exclude, however, that elements of this conception may be found in earlier philosophies. Now if we ask where Plato may have found empty space as a philosophical problem, only one answer is possible: in the Eleatic school. Once we accept that this was the historical origin of Plato's theory, we find this view confirmed by the terms in which he explains the theory. The whole description is framed on Eleatic and ontological views. The receptacle, as a receiving medium, is absolutely opposed to the εἴδη, the eternal ideas (51 A). The images of ideas, present in the receptacle, are the mathematical forms of the elements. The receptacle is characterized by its sameness and as a "this" (50 B, 49 D - E), but this is paradoxical, for it suggests that it is a subject in its own right, whereas it is only the spatial medium in which images of the ideas make their appearance. It is in the unfortunate condition of being so purely a μὴ ὄν that it comes near to substantiating the metaphysical notion of the μὴ ὄν which Plato wanted to convey by the theory of the *Sophistes*.

The question may be raised whether the conception of this spatial receptacle cannot have originated from the tradition of Ionian cosmology, because so many elements of the Ionian tradition are present in the *Timaeus*. The answer to this question must once more be found by consulting the internal structure of Plato's theory. If Plato's χώρα were a descendant of the ancient Anaximandrean ἄπειρον, it would have to be a first principle, which would be transformed into the various material substances by a process of condensation and rarefaction, or by aggregation and separation. The doctrine as a whole would have to be evolutionary. We should expect the substrate-matter to be present itself, be it in a transformed condition, in the many perceptible things of this world.

Plato knew the Ionian theories of evolution, as is evident from *Tim.* 49 B C, where he describes in detail the processes of liquefying and congealing, condensation and rarefaction, ignition and extinction. When beginning his account of these theories (49 A), he says that

208

his "third kind" is the "receptacle of all becoming, as a kind of nursing mother" (τιθήνη). If one should want to describe the receptacle as if it were a primordial mass from which things are split off, or a nursing-ground out of which the sensible world grew, nothing would be easier. One might even make use of Plato's own terminology to make him expound an Ionian evolutionary theory. It may be doubted whether, in that case, one would have read carefully enough.

The image of the τιθήνη is developed in even greater detail in 52 DE, where it is described as taking on the form of the four elements and appearing in all kinds of shapes. This would strengthen the impression that the substrate is absorbed or transformed into the existing things. The description in 52 DE is a more detailed repetition of that in 49 B - C, where it served as an introduction to the actual problem. Neither the Ionian theories nor the theory of the four elements can, in Plato's opinion, offer a satisfactory solution. The actual problem is: in what do things appear and out of what do they disappear? Plato explains this in 49 E. The expression he uses suggests that he does not take the "receptacle" in the sense of a primordial unqualified mass which is transformed into things, but in the sense of a medium in which they appear.

It is true that in this passage the prevailing impression is that we have to do with a mouldable stuff. The examples which Plato uses: the gold which is kneaded and given form, the ointment which is to receive the odours, have the same feature of a mouldable material in common. If we pass on to 52 B - C, where the same argument is repeated, we see that Plato gives a more detailed explanation of his intentions, entirely formulated in spatial concepts. Plato here uses the expressions χώρα, space, ἕδρα, seat, ἔν τινι τόπῳ, in a certain place. He says that an image, which is always a reproduction of an original, must for this reason come into existence in a medium different from itself (ἐν ἑτέρῳ, 52 C), or else it will be an absolute nothing (μηδὲν τὸ παράπαν). The expression *"in* a medium" occurs throughout the argument: it is found in 49 E (ἐν ᾧ), 50 C, 50 D, 52 B (ἔν τινι τόπῳ), 50 C (ἐν ἑτέρῳ). The images of the ideas "go in and out", as we find it expressed in 49 E (ἐν ᾧ φαντάζεται, ἐκεῖθεν ἀπόλλυται), 50 C (εἰσιόντα-ἐξιόντα). The substrate itself does not take part in the being of the sensible things. It only provides a seat for them to come into existence, while remaining itself completely outside of (πάντων ἐκτὸς εἰδῶν 50 E and 51 A), and untouched by the form (ἄμορφον ἁπασῶν τῶν ἰδεῶν 50 D). The term ὑποδοχή, "receptacle", is in harmony with this conception.

209

It is found in its verbal form in the explanation given by Plato in 50 B (δέχεται), where the substrate is described as τῆς τὰ πάντα δεχομένης σώματα φύσεως, "that which is to receive all sensible things."

The terms in which Plato gives his explanations, and the images he uses confirm the conclusion which was already drawn from the internal structure of the theory in our earlier argument. Plato's χώρα cannot be regarded as a continuation of the ancient ἄπειρον because in that case the substrate would have to be transformed into the sensible things and partake in their being. Plato, on the contrary, wants to describe a substrate underlying these transformations. The Ionian theories, well known to him, did not offer him a satisfactory solution, because he wanted to raise the question of the ultimate substratum of all material things. He tried to find an answer to this question by using the Eleatic methods of thinking. We may, tentatively, suppose that the most probable origin of Plato's theory of χώρα was the tradition of the Eleatic μὴ ὄν.

Neither the concept of ἄπειρον as Plato uses it nor his theory of χώρα can be compared to the theories of Democritus. The concept of ἄπειρον, as we shall see below, is taken by Plato in a mathematical and Pythagorean sense. His χώρα is probably a descendant of the Eleatic tradition. In the history of early Greek philosophy there is an ἄπειρον which is quite different from the concept used by Plato. It is the Ionian ἄπειρον, ultimately originating from Anaximander. This ἄπειρον is represented in the infinite cosmic space of Democritus, the κενόν or void in which the atoms move about. It is true that the word κενόν, and the designation of empty space as a μὴ ὄν as well, betray the presence of Eleatic patterns of thought, which had been incorporated into Ionian philosophy before Democritus. In its essentials, however, the atomic theory is Ionian, and, moreover, it has the characteristics of a physical theory. Plato's theory of matter is metaphysical and inspired by Eleatic philosophy. The difference between Plato and Democritus is determined by the tradition to which they belonged and from which they started.

Anaximander's ἄπειρον, whether by this or any other name, is absent in Plato. There is, however, a theory in Plato, in which the concept of an ἄπειρον plays an important part. It is found in the *Philebus*. The term ἄπειρον here has a meaning which is *toto caelo* different from Anaximander's conception. In the *Philebus* ἄπειρον is a principle of indeterminateness. The presence of an ἄπειρον in things means that their qualities are undetermined to such a degree that we

210

cannot say precisely what it is. Not until the changing proportions of these qualities have been fixed by a πέρας is there a well-determined being. At the moment when πέρας is introduced, the indeterminateness or ἄπειρον ceases to exist. In a general formula we can say that the qualities of things come into existence as a result of the interaction of a πέρας and an ἄπειρον. Van der Wielen (1941, 107 - 137) has plausibly argued, with the aid of texts from Simplicius and from Aristotle's *Physics*, that Plato had the mathematical idea of proportion in mind when formulating this theory. If a given line is divided into two parts by a point P, the division is unstable as long as the point P is moving along the line. At the moment P gets a fixed place, a stable proportion is introduced, and the division of the line has acquired determinateness or πέρας. The doctrine of πέρας-ἄπειρον of the *Philebus* therefore betrays a Pythagorean background. With the aid of a mathematical conception Plato defines two principles that have a metaphysical meaning. The ἄπειρον of the *Philebus* represents by no means an Ionian tradition, but is rather a result of Pythagorean and mathematical theory.

We may wonder if there is any relation between the ἄπειρον of the *Philebus* and the χώρα of the *Timaeus*. If the historical origin of the two concepts is different, we might expect the answer to be in the negative. On the other hand, Aristotle treats them as identical and considers both concepts as forerunners or representatives of his own ὕλη.

A comparison of the *Timaeus* with the *Philebus* seems to promise much indeed. We saw (above, p. 201) that the two dialogues run parallel as regards their treatment of the doctrine of the Nous (cf. Skemp 1942, 29 and 112). Next, the doctrine of the four causes, expounded in the *Philebus*, seems to present an analogy to the doctrine of the *Timaeus*, though it must be pointed out that the former dialogue has more abstract formulas suggesting a more general metaphysical validity of the theory. The concept of αἴτιον may be represented by the Demiurge of the *Timaeus*, the principle of πέρας has its parallel in the "forms and numbers" of the *Timaeus* (εἴδεσί τε καὶ ἀριθμοῖς, 53 B), the μικτόν corresponds more or less to the perceptible world, which is a generated image of the Ideas. Following this line we should have to identify the ἄπειρον of the *Philebus* with the χώρα = τὸ ἐν ᾧ of the *Timaeus*. This last step, however, is not too obvious.

Firstly, the way in which Plato puts forth his theory in the *Philebus* shows that he wants it to be understood in the sense of a

211

general ontological theory. This is not the case with χώρα, which is a spatial concept. Secondly, it is a remarkable fact that Plato's expositions in the *Philebus* do not give the impression of being a direct explanation of the theory of ideas. They are certainly not inconsistent with this theory, but the wording rather suggests that the discussion was an independent attempt at formulating general metaphysical principles. The theory of χώρα, on the contrary, has its place strictly within the framework of the theory of Ideas: χώρα is the receiving medium in which the images of the ideas appear.

Thirdly, the historical background of the two concepts is different. The set of opposites ἄπειρον-πέρας is Pythagorean in character. This makes it improbable that this ἄπειρον should have originated from the Eleatic void. Only if it were Eleatic could we attribute a spatial connotation to it and identify it with χώρα. Fourthly, the function of the ἄπειρον within the theory of the *Philebus* is completely different from that of χώρα within the theory of the *Timaeus*. The ἄπειρον is not an immanent principle of things in the sense that it is recognizable as a part of their substance. On the contrary, the ἄπειρον ceases to exist when it receives its determination from a πέρας. Therefore, its function is at least comparable to that of an immanent principle. The function of the χώρα is that of a nursing mother. To the Greek conception of motherhood this means that it is the necessary condition for things to come into existence. It is the space in which the perceptible things are realized as a necessary condition in the sense described above (p. 205; cf. De Vogel 1959, 22).

It seems reasonable, therefore, to maintain a distinction between the ἄπειρον of the *Philebus* and the χώρα of the *Timaeus*. The difference is that χώρα is a spatial concept, whereas the ἄπειρον is a metaphysical principle. Moreover, the concept of χώρα belongs to a theory which was framed in strict relation to the theory of ideas, whereas the ἄπειρον-theory of the *Philebus*, without contradicting Plato's central doctrine, is to a certain extent independent of it. This is confirmed by the later development of the ἄπειρον-theory, especially in the unwritten doctrine. For the theory in the *Philebus* the terms πέρας and ἄπειρον are used, the latter being synonymous of μᾶλλον καὶ ἧττον (25 C, 26 D). In the unwritten doctrine next to these terms the expression δυὰς ἀόριστος, the "undetermined Dyad", makes its appearance.

The new expression shows that the mathematical character of the concept was not lost. In the generalized version of the unwritten doctrine the theory was probably the last stepping-stone to Aristotle's theory of hylemorphism. It seems probable that Aristotle framed his theory on the example of the later version of Plato's theory of ἄπειρον and πέρας. The fact that it was the later version which Aristotle had in mind, explains why he informs us, that to Plato there were two kinds of matter: one in the sensible things, another in the Ideas themselves (*Met.* A 6, 988 a 10 - 13, and *Phys.* III 4, 203 a 9 - 10). In the latter passage the account has an unexpected historical truthfulness, because Aristotle does not say that Plato admitted two kinds of ὕλη or matter, but two kinds of indeterminateness: τὸ μέντοι ἄπειρον καὶ ἐν τοῖς αἰσθητοῖς καὶ ἐν ἐκείναις εἶναι.: "Plato says that the ἄπειρον is in the sensible things as well as in the ideas." Without abandoning the theory of Ideas, Plato, in his later years, developed a metaphysical theory which was to account for both corporeal and incorporeal being. The being of the sensible things as well as that of the Ideas could be analyzed into the ontological factors of an undetermined substrate (ἄπειρον, later δυὰς ἀόριστος) and a principle of determinateness (πέρας, later τὸ ἕν). The conception of a dual realm of being, was traditional in Plato's doctrine. He completed it by assuming the existence of a dual substrate.

There are two other fundamental theories of Plato which have been dealt with by Aristotle as if they could be identified with this couple of a determining principle and an undetermined one. These are the μὴ ὄν of the *Sophistes* and the χώρα of the *Timaeus*. We saw earlier in this chapter that the χώρα cannot be compared with Aristotle's concept of ὕλη, in contrast to the principle of the ἄπειρον, which directly prepared the way for it. The concept of χώρα probably has an Eleatic origin, and plays a part as a spatial receiving medium, which is not taken up into the constitution of things itself. Aristotle failed to see what χώρα in the *Timaeus* was intended to be. He supposed that Plato had designed it as a principle comparable to his own ὕλη and having the same function, as we can see from *Physics* IV 2, 209 b 11 - 13. Aristotle almost comes on the track of his own error when he adds that in his unwritten doctrine Plato gives quite a different description of the receiving substratum. In the unwritten doctrine the ἄπειρον of the *Philebus* must have performed the duties of an indeterminate principle, and with good reason it may be compared with Aristotle's theory of matter. The same cannot be said of the χώρα of the *Timaeus* (cf. Taylor 1928, 346 - 7, 400 - 407).

The second simplification which Aristotle brings about in Plato's system of thought, concerns the μὴ ὄν of the *Sophistes*. We can see from *Met.* N 2, 1089 a 2 - 26, that Aristotle assumes that the principles of ὄν and μὴ ὄν have the same value in Plato's system as εἶδος and ὕλη. In the text, at least, Aristotle attacks Plato as if this had been his intention. A defender of Aristotle could possibly point out that, in fact, Aristotle's matter is μὴ ὄν τι, a potential being which is not yet that which it must develop into. In this sense we are justified in saying that Aristotle's ὕλη is a μὴ ὄν τι. The reverse, however, is not true at all. It would be a gross mistake to identify the μὴ ὄν of the *Sophistes* with Aristotle's concept of ὕλη. Plato designed his theory to bring about an adjustment in his hitherto too strictly Eleatic views. It could not be maintained any longer that any kind of being, even the pure being of the Ideas could be confined within the limits of one concept. It appeared that no concept and no Idea existed autonomously without admitting the presence of any qualification different from its own. This means that every being has an element of otherness in itself. This is formulated by Plato in a theory in which the concept of μὴ ὄν coincides with that of ἕτερον. The terms form part of an ontological analysis, and it is out of the question that the μὴ ὄν should have the function of a kind of indeterminate substrate-matter.

The simplifications we have described are a current feature in Aristotle's method of interpreting. When he does not agree with some theory in Plato's work, he first gives an account of it which does not fit the facts. Then he gives an erroneous interpretation based on his own account and it is against the theory as he has described it, and the interpretation he has given it, that he launches his attack. The reader has the impression that in doing so Aristotle was inspired by the desire to prove that he had found the right solution of the problem. He supposes that any true solution must by its very nature contain whatever partial results may have been attained by others. His standard of judgement is whether or not a theory can be made into a part of his own system of thought.

To this practice objections can be made both from a historical and from a philosophical point of view. Philosophically the main difficulty is that by accepting Aristotle's criterion certain preconceived opinions are introduced into a philosophical system. In Aristotle's case the preconceived opinions are that his own system is the right one, and that the theories of his predecessors can be adapted to his system of thought. From a historical point of view it is, generally speaking, not necessary that the personal opinions of an author should influence his description of other philosophical doctrines. It could be imagined that

Aristotle should give an accurate account of Plato's intentions before criticizing them. This, however, is not the case, as the texts demonstrate only too clearly. Aristotle's method of working, together with his presuppositions, have influenced the accounts he gives of Plato's doctrines to such an extent that the account is often a downright falsification. It is the task of the historian of philosophy to separate what is sound from what is distorted by analyzing the texts according to the standards of historical and literary criticism.

In order to complete the discussion it may be interesting to compare the way Aristotle deals with Plato's theory to that of Plotinus. It is a remarkable fact that Plotinus incorporates into his theory of matter both the doctrine of χώρα and that of μὴ ὄν. The difference between him and Aristotle is, that the Stagirite thought they could not be incorporated into a sound theory, that he supposed Plato to have tried to do so, and that he reproaches Plato with this.

The method by which Plotinus incorporates both principles into his doctrine, shows that he at least did no violence to Plato's intentions, though there is clearly a difference in outlook. To Plotinus matter is not identical with space, but he deals with the concept of matter in spatial metaphors. Matter is the remotest border, where the emanation of light is giving way to darkness. Matter, therefore, has the function of a limit. It is not actually affected by the εἶδος, nor transformed by it, and it does not enter into the constitution of things. Thus, Plato's theory of χώρα is brought into agreement with the whole of Plotinus' philosophy.

The same may be said about the theory of μὴ ὄν. Matter is, to Plotinus, the most distant contrast to the ineffable One, out of which all being emanates. The One is characterized by having its place over and above all being, whereas matter is completely *infra* being. This means that matter is characterized in a most absolute degree as a not-being or μὴ ὄν. The philosopher who had his eyes open to the intentions of the master was not the disciple who for twenty years attended his lectures, but rather the philosopher who half a milennium afterwards brought the Platonic system to maturity, assigning it a place as one of the definite foundations of Western thought.

Mathematics and Timaeus

Ast 1835
Martin 1841
Sartorius 1886
Baeumker 1887
Shorey 1888
Cook Wilson 1889
Baeumker 1890, 1891
Rodier 1902
Rivaud 1905
Sachs 1917
Robin 1918
Gueroult 1924
Taylor 1926-7, 1928
Solmsen 1931
Robin 1933
Demos 1936
Vlastos 1939
Skemp 1942
Mugler 1948
Friedlaender 1949
Wilpert 1950, 1953

Morrow 1950
Solmsen 1950, II
Bruins 1951
Cherniss 1951, II; 1954, 1956
Ollerud 1951
Cornford 1952, I
Owen 1953
Heisenberg 1953
Brumbaugh 1954
Claghorn 1954
Markovic 1955
Wedberg 1955
Rivaud 1956
Hackforth 1959
Mugler 1960
Skemp 1960
Keyt 1961
Solmsen 1961
Witte 1964
Schulz 1966

Metaphysics and unwritten doctrine

Schneider 1884
Bellaar Spruyt 1885
Cherniss 1932
Stenzel 1933
de Vogel 1936
Wilpert 1941
de Vogel 1948
Ross 1951

de Vogel 1949, 1951, 1953
Malverne 1958
de Vogel 1959
Burkert 1962
Gaiser 1963
Allen 1964
Ilting 1965

GENERAL BIBLIOGRAPHY

I. TEXTS

Die Fragmente der Vorsokratiker, griechisch und deutsch von Hermann Diels. Achte Auflage hrsg. von Walther Kranz. 3 Teile. Berlin, 1956. (= DK = Diels-Kranz).

C. J. de Vogel, *Greek Philosophy. A Collection of Texts Selected and Supplied with Some Notes and Explanations*. (= *Gr. Ph.*) 3 vols. Leiden,
  I. Thales to Plato, 3d. ed., 1963.
  II. Aristotle, Early Peripatetic School, Early Academy, 1953.
  III. Hellenistic–Roman Period, 1959.

Orphicorum Fragmenta, collegit Otto Kern. Berolini, 1963 (Zweite Auflage, unveränderter Nachdruck der 1. Aufl., 1922).

Guilelmus Quandt, *Orphei Hymni*, edidit G. Quandt. Berolini, 1941 (New edition 1962).

Diogenis Laertii, *Vitae philosophorum*. Recognovit H. S. Long. 2 vol. Oxonii, 1964.

Doxographi Graeci collegit recensuit prolegomenis indicibusque instruxit Hermannus Diels. Editio tertia, exemplar editionis primae anni 1879 photomechanice impressum. Berolini 1958.

Ioannis Stobaei *Anthologium*. Recensuerunt C. Wachsmuth et O. Hense. Editio altera ex editione anni 1884 lucis ope expressa. 5 vol. Berolini 1958.

Platon, *Oeuvres Complètes*, tome VIII, 1re partie, *Parménide*, texte établi et traduit par Aug. Diès, Paris, 1950 (2e éd.).
2e partie, *Théétète*, texte établi et traduit par Aug. Diès, Paris, 1950 (2e éd.).
3e partie, *Le Sophiste*, texte établi et traduit par Aug. Diès, Paris, 1950 (2e éd.) (Collection des Universités de France, Assoc. Guill. Budé).

Platon, *Oeuvres Complètes*, tome IX, 2e partie, *Philèbe*. Texte établi et traduit par Aug. Diès. Paris, 1949 (Collection des Universités de France, Assoc. Guill. Budé).

217

Platon, Oeuvres Complètes, Tome X, *Timée – Critias*. Texte établi et traduit par Albert Rivaud. Paris, 1949 (Collection des Universités de France, Assoc. Guill. Budé).

E. B. England, *The Laws of Plato*. Text with introd. notes etc. 2 vol. Manchester-London, 1921.

Aristotle, *Metaphysics*. A revised text with introduction and commentary by W. D. Ross. 2 vol. Oxford, 1924, reprinted 1966.

Aristote, *Métaphysique*, trad. avec comm. par J. Tricot. Paris 1953, 2 vol.

Aristotle, *Physics*. A revised text with introduction and commentary by W. D. Ross. Oxford, 1936, reprinted 1960.

Aristotle, *On coming-to-be and passing-away* (*De generatione et corruptione*). A revised text with introduction and commentary, by H. H. Joachim, Oxford, 1922.

Aristotle, *On the Heavens* (De caelo). With an english translation by W. K. C. Guthrie. London-Cambridge Ma., 1939, reprinted 1953. (Loeb Class. Libr.)

Aristote, *Du ciel*. Texte établi et traduit par Paul Moraux. Paris 1965 (Coll. Univ. de France).

Aristotelis *Fragmenta Selecta*, recognovit W. D. Ross. Oxonii 1955.

Aristotelis qui fertur *De Melisso Xenophane Gorgia* libellus, edidit Hermannus Diels. Berlin, 1900 (Abh. Preuss. Akad. 25, 515). (= MXG).

Fritz Wehrli, *Die Schule des Aristoteles*, Heft VIII, *Eudemos von Rhodos*. Texte und Kommentar. Basel 1955.

Euclides. Opera omnia. Edd. J. L. Heiberg et H. Menge. 8 vol., Lipsiae 1883-1916. I-V = *Elementa*. Edidit et latine interpretatus est J. L. Heiberg, Lipsiae, 1883-1888.

Sir Thomas Heath, *The Thirteen Books of Euclid's Elements*, translated from the text of Heiberg. Second edition 1925, reprinted: Dover Publications, New York, 1956, 3 vol. (= Heath, *Euclid's Elements*).

Simplicii *in Aristotelis Physicorum libros quattuor Commentaria*, edidit Hermannus Diels. Berolini 1882-1895. (*Commentaria in Aristotelem Graeca*, edita consilio et auctoritate Academiae Litterarum Regiae Borussicae, vol. IX-X).

218

II. HANDBOOKS AND COLLECTED PAPERS

Theodor Gomperz, *Griechische Denker. Eine Geschichte der antiken Philosophie.* 2 vol. Leipzig 1911-12 (3. Aufl.).

Friedrich Ueberweg, *Grundriss der Geschichte der Philosophie des Altertums.* Elfte Auflage, hrsg. von Karl Praechter. Berlin, 1920.

Eduard Zeller, *Die Philosophie der Griechen in ihrer geschichtlichen Entwicklung dargestellt.* Sechste Auflage, hrsg. von Wilhelm Nestle. 6 Bde, Berlin 1919.

R. E. Allen (ed.), *Studies in Plato's Metaphysics.* London, 1965. (Reprints of articles by Cherniss, Cross, Allen, Cornford, Ryle, Runciman, Hicken, Ackrill, Lloyd, Vlastos, Geach, Owen, Cherniss, Morrow, Hackforth.) (= *reprint-volume Allen*).

Renford Bambrough (ed.), *New Essays on Plato and Aristotle.* London, 1965. (Essays by G. E. M. Anscombe, R. Bambrough, G. E. L. Owen, J. L. Ackrill, Gilbert Ryle, R. M. Hare, Gr. Vlastos, DMMc Kinnon).

John Burnet, *Early Greek Philosophy.* Fourth edition, London, 1930, reprinted 1952 (= *Burnet E.G.P.*).

J. Burnet, *Greek Philosophy. Thales to Plato.* London, 1914. Reprinted 1960. (= *Burnet G.P*).

I. Düring and G. E. L. Owen, *Aristotle and Plato in the Midfourth Century.* Papers of the Symposium Aristotelicum held at Oxford in August, 1957. Göteborg 1960. (Contains papers by Sir David Ross, Olof Gigon, Ingemar Düring, Suz. Mansion, Emile de Strycker, Richard Walzer, Paul Moraux, D. J. Allan, G. R. Morrow, G. E. L. Owen, D. A. Rees, J. B. Skemp, Fr. Solmsen, G. Verbeke, C. J. de Vogel and Paul Wilpert).

Hermann Fränkel, *Wege und Formen frühgriechischen Denkens.* Literarische und philosophiegeschichtliche Studien, hrsg. von Fr. Tietze. Zweite erweiterte Auflage. München, 1960. (Reprints of earlier publications).

Werner Jaeger, *The Theology of the Early Greek Philosophers* (Gifford Lectures 1936). Oxford, 1948. (= Jaeger, *Theol*).

L'infini et le réel. Dix-huitième semaine de Synthèse, Paris, oct. 1952. Exposés et discussions par M. P. Kucharski e.a. Centre International de Synthèse, Paris, 1955.

W. K. C. Guthrie, *A History of Greek Philosophy.* Vol. I. *The Earlier Presocratics and the Pythagoreans.* Cambridge 1962. Vol. II. *The Presocratic Tradition from Parmenides to Democritus.* Cambridge, 1965. (= *Guthrie*, 1962, 1965).

G. S. Kirk-J. E. Raven, *The Presocratic Philosophers. A Critical History with a Selection of Texts.* Cambridge 1957, reprint 1962 (= *Kirk-Raven*).

III. SPECIALIZED LITERATURE

AHLBERG   1917   Alf Ahlberg, *Materieproblemet i Platonismen. En historisk-kritisk Studie.* (Diss. Lund). Lund 1917.

ALLEN   1964   R. E. Allen, *The Interpretation of Plato's Parmenides: Zeno's paradox and the theory of forms.* Journal History Philosophy 2, 1964, 143-155.

AST   1835   Fr. Ast, *Ueber die Materie im platonischen Timaeus.* Abh. Bayerischen Ak. der Wiss., philos.-philol. Classe, Bd. I, München 1835, S. 44-54.

BAEUMKER   1887   Cl. Baeumker, *Die Ewigkeit der Welt bei Platon.* Philos. Monatshefte 23, 1887, 513-529.

–   1890   Clemens Baeumker, *Das Problem der Materie in der griechischen Philosophie.* Münster, 1890.

–   1891   Cl. Baeumker, *Noch einmal zu Platon's Timaeus 51 E - 52 B* Philos. Jahrb. Görres-Ges. 4, 1891, 256-259.

BAILEY   1928   Cyril Bailey, *The Greek Atomists and Epicurus.* Oxford 1928.

BALLAUFF   1953   Theodor Ballauff, *Vom Ursprung. Interpretationen zu Thales' und Anaximanders Philosophie.* Tijdschr. v. Philos. 15, 1953, 18-70.

BARGRAVE-WEAVER   1959   D. Bargrave-Weaver, *The Cosmogony of Anaxagoras.* Phronesis 4, 1959, 77-91.

BARNETT   1945   R. D. Barnett, *The Epic of Kumarbi and the Theogony of Hesiod.* Journal of Hellenic Studies 65, 1945, 100-101.

BECKER   1936   Oskar Becker, *Die Lehre vom Geraden und Ungeraden im neunten Buch der euklidischen Elemente.* Quellen und Studien zur Geschichte der Mathematik, Astronomie und Physik, B: Studien, 3, 1936, 533-553.

–   1957, I   Oskar Becker, *Zwei Untersuchungen zur antiken Logik.* Wiesbaden 1957 (Klass-phil. Studien, 17).

–   1957, II   Oskar Becker, *Das mathematische Denken der Antike.* Göttingen 1957. Review: Gnomon 1958, 81-87 by Kurt von Fritz.

–   1959   Oskar Becker, *Die Archai in der griechischen Mathematik. Einige ergänzende Bemerkungen zum Aufsatz K. von Fritz.* Archiv für Begriffsgeschichte 4, 1959, 210-266.

BELLAAR SPRUYT   1885   C. Bellaar Spruyt, *Over de betekenis der woorden ἄπειρον en πέρας in Plato's Philebus.* Versl. en Meded. Kon. Akad. III, 2, 8-38. Amsterdam 1885.

BERNARDETE   1964   José A. Benardete. *Infinity. An essay in metaphysics.* Oxford 1964.

BETH   1953   Evert W. Beth, *The Prehistory of Research into Foundations.* British Journal Philos. of Science, III 1953, 58-81.

| | 1959 | E. W. Beth, *The Foundations of Mathematics. A Study in the Philosophy of Science.* Amsterdam 1959. |

BIANCHI 1960 Ugo Bianchi, *Teogonie e Cosmogonie.* Roma 1960.

BIGNONE 1916 E. Bignone, *Empedocle. Studio critico, traduzione e commento delle testimonianze e dei frammenti.* Torino 1916.

BOEDER 1964 H. Boeder, *Milesische Philosophie.* Archiv für Begriffsgeschichte 9, 1964, 53-58.

BOEHM 1905 Fr. Boehm, *De symbolis Pythagoreis.* Diss. Berlin 1905.

BOLLINGER 1925 Jenny Bollinger, *Die sogenannten Pythagoreer des Aristoteles.* Zürich 1925 (diss).

BOLZANO 1851 Bernard Bolzano, *Paradoxien des Unendlichen.* Hrsg. von Alois Höfler, mit Anm. versehen von Hans Hahn. Hamburg 1955 (Philos. Bibl. 99) (Photostatic repr. of ed. 1851).

BOOTH 1957 N. B. Booth, *Were Zeno's arguments a reply to attacks upon Parmenides? Were Zeno's arguments directed against the Pythagoreans?* Phronesis, 2, 1957, 1-9, 90-103.

BOUSSOULAS 1959 N. Boussoulas, *Les Pythagoriciens. Essai sur la structure du Mélange dans la pensée présocratique.* Revue métaph. morale, 64, 1959, 385-395.

BRANDON 1963 S. G. F. Brandon, *Creation Legends of the Ancient Near East.* London 1963.

BRENDEL 1936 Otto Brendel, *Symbolik der Kugel.* Mitt. deutsch. arch. Inst. Röm. Abt. 51, 1936, 1-95.

BROCHARD 1888 V. Brochard, *Les arguments de Zénon d'Elée contre le mouvement.* Compte rendu de l'Académie des sciences morales 1888, N.S. 29, 555-568 in: *Etudes de philosophie ancienne et de philosophie moderne,* Paris 1954, p. 3-14.

| | 1893 | V. Brochard, *Les prétendus sophismes de Zénon d'Elée.* Revue de Métaphysique et de Morale, I, 1893, 209-215. in: *Etudes de philosophie ancienne et de philosophie moderne.* Paris 1954, p. 15-22. |

| | 1900 | V. Brochard, *Le devenir dans la philosophie de Platon.* (Congrès intern. de philos. 1900), in: V. Brochard, *Etudes de philosophie ancienne et de philosophie moderne,* Paris 1954, 95 - 112. |

BRÖCKER 1943 W. Bröcker, *Die Lehre des Anaxagoras.* Kant-Studien NF 42, Heft 1-3, 1942-43, 176-189.

| | 1964 | Walter Bröcker, *Parmenides.* Archiv für Begriffsgeschichte, 9, 1964, 79-86. |

BRUINS 1951 E. M. Bruins, *La chimie du Timée.* Revue métaph. morale, 56, 1951, 269-282.

BRUMBAUGH 1954 Robert S. Brumbaugh, *Plato's mathematical imagi-*

nation. The mathematical passages in the dialogues and their interpretation. Bloomington 1954. (Indiana Univ. Publ., Humanities: 29).

BRUNSCHVICQ   1947   Léon Brunschvicq, *Les étapes de la philosophie mathématique.* Paris 1947.

BURKERT   1962   Walter Burkert, *Weisheit und Wissenschaft, Studien zu Pythagoras, Philolaos und Platon.* Nürnberg, 1962 (Erlanger Beiträge X).

–   1963   W. Burkert, *Iranisches bei Anaximandros.* Rheinisches Museum 106, 1963, 97-134.

CAJORI   1915   Florian Cajori, *The History of Zeno's Arguments on Motion: Phases in the Development of the Theory of Limits.* American Mathematical Monthly 22, 1915 p.1-6, 39-47, 77-82, 109-115, 143-149, 179-186, 215-220, 253-258, 292-297.

CALOGERO   1932   Guido Calogero, *Studi sull' Eleatismo.* Roma 1932. (Pubblicazioni della scuola di filosofia della R. Universitá di Roma, III).

CANTOR   1907   Moritz Cantor, *Vorlesungen über Geschichte der Mathematik.* Zwei Bände, Leipzig 1907-1913.

CAPELLE   1919   Wilh. Capelle, *Anaxagoras.* Neue Jahrb. klass. Altertum 43, 1919, 81-102, 169-198.

CHERNISS   1932   H. Fr. Cherniss, *Parmenides and the Parmenides of Plato.* Am. Journal Philology 53, 1932, 122-138.

–   1935   H. Cherniss, *Aristotle's Criticism of Presocratic Philosophy.* Baltimore 1935.

–   1944   Harold Cherniss, *Aristotle's Criticism of Plato and the Academy.* Vol. I, Baltimore 1944, second printing 1946.

–   1945   H. Cherniss, *The Riddle of the Early Academy.* New York, 1962 (reissued from first impression 1945).

–   1951, I   H. Cherniss, *The Characteristics and Effects of Presocratic Philosophy.* Journal History Ideas 12, 1951, 319-345.

–   1951, II   H. Fr. Cherniss, *Plato as Mathematician.* Review of Metaphysics 4, 1951, 395-425 (about: Mugler 1948).

–   1954   H. Fr. Cherniss, *The sources of evil according to Plato.* Proceedings Am. Philos. Society 98, 1954, 23-30.

–   1956   H. Fr. Cherniss, *Timaeus 52 C 2-5.* Mélanges Diès, Paris 1956, 49-60.

CLAGHORN   1954   George S. Claghorn, *Aristotle's Criticism of Plato's Timaeus.* The Hague 1954.

CLASSEN   1962   C. J. Classen, *Anaximander.* Hermes 90, 1962, 159-172.

CLEMEN   1939   Carl Clemen, *Die phönikische Religion nach Philon von Byblos.* Leipzig 1939 (Mitt. vorderas-aeg. Ges. 42, 3).

COHN   1896   Jonas Cohn, *Geschichte des Unendlichkeitsproblems im*

222

		abendländischen Denken bis Kant. Leipzig 1896, Nachdruck Darmstadt 1960.
COOK WILSON	1889	J. Cook Wilson, *On the Interpretation of Plato's Timaeus. Critical Studies with special reference to a recent edition.* London 1889.
CORNFORD	1912	F. M. Cornford, *From Religion to Philosophy. A Study in the Origins of Western Speculation.* London 1912. Reprinted New York 1957 (Harper Torchbooks).
–	1922-23	F. M. Cornford, *Mysticism and Science in the Pythagorean Tradition.* Class. Qu. 16, 1922, 137-150 17, 1923, 1- 12
–	1926	F. M. Cornford, *Mystery Religions and Pre-Socratic Philosophy.* The Cambridge Ancient History, IV 522-578. Cambridge 1960 (first edition 1926).
–	1930	F. M. Cornford, *Anaxagoras' Theory of Matter.* Classical Quarterly 24, 1930, 14-30, 83-95.
–	1933	F. M. Cornford, *Parmenides' Two Ways.* Class. Qu. 27, 1933, 97-111.
–	1934	F. M. Cornford, *Innumerable Worlds in Presocratic Philosophy.* Class. Qu. 28, 1934, 1-16.
–	1936	F. M. Cornford, *The Invention of Space.* in: Essays in Honour of Gilbert Murray 1936, 215-235.
–	1939	F. M. Cornford, *Plato and Parmenides. Parmenides' Way of Truth and Plato's Parmenides Translated with an Introduction and a Running Commentary.* London 1939 (second ed. 1950).
	1952, I	F. M. Cornford, *Plato's Cosmology. The Timaeus of Plato translated with a running commentary.* London 1937, third edition, 1952.
–	1952, II	F. M. Cornford, *Principium Sapientiae.* The *Origins of Greek Philosophical Thought.* Cambridge 1952 (edited by W. K. C. Guthrie).
DE CORTE	1958	M. de Corte, *Mythe et Philosophie chez Anaximandre.* Laval théologique et philosophique 14, 1958, 9-29.
COVOTTI	1897	Aurelio Covotti, *Le teorie dello spazio e del tempo nella filosofia greca fin ad Aristotele.* Annali Scuola Normale Superiore di Pisa, 1897.
COXON	1934	A. H. Coxon, *The Philosophy of Parmenides.* Class. Qu. 28, 1934, 134-144.
CROISSANT	1937	Jeanne Croissant, *La conception du continu en Grèce avant la découverte du calcul infinitésimal.* Travaux IXe Congrès Philos. fasc. VI, chap. V, 181-192. Paris 1937.
–	1944	Jeanne Croissant, *Matière et changement dans la physique ionienne.* L'antiquité classique 13, 1944, 61-94.

DAVISON 1953 J. A. Davison, *Protagoras, Democritus and Anaxagoras*. Classical Quarterly 47, 1953, 33-45

DEICHGRÄBER 1938 K. Deichgräber, *Xenophanes περὶ φύσεως*. Rheinisches Museum 87, 1938, 1-31.

DELATTE 1922 A. Delatte, *La vie de Pythagore de Diogène Laerce*. Bruxelles 1922. (Acad. R. Belge, Mémoires Classe des Lettres, II 17 fasc. 2).

DEMOS 1936 R. Demos. *The Receptacle*. Philosophical Review 45, 1936, 535-557.

DETIENNE 1964 M. Detienne, *Les origines religieuses de la notion d'intellect. Hermotime et Anaxagore*. Revue philosophique France Etranger 154, 1964, 167-178.

DIELS 1897 Hermann Diels, *Parmenides' Lehrgedicht, griechisch und deutsch*. Berlin 1897.

– 1899 H. Diels, *Elementum. Eine Vorarbeit zum griechischen und lateinischen Thesaurus*. Leipzig 1899.

DODDS 1945 E. R. Dodds, *Plato and the Irrational*. Journal of Hellenic Studies 65, 1945, 16-25.

DOLIN 1962 E. F. Dolin, *Parmenides and Hesiod*. Harvard Studies Class. Philol., 66, 1962, 93-98.

DÖRFLER 1912 Jos. Dörfler, *Die kosmogonischen Elemente in der Naturphilosophie des Thales*. Archiv für Geschichte der Philosophie 25, 1912, 305-331.

– 1916 J. Dörfler, *Ueber den Ursprung der Naturphilosophie Anaximanders*. Wiener Studien 38, 1916, 189-226.

DORNSEIFF 1937 Fr. Dornseiff, *Altorientalisches in Hesiods Theogonie*. L'Antiquité classique 6, 1937, 231-258.

– 1956 Franz Dornseiff, *Antike und alter Orient. Interpretationen*. Leipzig 1956. (= Kleine Schriften I).

DIJKSTERHUIS 1930 E. J. Dijksterhuis, *De elementen van Euclides*. 2 dn. Groningen 1929-30.

– 1935 E. J. Dijksterhuis, *Prae-helleense wiskunde*. De Gids 99, 1935, 2, 209-230, 337-349; 3, 41-58.

EISLER 1910 Robert Eisler, *Weltenmantel und Himmelszelt. Religionsgeschichtliche Untersuchungen zur Urgeschichte des antiken Weltbildes*. München 1910.

EISSFELDT 1952 Otto Eissfeldt, *Sanchunjaton von Berut und Ilumilku von Ugarit*. Halle 1952. (Beiträge Religionsgesch. Altert., Heft 5).

FERGUSON 1964 John Ferguson, *Two notes on the Preplatonics (Empedocles 31 A 30, Anaxagoras 59 B 11)*. Phronesis 9, 1964, 98-106.

FESTUGIÈRE 1945 A. J. Festugière, *Les "mémoires pythagoriques" cités par Alexandre Polyhistor*. Revue ét. gr., 1945, 1-65.

FRANK 1923 Erich Frank, *Plato und die sogenannten Pythagoreer*. Halle a.S. 1923. Nachdruck Tübingen 1962.

FRÄNKEL 1930 Hermann Fränkel, *Parmenidesstudien*. Göttinger Nachrichten 1930, 153-192. Reprinted: H. Fränkel,

224

Wege und Formen frühgriechischen Denkens, München 1960, 157-197.

– 1960   Hermann Fränkel, *Zenon von Elea im Kampf gegen die Idee der Vielheit*. in: *Wege und Formen frühgriechischen Denkens*, München 1960, 198-236.

– 1962   Hermann Fränkel, *Dichtung und Philosophie des frühen Griechentums*. Zweite, überarbeitete Auflage, München 1962.

FRANKFORT   1949   H. Frankfort, J. Wilson, Th. Jacobsen, *Before Philosophy*. Harmondsworth 1949. (Pelican Books).

FREUDENTHAL   1957   H. Freudenthal, *Zur Geschichte der Grundlagen der Geometrie, zugleich eine Besprechung der 8. Auflage von Hilberts Grundlagen der Geometrie*. Nieuw Archief voor Wiskunde, 5, 1957, 105-142.

– 1966   H. Freudenthal, *Y avait-il une crise des fondements des mathématiques dans l'Antiquité?* Bulletin Société Math. Belgique, 18, 1966, 43-55.

FRIEDLAENDER   1949   P. Friedlaender, *Structure and destruction of the atom according to Plato's Timaeus*. Univ. of California Publications in Philosophy vol. 16, no. 11, 1949, 225-240 (with 4 plates).

VON FRITZ   RE   Kurt von Fritz,
art. *Xenophanes*, in: Pauly-Wissowa RE
art. *Theaitetos 2*, in: Pauly-Wissowa RE
art. *Theodoros 31*, in: Pauly-Wissowa RE
art. *Oinopides*, in: Pauly-Wissowa RE
art. *Pythagoras-Pythagoreer*, in: Pauly-Wissowa RE

– 1932   Kurt von Fritz, *Platon, Theaetet, und die antike Mathematik*. Philologus 87, 1932, 40-62, 136-178.

– 1945   Kurt von Fritz, *The Discovery of Incommensurability by Hippasus of Metapontum*. Annals of Mathematics 46, 1945, 242-264.

1945-6   Νοῦς, νοεῖν, *and their Derivatives in Presocratic Philosophy*.
Classical Philology 40, 1945, 223-242
                              41, 1946, 12- 34

– 1952   Kurt von Fritz, *Der gemeinsame Ursprung der Geschichtsschreibung und der exakten Wissenschaften bei den Griechen*. Philosophia naturalis 2, 1952 200-223, 376-379.

– 1955   Kurt von Fritz, *Die* ΑΡΧΑΙ *in der griechischen Mathematik*. Archiv für Begriffsgeschichte I, 1955, 13-103.

– 1959   Kurt von Fritz, *Gleichheit, Kongruenz und Ähnlichkeit in der antiken Mathematik bis auf Euklid*. Archiv für Begriffsgeschichte 4, 1959, 7-81.

– 1961   Kurt von Fritz, *Der Beginn universalwissenschaft-*

licher Bestrebungen und der Primat der Griechen.
Studium Generale 14, 1961, 546-583, 600-637.

– 1963 Kurt von Fritz, *Philosophie und sprachlicher Ausdruck bei Demokrit, Platon und Aristoteles.* Darmstadt 1963.

– 1964 Kurt von Fritz, *Der* Νοῦς *des Anaxagoras.* Archiv für Begriffsgeschichte, 9, 1964, 87-102.

GAISER 1963 Konrad Gaiser, *Platons ungeschriebene Lehre*, Stuttgart 1963.

GAYE 1910 R. K. Gaye, *On Aristotle Physics Z IX, 239 b 33-240 a 18 = Zeno's Fourth Argument against Motion.* Journal of Philology (London-Cambridge), 31, 1910, 95-116.

GERSHENSON-
GREENBERG 1961 D. E. Gershenson-D. A. Greenberg, *Melissus of Samos in a new light: Aristotle's Physics 186 a 10-16.* Phronesis 6, 1961, 1-9.

– 1964 D. E. Gershenson-D. A. Greenberg, *Anaxagoras and the Birth of Physics.* New York, 1964.

GHYKA 1952 Matila Ghyka, *Philosophie et mystique du nombre.* Paris 1952.

MC.GIBBON 1964 D. McGibbon, *The Atomists and Melissos.* Mnemosyne 17, 1964, 248-255.

GIGON 1936 O. Gigon, *Zu Anaxagoras.* Philologus 91, 1936, 1-41.

– 1945 Olof Gigon, *Der Ursprung der griechischen Philosophie. Von Hesiod bis Parmenides.* Basel 1945.

– 1954 Olof Gigon, *Die Theologie der Vorsokratiker* in: *La Notion du Divin depuis Homère jusqu'à Platon,* Entretiens Fondation Hardt, I, Genève 1954, 127-166.

GILBERT 1909 Otto Gilbert, *Aristoteles' Urteile über die pythagoreische Lehre.* Archiv Gesch. Philos. 22, 1909, 28-48, 145-165.

GOMPERZ 1924 H. Gomperz, *Psychologische Beobachtungen an griechischen Philosophen. Parmenides-Sokrates.* Imago 10, 1924, 1-92.

– 1932 H. Gomperz, Ἀσώματος, Hermes 67, 1932, 155-167.

– 1933 H. Gomperz, Ὄψις τῶν ἀδήλων τὰ φαινόμενα. Hermes 68, 1933, 341-343.

GOTTSCHALK 1965 H. B. Gottschalk, *Anaximander's Apeiron.* Phronesis 10, 1965, 37-53.

GRÜNBAUM 1952 Adolf Grünbaum, *A consistent conception of the extended linear continuum as an aggregate of unextended elements.* Philosophy of Science (Baltimore), 19, 1952, 288-306.

– 1955 Adolf Grünbaum, *Modern Science and Refutation of the Paradoxes of Zeno.* The Scientific Monthly 81, 5, 234-239 (nov. 1955).

– 1963 Ad. Grünbaum, *Philosophical Problems of Space and Time.* New York 1963. (Borzoi Books).

GUAZZONI FOÁ 1960 Virg. Guazzoni Foá, *Dall'* ἄπειρον *di Anassimandro*

226

		all' ἀτέλεστον *di Parmenide*. Giornale di Metafisica (Genova), 15, 1960, 465-474.
–	1961	Virg. Guazzoni Foá, *Senofane e Parmenide in Platone*. Giornale di Metafisica (Genova), 16, 1961, 467-476.
–	1966	Virg. Guazzoni Foá, *Un ripensamento sulla* σφαίρη *di Parmenide*. Giornale di Metafisica 21, 1966, 344-354.
GUEROULT	1924	M. Gueroult, *Le Xe livre des lois et la dernière forme de la physique platonicienne*. Revue ét. gr. 37, 1924, 27-78.
GUTHRIE	1934	W. K. C. Guthrie, *Orpheus and Greek Religion. A Study of the Orphic Movement*. New York 1966. (First ed. 1934).
–	1957	W. K. C. Guthrie, *In the Beginning. Some Greek Views on the Origin of Life and the Early State of Man*. London 1957.
HACKFORTH	1959	R. Hackforth, *Plato's Cosmogony. (Timaeus 27 D)* Class. Qu. 9, 1959, 17-22.
HAMMER-JENSEN	1910	Ingeborg Hammer-Jensen, *Demokrit und Platon*. Archiv Gesch. Philos., 23, 1910, 92-105, 211-229.
HASSE-SCHOLZ	1928	Helmut Hasse und Heinrich Scholz, *Die Grundlagenkrisis der griechischen Mathematik*. Berlin 1928 (Pan-Bücherei, Philos. 3).
HEATH	1921	Sir Thomas Heath, *A History of Greek Mathematics*. Oxford 1921, 2 vol. Reprinted 1960.
–	1931	Sir Thomas Heath, *A Manual of Greek Mathematics*. New York 1963 (Dover Publications). (First ed. Oxford 1931).
HEEMERT VAN	1963	A. van Heemert, *Wiskunde en eeuwige waarheden*. Groningen 1963 (openbare les).
HEIDEL	1901	W. A. Heidel, Πέρας *and* ἄπειρον *in the Pythagorean Philosophy*. Archiv Gesch. Philos. 14, 1901, 384-399.
–	1940	W. A. Heidel, *The Pythagoreans and Greek Mathematics*. American Journal of Philology, 61, 1940, 1-33.
–	1942	W. A. Heidel, *The Babylonian Genesis*. Chicago 1942, second ed. 1951.
HEISENBERG	1953	W. Heisenberg, *Platons Vorstellungen von den kleinsten Bausteinen der Materie und die Elementarteilchen der modernen Physik*. In: Im Umkreis der Kunst, Festschrift E. Preetorius, 1953, 137-140.
HEITSCH	1966	Ernst Heitsch, *Das Wissen des Xenophanes*. Rhein. Mus. Philol. 109, 1966, 193-235.
HELLER	1958	Siegfried Heller, *Die Entdeckung der stetigen Teilung durch die Pythagoreer*. Abh. Akad. Berlin, Kl. f. Math. Phys. u. Technik 1958, 6.
HERTER	1957	Hans Herter, *Bewegung der Materie bei Platon*. Rhein. Mus. für Philologie 100, 1957, 327-347.

227

HÖLSCHER   1953   Uvo Hölscher, *Anaximander und die Anfänge der griechischen Philosophie*. Hermes 81, 1953, 257-277, 385-418.

–   1965   Uvo Hölscher, *Weltzeiten und Lebenszyklus. Eine Nachprüfung der Empedokles-Doxographie*. Hermes 93, 1965, 7-33.

HOOYKAAS   1933   R. Hooykaas, *Het begrip element in zijn historisch-wijsgerige ontwikkeling*. Diss. Utrecht 1933.

–   1947   R. Hooykaas, *Het ontstaan van de chemische atoomleer*. Ts. v. Philos. 9, 1947, 63-136.

HOWALD   1934   E. Howald, *Leukippos*. Festschrift Joel, Basel 1934, 159-164.

ILTING   1964   K. H. Ilting, *Zur Philosophie der Pythagoreer*, Archiv für Begriffsgeschichte, 9, 1964, 103-132.

–   1965   K. H. Ilting, *Aristoteles über Platons philosophische Entwicklung*. Zeitschr. philos. Forschung, 19, 1965, 377-392.

JAEGER   1920   F. M. Jaeger, *Elementen en atomen eens en thans. Schetsen uit de ontwikkelingsgeschiedenis der elementenleer en atomistiek*. Groningen 1920.

JÖHRENS   1939   O. Jöhrens, *Die Fragmente des Anaxagoras*. Bochum 1939 (diss. Göttingen).

JUNGE   1958   Gustav Junge, *Von Hippasus bis Philolaus. Das Irrationale und die geometrischen Grundbegriffe*. Classica et Mediaevalia 19, 1958, 41-72.

KAHN   1958   C. H. Kahn, *Anaximander and the Arguments concerning the ἄπειρον at Phys. 203 b 4-15*. Festschrift Ernst Kapp, Hamburg, 1958, 19-29.

–   1960   C. H. Kahn, *Anaximander and the Origins of Greek Cosmology*. New York, 1960.

KERÉNYI   1950   K. Kerényi, *Pythagoras und Orpheus. Präludien zu einer zukünftigen Geschichte der Orphik und des Pythagoreismus*. Zürich, 3. Aufl., 1950. (Albae Vigiliae, NF. 9).

KERSCHENSTEINER   1962   Jula Kerschensteiner, *Kosmos. Quellenkritische Untersuchungen zu den Vorsokratikern*. München 1962 (Zetemata, 30).

KEYT   1961   David Keyt, *Aristotle on Plato's receptacle*. American Journal Philology, 82, 1961, 291-300.

KIRK   1955   G. S. Kirk, *Some problems in Anaximander*. Classical Quarterly 49, 1955, 21-38.

–   1960   G. S. Kirk, *Popper on Science and the Presocratics*. Mind 69, 1960, 318-339.

KIRK-STOKES   1960   G. S. Kirk and Michael C. Stokes, *Parmenides' Refutation of Motion*. Phronesis 5, 1960, 1-4.

KLOWSKI   1966   J. Klowski, *Das Entstehen der Begriffe Substanz und Materie*. Archiv Gesch. Philos. 48, 1966, 2-42.

–   1967   J. Klowski, *Zum Entstehen der Begriffe Sein und*

		Nichts und der Weltentstehungs- und Weltschöpfungstheorieën im strengen Sinne. Archiv Gesch. Philos. 49, 1967, 121-148.
KRANZ	1912, I	W. Kranz, *Empedokles und die Atomistik.* Hermes 47, 1912, 18-42.
–	1912, II	W. Kranz, *Die ältesten Farbenlehren der Griechen.* Hermes 47, 1912, 126-140.
–	1916	Walther Kranz, *Ueber Aufbau und Bedeutung des parmenideischen Gedichtes.* Sitzber. preuss. Akad., Berlin 1916, 1158-1176.
–	1949	W. Kranz, *Empedokles. Antike Gestalt und romantische Neuschöpfung.* Zürich 1949.
–	1954	W. Kranz, *Die Entstehung des Atomismus.* Convivium, Festgabe Konrat Ziegler, Stuttgart 1954, 14-40.
–	1957	Walther Kranz, *Kosmos.* Archiv für Begriffsgeschichte, Band 2, Teil 1-2. Bonn 1955-7.
KRAUS	1949	Walther Kraus, *Das Wesen des Unendlichen bei Anaximander.* Rheinisches Museum 1949, 364-379.
KUCHARSKI	1955	P. Kucharski, *Aux frontières du platonisme et du pythagorisme. A propos d'un passage du De Anima d'Aristote. (404 b 18-27).* Archives de Philosophie, 19, 1955, 7-43.
–	1959	P. Kucharski, *Les principes des pythagoriciens et la dyade de Platon.* Archives de Philosophie 1959, 175-191, 385-431.
–	1964	P. Kucharski, *Anaxagore et les idées biologiques de son siècle.* Revue philosophique France Etranger, 154, 1964, 137-166.
LAEMMLI	1962	Franz Laemmli, *Vom Chaos zum Kosmos. Zur Geschichte einer Idee.* Basel 1962, 2 Teile (Text-Anm). (Schweiz. Beitr. Altertumsw., Heft 10).
LANZA	1963	Diego Lanza, *Le omeomerie nella tradizione dossografica anassagorea.* La Parola del Passato, 18, 1963, 256-293.
LASSERRE	1966	François Lasserre, *The Birth of Mathematics in the Age of Plato.* Cleveland and New York 1966 (Meridian Books).
LASSWITZ	1890	Kurd Lasswitz, *Geschichte der Atomistik.* 2 Teile. Hamburg-Leipzig, 1890.
LEE	1936	H. D. P. Lee, *Zeno of Elea. A Text, with Translation and Notes.* Cambridge 1936.
–	1965	Harold Lee, *Are Zeno's paradoxes based on a mistake?* Mind 74, 1965, 563-570.
LÉVY	1926	Isidore Lévy, *Recherches sur les sources de la légende de Pythagore.* Paris 1926.
LINFORTH	1941	Ivan M. Linforth, *The Arts of Orpheus.* Berkeley 1941.
LLOYD	1967	G. E. R. Lloyd, *Popper versus Kirk: A Controversy*

in the Interpretation of Greek Science. British Journal Philos. Science, 18, 1967, 21-38.

LOENEN   1951   J. H. Loenen, *De Nous in het systeem van Plato's philosophie.* Amsterdam 1951 (Diss.).

–   1954   J. H. Loenen, *Was Anaximander an evolutionist?* Mnemosyne 7, 1954, 215-232.

–   1959   J. H. Loenen, *Parmenides Melissus Gorgias. A Reinterpretation of Eleatic Philosophy.* Assen 1959.

LONG   1963   A. A. Long, *The Principles of Parmenides' Cosmogony.* Phronesis 8, 1963, 90-107.

LORIA   1914   Gino Loria, *Le scienze esatte nell'antica grecia.* Seconda edizione, Milano 1914.

LUMPE   1952   Ad. Lumpe, *Die Philosophie des Xenophanes von Kolophon.* München 1952 (diss.).

–   1955   Ad. Lumpe, *Der Terminus* Ἀρχή *von den Vorsokratikern bis auf Aristoteles.* Archiv für Begriffsgesch., I, 1955, 104-116.

–   1962   Ad. Lumpe, *Elementum.* Archiv für Begriffsgeschichte 7, 1962, 285-293.

LURIA   1933   S. Luria, *Die Infinitesimalmethode der antiken Atomisten.* Qu. u. St. Gesch. Mathem., Abt. B: Studien, II 1933, 106-180.

–   1936   S. Luria, *Zur Leukippfrage.* Symbolae Osloenses fasc. 15, 1936, 19-22.

LUTHER   1966   Wilh. Luther, *Wahrheit, Licht und Erkenntnis in der griechischen Philosophie bis Demokrit.* Archiv für Begriffsgeschichte 10, 1966, 1-240.

MADDALENA   1940   Antonio Maddalena, *Sulla cosmologia ionica da Talete a Eraclito.* Padova 1940 (Pubbl. Fac. Lettere, 19).

MALVERNE   1958   Lucien Malverne, *Remarques sur le Sophiste.* Revue Métaph. Morale 63, 1958, 149-166.

MANSFELD   1964   J. Mansfeld, *Die Offenbarung des Parmenides und die menschliche Welt.* Assen 1964. (Diss.).

MARKOVIC   1955   Zeljko Markovic, *La théorie de Platon sur l'Un et la Dyade indéfinie et ses traces dans la mathématique grecque.* Revue d'histoire des sciences et de leurs applications, 8, 1955, 289-297.

MARTIN   1841   Th. H. Martin, *Études sur le Timée de Platon.* 2 vol. Paris 1841.

MATHEWSON   1958   R. Mathewson, *Aristotle and Anaxagoras: An Examination of F. M. Cornford's Interpretation.* Classical Quarterly 52, 1958, 67-81.

MATSON   1963   W. J. Matson, *Democritus, fragment 156.* Class. Qu. 13, 1963, 26-29.

MAU   1949   Jürgen Mau, *Studien zur erkenntnistheoretischen Grundlage der Atomlehre im Altertum.* Wissensch. Zs. der Humboldt-Univ., II, 1952-3, Heft 3, 1-20 (= Inauguraldiss. Berlin 1949).

–   1954   Jürgen Mau, *Zum Problem des Infinitesimalen bei den antiken Atomisten*. Berlin 1954. (Deutsche Akad. d. Wiss. zu Berlin, Veröffentl. No. 4).

MÉAUTIS   1922   Georges Méautis, *Recherches sur le Pythagorisme*. Neuchâtel 1922. (Recueil Trav. Fac. Lettres, 9).

VAN MELSEN   1948   A. G. van Melsen, *De betekenis der wijsgerige corpuscula-theorieën voor het ontstaan der chemische atoomleer*. Ts. Philos. 10, 1948, 673-716.

–   1952   A. G. van Melsen, *From Atomos to Atom. The History of the Concept Atom*. (Duquesne Studies, Philos. Series 1) Pittsburgh Pa. 1952.

–   1962   A. G. M. van Melsen, *De geschiedenis van het begrip atoom. Van atomos naar atoom*. Utrecht 1962 (Aula-boeken) (eerste druk 1949).

MERLAN   1966   Philip Merlan, *Neues Licht auf Parmenides*. Archiv Gesch. Philos. 48, 1966, 267-276.

MICHEL   1950   Paul-Henri Michel, *De Pythagore à Euclide. Contribution à l'histoire des mathématiques pré-euclidiennes*. Paris 1950.

MILHAUD   1900   G. Milhaud, *Les philosophes-géomètres de la Grèce. Platon et ses prédécesseurs*. Paris 1900. (nouv. impr. 1934).

–   1906   G. Milhaud, *Études sur la pensée scientifique chez les grecs et les modernes*. Paris 1906.

–   1911   G. Milhaud, *Nouvelles études sur l'histoire de la pensée scientifique*. Paris 1911.

MONDOLFO   1952   Rodolfo Mondolfo, *El infinito en el pensamiento de la antigüedad clásica*. Buenos Aires 1952.

MOORHOUSE   1962   A. C. Moorhouse, Δέν *in classical Greek*. Class. Qu. 12, 1962, 235-238.

MORRISON   1956   J. S. Morrison, *Pythagoras of Samos*. Class. Qu. 50, 1956, 135-156.

MORROW   1950   Glenn R. Morrow, *Necessity and Persuasion in Plato's Timaeus*. Philos. Review 59, 1950, 147-163. Also in: reprint-volume Allen, 421-437.

MUGLER   1948   Charles Mugler, *Platon et la recherche mathématique de son époque*. Strasbourg-Zürich, 1948. (Review: Mnemosyne 1949, 346-349, van der Wielen).

–   1956   Ch. Mugler, *Le problème d'Anaxagore*. Revue ét. gr. 69, 1956, 314-376.

–   1960   Charles Mugler, *La physique de Platon*. Paris 1960. (Études et comm., 35).

–   1963   Ch. Mugler, *L'invisibilité des atomes*. Revue ét. gr. 76, 1963, 397-403.

NABER   1908   H. A. Naber, *Das Theorem des Pythagoras*. Haarlem, 1908.

NATORP   1884   Paul Natorp, *Forschungen zur Geschichte des Erkenntnisproblems im Altertum. Protagoras, Demokrit,*

		Epikur und die Skepsis. Berlin 1884, Nachdruck Hildesheim 1965.
–	1890, I	*Aristipp in Platons Theätet.* Archiv Gesch. Philos. 3, 1890, 347-362.
–	1890, II	P. Natorp, *Demokrit-Spuren bei Platon.* Archiv Gesch. Philos. 3, 1890, 515-531.
NEUGEBAUER	1952	O. Neugebauer, *The exact sciences in antiquity.* Princeton 1952, second edition: Rhode Island 1957.
NILSSON	1935	Martin P. Nilsson, *Early Orphism and kindred religious movements.* Harvard Theol. Review 28, 1935, 181-230.
OLLERUD	1951	Anders Ollerud, *L'idée de macrocosmos et de microcosmos dans le Timée de Platon. Étude de mythologie comparée.* Uppsala 1951, diss.
OWEN	1953	G. E. L. Owen, *The Place of the Timaeus in Plato's Dialogues.* Class. Qu. 3, 1953, 79-95. Also in: Reprint-volume Allen, 313-338.
–	1958	G. E. L. Owen, *Zeno and the Mathematicians.* Proceedings Aristotelian Society, 58, 1957-58, 199-222.
–	1960	G. E. L. Owen, *Eleatic Questions.* Class. Qu. 54, 1960, 84-101.
PATIN	1899	A. Patin, *Parmenides im Kampfe gegen Heraklit.* Jahrbücher für classische Philologie 25 Suppl. Bd. Leipzig 1899, 489-660 (*Review*: Paul Shorey in: Amer. J. of Philology 21, 1900, 77-86).
PECK	1926	A. L. Peck, *Anaxagoras and the parts.* Class. Qu. 20, 1926, 57-71.
–	1931	A. L. Peck, *Anaxagoras: Predication as a Problem in Physics.* Classical Quarterly 25, 1931, 27-37, 112-120.
PHILIP	1966	J. A. Philip, *Pythagoras and early Pythagoreanism.* Toronto 1966. (Phoenix Journal, Suppl. Vol. 7).
PHILIPPSON	1929	R. Philippson, *Democritea.* Hermes 64, 1929, 167-183.
POHLENZ	1918	M. Pohlenz, *Das zwanzigste Kapitel von Hippokrates' de Prisca Medicina.* Hermes 53, 1918, 396-421.
POPPER	1953	K. R. Popper, *The Nature of Philosophical Problems and their Roots in Science. Plato and the Crisis in Early Greek Atomism.* British Journal for the Philosophy of Science, 3, 1953, 124-156.
–	1958	K. R. Popper, *Back to the Presocratics.* Proceedings Aristotelian Society, 1958-9, 1-24.
PRAUSS	1966	G. Prauss, *Platon und der logische Eleatismus.* Berlin 1966.
PRÜMM	1956	Karl Prümm, *Die Orphik im Spiegel der neueren Forschung.* Zeitschr. Kathol. Theologie, 78, 1956, 1-40.
RAVEN	1948	J. E. Raven, *Pythagoreans and Eleatics.* Cambridge, 1948. (Review: Mnemosyne 1949, 341-3 by Verdenius, Gnomon 1953, 29-35 by Vlastos).
–	1954	J. E. Raven, *The Basis of Anaxagoras' Cosmology.* Class. Qu. 48, 1954, 123-137.

232

REIDEMEISTER 1949 K. Reidemeister, *Das exakte Denken der Griechen. Beiträge zur Deutung von Euklid, Plato, Aristoteles.* Hamburg 1949. (Review: Philos. Rundschau, 1, 1953-4, 185-187 von O. Becker).

REINHARDT 1912 K. Reinhardt, *Hekataios von Abdera und Demokrit.* Hermes 47, 1912, 492-513.

– 1916 Karl Reinhardt, *Parmenides und die Geschichte der griechischen Philosophie.* Bonn 1916.

– 1950 Karl Reinhardt, *Empedokles, Orphiker und Physiker.* Classical Philology, 45, 1950, 170-179.

RENAN 1858 E. Renan, *Mémoire sur l'origine et le caractère véritable de l'histoire phénicienne qui porte le nom de Sanchoniathon.* Mémoires de l'Institut Impérial de France, Académie des Inscriptions et Belles-Lettres XXIII 1858, deuxième partie, p. 241-334.

REY 1930 Abel Rey, *La science orientale avant les grecs.* (La science dans l'antiquité, I). Paris 1930, réimpr. 1942. (L'évolution de l'humanité).

– 1933 Abel Rey, *La jeunesse de la science grecque.* (La science dans l'antiquité II). Paris 1933 (Évol. hum.).

– 1939 Abel Rey, *La maturité de la pensée scientifique en Grèce.* (La science dans l'antiquité III). Paris, 1939 (Évol. hum.).

RIVAUD 1905 Albert Rivaud, *Le problème du devenir et la notion de la matière dans la philosophie grecque depuis les origines jusqu'à Theophraste.* (Thèse). Paris 1905.

– 1956 Alb. Rivaud, *Espace et changement dans le Timée de Platon.* Mélanges Diès, Paris 1956, 209-214.

ROBIN 1918 L. Robin, *Études sur la signification et la place de la physique dans la philosophie de Platon.* Revue philos. France Etranger, 86, 1918, 175-230, 370-415. Reprinted: L. Robin, *La pensée hellénique des origines à Epicure,* Paris 1942, 231-336.

– 1933 L. Robin, *L'atomisme ancien.* Revue de synthèse historique, 6, 1933, 205-218. Reprinted: L. Robin, *La pensée hellénique des origines à Epicure,* Paris 1942, 67-80.

– 1948 Léon Robin, *La pensée grecque et les origines de l'esprit scientifique.* Paris 1948. (Évol. hum).

RODIER 1902 G. Rodier, *Les mathématiques et la dialectique dans le système de Platon.* Archiv Gesch. Philos. 15, 1902, 479-490.

ROMANO 1965 Francesco Romano, *Anassagora.* Padova 1965. (Pubbl. Istituto Univ. di Magistero di Catania, Serie Filosofica, N. 52).

ROSS 1951 Sir David Ross, *Plato's Theory of Ideas.* Oxford 1951.

ROSTAGNI 1914 August. Rostagni, *Pitagora ed i Pitagorici in Timeo.* Atti R. Acad. delle Scienze di Torino, 49, 1913-14, 373-395.

233

–   1924   Augusto Rostagni, *Il verbo di Pitagora*. Torino 1924.

ROUGIER   1959   Louis Rougier, *La religion astrale des pythagoriciens*.
                         Paris 1959. (Coll. Mythes et religions).

DE RIJK   1947   L. M. de Rijk, *Aristoteles en de eleatische bewegings-
                         antinomieën*. Ts. v. Filos. 9, 1947, 171-202.

SACHS   1917   Eva Sachs, *Die fünf platonischen Körper. Zur Ge-
                         schichte der Mathematik und der Elementenlehre
                         Platons und der Pythagoreer*. Berlin 1917. (Philol.
                         Unters. 24).

SAMBURSKY   1956   S. Sambursky, *The Physical World of the Greeks*.
                         London 1956.

–   1959   S. Sambursky, *A Democritean Metaphor in Plato's
                         Kratylos*. Phronesis 4, 1959, 1-4.

SARTORIUS   1886   M. Sartorius, *Die Realität der Materie bei Plato*.
                         Philosophische Monatshefte 22, 1886, 129-167.

SCHNEIDER   1884   Gustav Schneider, *Die platonische Metaphysik auf
                         Grund der im Philebos gegebenen Prinzipien in ihren
                         wesentlichen Zügen dargestellt*. Leipzig 1884.

SCHOTTLAENDER   1929   R. Schottländer, *Nus als Terminus*. Hermes 64,
                         1929, 228-242.

SCHRAMM   1962   M. Schramm, *Die Bedeutung der Bewegungslehre des
                         Aristoteles für seine beiden Lösungen der zenonischen
                         Paradoxie*. Frankfurt a.M. 1962 (Philos. Abh. XIX).

SCHRECKENBERG   1964   H. Schreckenberg, *Ananke. Untersuchungen zur
                         Geschichte des Wortgebrauchs*. München 1964. Zete-
                         mata, 36).

SCHULZ   1905   Wolfg. Schulz, *Pythagoras und Heraklit*. Leipzig-
                         Wien, 1905. (Studien zur antiken Kultur, 1).

–   1907   Wolfg. Schulz, *Altjonische Mystik*. Wien und Leipzig,
                         1907. (Studien zur antiken Kultur, Heft 2 u. 3).

SCHULZ   1966   D. J. Schulz, *Das Problem der Materie in Platons
                         "Timaios"*. Bonn 1966 (Abh. z. Philos., Psych. u.
                         Pädag., 31).

SCHWABL   1950   Hans Schwabl, *Parmenides. Die Einheit seines Lehr-
                         gedichtes*. Wien 1950 (diss.).

–   1953   Hans Schwabl, *Sein und Doxa bei Parmenides*. Wiener
                         Studien 66, 1953, 50-75.

–   1963   Hans Schwabl, *Hesiod und Parmenides. Zur Formung
                         des parmenideischen Prooimions*. Rheinisches Mu-
                         seum 109, 1963, 134-142.

–   1964   H. Schwabl, *Anaximander. Zu den Quellen und seiner
                         Einordnung im vorsokratischen Denken*. Archiv für
                         Begriffsgeschichte 9, 1964, 59-72.

SELIGMANN   1962   P. Seligmann, *The ΑΠΕΙΡΟΝ of Anaximander. A
                         Study in the Origin and Function of Metaphysical
                         Ideas*. London, 1962.

SHOREY   1888   Paul Shorey, *The Interpretation of the Timaeus*.
                         American Journal Philol. 9, 1888.

SKEMP 1942 J. B. Skemp, *The Theory of Motion in Plato's later Dialogues*. Cambridge 1942. (Cambridge Classical Studies). Enlarged edition: Amsterdam 1967.

– 1960 J. B. Skemp, Ὕλη and ὑποδοχή in: *Aristotle and Plato in the midfourth century*, papers edited by I. Düring and G.E.L. Owen, Göteborg, 1960, 201-212.

SOLMSEN 1931 Fr. Solmsen, *Platos Einfluss auf die Bildung der mathematischen Methode*. Quellen und Studien zur Geschichte der Mathematik, Abt. B: Studien I 1931, 93-107.

– 1950, I Fr. Solmsen, *Tissues and the Soul*. Philos. Review, 59, 1950, 435-468.

– 1950, II Fr. Solmsen, *Chaos and apeiron*. Studi italiani di filologia classica, 24, 1950, 235-248.

– 1961 Fr. Solmsen, *Aristotle's word for matter*, in: *Didascaliae, Studies in honour of Anselm Albareda*, New York, 1961, 395-408.

– 1965 F. Solmsen, *Love and Strife in Empedocles' Cosmology*. Phronesis, X, 1965, 109-148.

STEINMETZ 1966 P. Steinmetz, *Xenophanesstudien*. Rhein. Mus. Philol. 109, 1966, 13-73.

STENZEL 1920 J. Stenzel, *Platon und Demokritos*. Neue Jahrb. klass. Alt. 45, 1920, 89-100 (also in: *Kleine Schriften*, Darmstadt 1956, 60-71).

– 1933 J. Stenzel, *Zahl und Gestalt bei Platon und Aristoteles*. Zweite erweiterte Auflage, Leipzig-Berlin 1933 (1. Aufl. 1924).

STOKES 1962 M. C. Stokes, *Hesiodic and Milesian Cosmogonies*. Phronesis 7, 1962, 1-37
8, 1963, 1-34

– 1965 M. C. Stokes, *On Anaxagoras*. Archiv. Gesch. Philos. 47, 1965, 1-19: Part I: *Anaxagoras' Theory of Matter*. 217-250: Part II: *The Order of Cosmogony*.

STRANG 1963 Colin Strang, *The Physical Theory of Anaxagoras*. Archiv Gesch. Philos. 45, 1963, 101-118.

SZABÓ 1951 A. Szabó, *Beiträge zur Geschichte der griechischen Dialektik*. Acta Antiqua Academiae Scientiarum Hungaricae 1, 1951, 377-410.

– 1954, I A. Szabó, *Zur Geschichte der Dialektik des Denkens*. Acta Antiqua Academiae Scientiarum Hungaricae, 2, 1954, 17-62.

– 1954, II *Zum Verständnis der Eleaten*. Acta Antiqua Academiae Scientiarum Hungaricae, 2, 1954, 243-289.

– 1955 A. Szabó, *Eleatica*. Acta Antiqua Academiae Scientiarum Hungaricae, 3, 1955, 67-103.

– 1956 A. Szabó, *Wie ist die Mathematik zu einer deduktiven Wissenschaft geworden?* Acta Antiqua Academiae Scientiarum Hungaricae 4, 1956, 109-152.

	1958	A. Szabó, *Die Grundlagen in der frühgriechischen Mathematik.* Studi italiani di filologia classica 30, 1958, 1-51.
	1960	Árpád Szabó, *Anfänge des euklidischen Axiomensystems.* Archive for History of Exact Sciences 1, 1960, 37-106.
	1964	Árpád Szabó, *Ein Beleg für die voreudoxische Proportionenlehre?* Archiv für Begriffsgeschichte 9, 1964, 151-172.
	1967	Árpád Szabó, *Greek Dialectic and Euclid's axiomatics,* in: *Problems in the Philosophy of Mathematics,* Proceedings Colloquium London 1965, edited by Imre Lakatos, Amsterdam 1967 (Studies in Logic and the Foundations of Mathematics), p. 1-8, followed by discussions with Kneale, Whitrow, Popper a.o., p. 9-27.
TANNERY	1887	Paul Tannery, *Pour l'histoire de la science hellène. De Thalès à Empédocle.* Paris 1887.
TATE	1936	J. Tate, *On Plato: Laws X 889 CD.* Class. Qu. 30, 1936, 48-54.
TAYLOR	1926	A. E. Taylor, *Two Pythagorean Philosophemes. I The connexion* τὸ ἄρτιον *and bisection ad infinitum.* II. *The One and the 'Gnomons'.* Classical Review 40, 1926, 149-151.
	1926-7	*Forms and Numbers. A Study in Platonic Metaphysics.* Mind 35, 1926, 419-440 36, 1927, 12- 33.
	1928	A. E. Taylor, *A Commentary on Plato's Timaeus.* Oxford 1928.
THEILER	1924	W. Theiler, *Zur Geschichte der teleologischen Naturbetrachtung bis auf Aristoteles.* Diss. Basel, 1924.
THESLEFF	1961	Holger Thesleff, *An Introduction to the Pythagorean Writings of the Hellenistic Period.* Åbo 1961. (Acta Acad. Aboensis, Hum, 24, 3).
TIMPANARO CARDINI	1958-1962-1964	Maria Timpanaro Cardini, *Pitagorici. Testimonianze e Frammenti.* Firenze, I, 1958; II, 1962; III, 1964 (Bibl. di Studi Superiori, 28, 41, 45).
TOEPLITZ	1925	Otto Toeplitz, *Mathematik und Antike.* Die Antike I 1925, 175-203.
	1931	Otto Toeplitz, *Das Verhältnis von Mathematik und Ideenlehre bei Plato.* Quellen und Studien zur Geschichte der Mathematik, Abt. B: Studien I 1931, 3-33.
TOULMIN-GOODFIELD	1959	Stephen Toulmin, June Goodfield, *The Architecture of Matter.* London 1962 (Reprinted 1965 Pelican Books).
TUMARKIN	1943	Anna Tumarkin, *Der Begriff des Apeiron in der griechischen Philosophie.* Jahrb. d. Schweizer Philos. Ges., 3, 1943, 55-71.

236

UNTERSTEINER   1955, I   Mario Untersteiner, *Senofane, testimonianze e frammenti*. Firenze 1955. (Review: Gnomon, 29, 1957, 127-131, Kerferd).

–   1955, II   Mario Untersteiner, *L'essere di Parmenide è* OYΛON *non* EN. Rivista critica di storia della filosofia, 10, 1955, 5-23.

–   1956   Mario Untersteiner, *Senofane. Testimonianze e Frammenti*. Introduzione, Traduzione e Commento. Firenze 1956. (Bibl. di Studi Superiori 33).

–   1958   Mario Untersteiner, *Parmenide. Testimonianze e Frammenti*. Introduzione, Traduzione e Commento Firenze 1958. (Bilbl. di Studi Superiori 38)

–   1963   Mario Untersteiner, *Zenone. Testimonianze e Frammenti*. Introduzione, Traduzione e Commento. Firenze 1963. (Bibl. di Studi Superiori 46).

VERDENIUS   1942   W. J. Verdenius, *Parmenides. Some comments on his poems*. Utrecht 1942.

VIRIEUX-REYMOND   1956   Antoinette Virieux-Reymond, *Quelques étapes importantes dans la formation de la notion d'infini au cours de l'antiquité*. Actes VIIIe Congrès International d'Histoire des Sciences, 1956, 45-51.

VLASTOS   1939   Gregory Vlastos, *The disorderly motion in the Timaeus*. Class. Qu. 33, 1939, 71-83 (also in reprint-volume Allen, 379-399).

   1945-46   Gr. Vlastos, *Ethics and Physics in Democritus*.
Philos. Review 54, 1945, 578-592
                55, 1946, 53- 64.

–   1950   Gr. Vlastos, *The Physical Theory of Anaxagoras*. Philos. Review 59, 1950, 31-57.

–   1952   Gregory Vlastos, *Theology and Philosophy in Early Greek Thought*. Philos. Quarterly 2, 1952, 97-123.

–   1953   G. Vlastos, *Review of: J. E. Raven, Pythagoreans and Eleatics*. Gnomon 25, 1953, 29-35.

–   1966, I   Gregory Vlastos, *A Note on Zeno's Arrow*. Phronesis XI, 1966, 3-18.

–   1966, II   Gr. Vlastos, *Zeno's Race Course*. J. Hist. Philos. 4, 1966, 95-108.

DE VOGEL   1936   C. J. de Vogel. *Een keerpunt in Plato's denken*. Amsterdam 1936 (diss. Utrecht).

–   1948   C. J. de Vogel, *La dernière phase du Platonisme et l'interprétation de M. Robin*. in: Studia Vollgraff, Amsterdam 1948, 165-178.

–   1949   C. J. de Vogel, *Problems concerning later Platonism*. Mnemosyne 1949, 197-216, 299-318.

–   1951   C. J. de Vogel, *Examen critique de l'interprétation traditionelle du platonisme*. Revue métaph. morale 1951, 249-268.

–   1953   C. J. de Vogel, *Platon a-t-il ou n'a-t-il pas introduit le mouvement dans son monde intelligible? Critique des interprétations modernes de Soph. 249 a et de Tim. 31 b.* Actes XIe Congrès Intern. Philos., Bruxelles 1953, vol. 12, 61-67.

– 1959 C. J. de Vogel, *La théorie de l' ἄπειρον chez Platon et dans la tradition platonicienne.* Revue philos. France Étranger 84, 1959, 21-39.

– 1966 C. J. de Vogel, *Pythagoras and early Pythagoreanism. An interpretation of neglected evidence on the philosopher Pythagoras.* Assen 1966.

VOGT 1909 H. Vogt, *Die Geometrie des Pythagoras.* Bibliotheca Mathematica, 3. Folge, 9. Bd., Leipzig 1908-09, 15-54.

– 1910 H. Vogt, *Die Entdeckungsgeschichte des Irrationalen nach Plato und anderen Quellen des 4. Jahrh.* Bibliotheca Mathematica, 3. Folge, 10 Bd., Leipzig 1909-10, 97-155.

– 1914 H. Vogt, *Zur Entdeckungsgeschichte des Irrationalen.* Bibliotheca Mathematica, 3. Folge, 14 Bd., Leipzig 1913-14, 9-29.

VOLLGRAFF 1949 W. Vollgraff, *Elementum.* Mnemosyne, 1949, 89-115.

VAN DER WAERDEN 1941 B. L. van der Waerden, *Zenon und die Grundlagenkrise der griechischen Mathematik.* Mathematische Annalen 117, 1940-41, 141-161.

– 1943 B. L. van der Waerden, *Die Harmonielehre der Pythagoreer.* Hermes 78, 1943, 163-199.

– 1948 B. L. van der Waerden, *Die Arithmetik der Pythagorëer.* Mathematische Annalen 120, 1947-49, 127-153, 676-700.

– 1951 B. L. van der Waerden, *Die Astronomie der Pythagoreer.* Amsterdam 1951. (Kon. Akad. afd. Nat. I 20, 1). Review: Gnomon 25, 1953, 35-39 by Oskar Becker.

– 1953 B. L. van der Waerden, *Das grosse Jahr des Orpheus.* Hermes 81, 1953, 481-483.

– 1966 B. L. van der Waerden, *Erwachende Wissenschaft. Ägyptische, Babylonische und Griechische Mathematik.* Aus dem Holländischen übersetzt mit Zusätzen des Verfassers. Basel-Stuttgart 1966. (first impression: Groningen 1950, in Dutch).

WEDBERG 1955 A. Wedberg, *Plato's Philosophy of Mathematics.* Stockholm 1955.

WEST 1963 M. L. West. *Three presocratic cosmologies.* (Alcman, Pherecydes, Thales) Classical Quarterly 13, 1963, 154-176.

WHITROW 1961 G. J. Whitrow, *The Natural Philosophy of Time.* London-Edinburgh 1961. (p.135-152: Zeno's Paradoxes).

VAN DER WIELEN 1941 W. van der Wielen, *De ideegetallen van Plato.* diss. Amsterdam, 1941.

WILPERT   1941   P. Wilpert, *Neue Fragmente aus* Περὶ ταγαθοῦ. Hermes 76, 1941, 225-250.

–   1950   Paul Wilpert, *Die Elementenlehre des Platon und Demokrit.* Festschrift Aloys Wenzl, München, 1950, 49-66.

–   1953   P. Wilpert, *Eine Elementenlehre im platonischen Philebos.* in: Studies Robinson 2, 573-582. St. Louis, 1953.

WITTE   1964   Bernd Witte, *Der* εἰκὼς λόγος *in Platos Timaios. Beitrag zur Wissenschaftsmethode und Erkenntnistheorie des späten Plato.* Archiv Gesch. Philos. 46, 1964, 1-16.

ZELLER   1892   E. Zeller, *Plato's Mitteilungen über frühere und gleichzeitige Philosophen.* Archiv für Geschichte der Philosophie 5, 1892, 165-184.

ZEUTHEN   1910   H. G. Zeuthen, *Sur la constitution des livres arithmétiques des Eléments d'Euclide et leur rapport à la question de l'irrationalité.* Oversigt over det klg. danske Videnskabernes Selskabs forhandlingen. Bulletin de l'Acad. Royale de Danemark. Copenhague, 1910, 395-437.

–   1913   H. G. Zeuthen, *Sur les connaissances géométriques des grecs avant la réforme platonicienne de la géométrie.* Oversigt over det klg. danske Videnskabernes Selskabs forhandlingen. Bulletin de l'Ac. Royale de Danemark 1913, 431-473.

–   1915   H. G. Zeuthen, *Sur l'origine historique de la connaissance des quantités irrationelles.* Oversigt over det klg. danske Videnskabernes Selskabs forhandlingen. Bulletin de l'Ac. Royale de Danemark, 1915, 333-362.

ZIEGLER   RE   Konrat Ziegler,
art. *Orpheus*, in: Pauly-Wissowa RE.
art. *Orphische Dichtung*, in: Pauly-Wissowa RE.

INDEX NOMINUM

INDEX RERUM

244

INDEX LOCORUM